Praise for *It's All Connected*

It's All Connected provides clear illustrations of the key principles of design of the new Common Core State Standards: focus and coherence. The lessons offer middle-school teachers the resources to focus on a key concept of mathematics, proportional reasoning, and create coherence by deliberately making connections among the concepts studied. In addition, each lesson offers the pedagogical support teachers need to differentiate their instruction for their students who are struggling, for those who are on-track, and for those ready for going beyond.

Harold Asturias
Director, Center for Mathematics Excellence and Equity
Lawrence Hall of Science, University of California, Berkeley

It's All Connected supports students in areas that are central to students' success in mathematics. The lessons help students explore the relationships among difficult mathematics concepts and engage students in appealing situations to deepen their understandings. For example, the lesson "Zapping Zombies" takes advantage of the interest and the imagination of students at this level. Having fun and learning at the same time—a great concept!

Glenda Lappan
University Distinguished Professor, Michigan State University
Past President, National Council of Teachers of Mathematics

If proportional reasoning has always baffled you, this book will help to unlock its mysteries. *It's All Connected* offers a brilliant collection of lessons that provide engaging context, thought-provoking questions, and insightful guidance for teachers. Carmen's commitment to having students understand mathematics by making connections to big ideas such as proportional reasoning is apparent in this thought-out resource. Both teachers and students will enjoy doing math this way! Everyone wins with this book. I am recommending this book to all the math teachers in our district. Kudos to Carmen!

Edwina Henslee
Middle School Mathematics Curriculum Coordinator, Hobbs, New Mexico

It's All Connected presents a powerful study in proportional reasoning, capturing the essence of foundational pieces of mathematical understanding crucial to the success of students in high school, college and/or a career of their choice. The resource reinforces "mathematical understandings" endorsed by the Common Core State Standards and NCTM. Additionally these lessons help develop the Standards for Mathematical Practices found in the Common Core State Standards. These practices promote rich mathematical learning. I highly recommend *It's All Connected* to teachers looking for well-thought-out lessons for their students.

Karen Sisco Snow
Math Consultant, Houston, Arkansas

It's All Connected clearly highlights, through questioning strategies, ways to prevent or correct misconceptions. In particular, the questions that differentiate instruction with struggling and on-task students provide teachers with concrete tools to facilitate learning. The additional questions to extend student thinking provide challenges for those opportune moments with stronger learners. Having had the chance to observe Carmen in the classroom, I know how successful she is in teaching these concepts to middle-school students.

Cynthia L. Schneider
Researcher, Austin, Texas

Carmen is one of the best connectors of ideas that I have ever met. She not only sees how the mathematical pieces fit together, she helps the rest of us make sense of those connections. Most of all, Carmen is the ultimate teacher. She is as committed to her own continued learning as she is to that of her students. She has great intuition with students and, like a great teacher, she listens to her students and she seems to know the right questions to ask to get them thinking just a bit harder.

Cathy Seeley
Author, Faster Isn't Smarter: Messages About Math, Teaching,
and Learning in the 21st Century
Past President, National Council of Teachers of Mathematics
Senior Fellow, Charles A. Dana Center, The University of Texas at Austin

Grades
6–8

It's All
Connected

The Power of
PROPORTIONAL REASONING
to Understand Mathematics Concepts

Carmen Whitman

FOREWORD BY CATHY SEELEY

Math Solutions
Sausalito, California, USA

Math Solutions
150 Gate 5 Road
Sausalito, California, USA 94965
www.mathsolutions.com

Library of Congress Cataloging-in-Publication Data
CIP is on file with the Library of Congress.
ISBN 978-1-935099-24-6

Editor: Jamie Ann Cross
Production Service: MATHQueue, Inc.
Production Coordinator: Melissa L. Inglis-Elliott
Interior design: Tristann Jones
Cover design: Susan Barclay/Barclay Design
Cover image: "Abstract" by Simon Greig. © Simon Greig. All rights reserved.
http://ideas.veer.com/members/0610065.

Printed in the United States of America on acid-free paper
15 14 13 12 11   ML   1 2 3 4 5

A Message from Math Solutions

We at Math Solutions believe that teaching math well calls for increasing our understanding of the math we teach, seeking deeper insights into how students learn mathematics, and refining our lessons to best promote students' learning.

Math Solutions shares classroom-tested lessons and teaching expertise from our faculty of professional development consultants as well as from other respected math educators. Our publications are part of the nationwide effort we've made since 1984 that now includes

- more than five hundred face-to-face professional development programs each year for teachers and administrators in districts across the country;
- professional development books that span all math topics taught in kindergarten through high school;
- videos for teachers and for parents that show math lessons taught in actual classrooms;
- on-site visits to schools to help refine teaching strategies and assess student learning; and
- free online support, including grade-level lessons, book reviews, inservice information, and district feedback, all in our Math Solutions Online Newsletter.

For information about all of the products and services we have available, please visit our website at *www.mathsolutions.com.* You can also contact us to discuss math professional development needs by calling (800) 868-9092 or by sending an email to *info@mathsolutions.com.*

We're always eager for your feedback and interested in learning about your particular needs. We look forward to hearing from you.

Contents

Proportionality may be the most important connecting idea in all of school mathematics. However, there was a time when I didn't even realize what I didn't know about this critical and powerful topic. I had learned lots of mathematics on my way to a degree in the subject from an engineering institution. Yet none of my mathematics courses had helped me think deeply about the fundamental notions of proportional relationships that deepen our understanding of numbers and lead to making sense of algebra. When I began teaching junior high school mathematics forty years ago, I dutifully taught the unit on ratios, proportions, and percent without thinking too much about the underlying ideas. I was perfectly content to teach my students how to cross-multiply to solve a proportion and how to solve three types of percent problems.

At some point in my continued learning and my work with other teachers, I started hearing conversations about "big ideas" in mathematics. I liked the possibility that we could zoom out from the day's lesson to look at ideas that might cross multiple topics and could even connect apparently different mathematical skills with each other. And when the subject of proportional relationships was used as an example of this kind of connecting thread, I'm sure I physically hit my forehead with my hand in disbelief that I had gone so long not seeing what now seems obvious about the central role proportionality can play in a person's development of mathematical thinking and proficiency. As Carmen relates in "About This Resource," I, too, wanted a "do-over" with my former students—I realized that I could teach middle school mathematics much more effectively building on a broader and deeper way of thinking about the development of proportional understanding.

Proportionality starts small and just keeps getting bigger. Even though we focus on the development of proportional understanding at middle school, its seeds appear in the elementary grades as students notice patterns in the multiplication tables or make generalizations about relationships, like observing that for each candy bar they sell, their band fund grows by $2. As students work with fractions, the role of proportionality becomes more central in exploring how to represent a fraction with equivalent names. Then in middle school, suddenly proportional relationships are everywhere—in working with commissions, taxes, scale drawings, similarity, and the list goes on. The big payoff comes when students can take what they know about proportionality and use it to make sense of linear relationships in algebra, understanding the fundamental proportionality represented in a constant rate of change. This understanding of *slope* helps students start to explore and separate different types of functions, realizing that some are based on a constant rate of change and some are not. It may not be an exaggeration to suggest that, with this understanding, a door to higher-level mathematics can open for many students, as linear relationships underlie many advanced mathematical ideas all the way to calculus. And along this journey, helping students "get" proportionality can keep them more engaged in the mathematics they are learning as we challenge them and help them make sense of connections that link what they learn today with what they learned last week. Wow.

Carmen Whitman is one of the best connectors of ideas that I have ever met. She not only sees how the mathematical pieces fit together, she helps the rest of us make sense of those connections. Most of all, Carmen is the ultimate teacher. She is as committed to her own continued learning as she is to that of her students. She has great intuition with students and, like a great teacher, she listens to her students and she seems to know the right questions to ask to get them thinking just a bit harder. In this wonderful book, Carmen offers us our own opportunity to think just a bit harder and to put into practice what we learn so that students can realize their potential in the mathematical learning that comes from "getting" proportionality. I'm absolutely delighted to see some of Carmen's wisdom shared in this way, and I know you will enjoy this wonderful learning adventure!

—Cathy Seeley

Senior Fellow, Charles A. Dana Center, The University of Texas at Austin

Past President, National Council of Teachers of Mathematics

Author, *Faster Isn't Smarter: Messages About Math, Teaching, and Learning in the 21st Century*

Dedication

For my mother, Mary L. Silvas, who piqued my curiosity,
my father, Guadalupe, who made sense of it all, and my daughter, Catrina,
who gives me a reason to want to be better.
Pinkies with Pride

Acknowledgments

▶ Emma Trevino—a special thanks for the continuous inspiring conversations, for allowing me to share my thoughts, for being patient when I made no sense, and understanding when I needed to vent. Your ideas are endless; your wisdom is exceptional; and I highly respect your judgment.

▶ Vicki Massey—your questions and comments were thought provoking and your perspective pushed me to produce a better product.

▶ James Whitman—your tireless effort helped to get it done correctly.

My Story

I remember sitting in a class while in middle school and thinking, "Just another day of sitting here doing exactly what my teachers want me to do." I was a decent student; I did everything I was told to do but did not put forth the effort I should have in order to excel. It wasn't until my last year in middle school that I had a sudden realization: I needed to quit doing just OK and start trying to do the best I could. That year I had great caring and knowledgeable teachers who made an impact on my motivation to learn; it was then that I decided I wanted to be a teacher who made a significant difference in my student's lives.

At the beginning of my teaching career, I had the opportunity to work with students in a very non-traditional setting. I was able to take students from varied backgrounds and help them move forward. In my mind, it did not matter if these students had not memorized their multiplication facts or they did not know how to find common denominators—they were going to learn math. We definitely struggled; to this day I sometimes want to call back some of my students and teach them again; as I've worked with additional students I've learned so much more about the art of teaching. Occasionally, I run into former students who tell me, "I became a math teacher because of you!" and I wonder when along my career path I had taught them. Twenty years ago I was a different kind of math teacher. Did they become a teacher like I was when I started teaching or did they realize that a change in teaching methodology was needed to connect more effectively with students? I hope for the latter, and that I inspired them to find their own paths to reaching children.

> Teaching isn't about finding the perfect worksheet or using manipulatives; it is about helping my students make sense of the mathematics and asking the right questions to help them understand it.

It wasn't until I started using the curriculum *Connected Mathematics* that I gained insight into and discovered the importance of my students understanding mathematics and not just learning procedures. Teaching isn't about finding the perfect worksheet or using manipulatives; it is about helping my students make sense of the mathematics and asking the right questions to help them understand it. I finally started really listening to students and their questions. I remember one student asking, "Why do you tell me to reduce the fraction and then tell me they are equivalent?" I realized that this student was doing just as I had in middle school—doing what the teacher wanted but not necessarily knowing why. However, there was a difference; he unlike I, was brave enough to ask why. Changing the way I taught was not easy; in fact,

> This resource, *It's All Connected*, illustrates what I've learned in my teaching career: the value of using working knowledge to make connections with new concepts as they are studied.

it was the most difficult thing I have ever done. I did not always have answers to all the questions asked by my students; but when I realized that was OK. I became a better teacher. Becoming a learner along with my students helped us build a community of learners. I listened and asked questions as a way of helping my students succeed. I continually asked myself, "How can I help my students make the connections between the mathematics concepts I am trying to teach?"

This resource, *It's all Connected,* illustrates what I've learned in my teaching career: the value of using working knowledge to make connections with new concepts as they are studied.

Why Focus on Proportionality?

The ability to reason proportionally is at the forefront of middle school mathematics. As middle school students develop the ability to reason proportionally and represent proportional relationships in a variety of ways, they continually encounter opportunities to apply this knowledge across all strands of mathematics. The National Council of Teachers of Mathematics (NCTM) *Principal and Standard for School Mathematics* states, "Facility with proportionality develops through work in many areas of the curriculum, including ratio and proportion, percent, similarity, scaling, linear equations, slope, relative frequency histograms, and probability. The understanding of proportionality should also emerge through problem solving and reasoning, and it is important in connecting mathematical topics and in connecting mathematics and other domains such as science and art." Teaching proportionality-infused lessons throughout the five content strands—Number and Operations, Algebraic Reasoning, Geometry, Measurement, and Probability and Statistics—helps students make connections among concepts. By including proportionality, proportional relationships and proportional reasoning in all these lessons, we can begin to think of proportionality as the "big idea" that helps us to make this unifying connection across all strands. Teachers can further help students see middle-school mathematics not as separate and unrelated concepts, but as concepts that revolve around a unifying idea or skill.

> By including proportionality, proportional relationships and proportional reasoning in all these lessons, we can begin to think of proportionality as the "big idea" that helps us to make this unifying connection across all strands.

Throughout my years of teaching, as we moved from one content strand to another, students often did not see the connection among the topics. Frequently students viewed each new topic as another unrelated or separate concept with no mathematical connection to anything previously studied. Upon reflection, I resolved to use lessons and teaching strategies that made these mathematical connections more evident, so that students would recognize the purpose and value of their prior knowledge, and subsequently use that knowledge as a tool to build a strong foundation in middle school mathematics.

What Kinds of Lessons Are Included?

I have included eighteen lessons that together address the five content strands of middle-school mathematics. These lessons have goals that can typically be found in standards throughout the middle grades. Each lesson incorporates various strategies and the language my students have used when exploring these topics. Ideally we want middle school curriculum to move away from the limiting view of proportionality traditionally promoted—when we "set up the proportion and solve for x"—to a more inclusive view. This inclusive view encompasses a variety of student-driven strategies, making use of and connecting to students' prior learning. As students learn new concepts, we want them to use the mathematics they already know to evaluate each new situation. Considering whether a situation is proportional or non-proportional will sometimes help students begin to reason towards a solution. Thinking this way also helps students build a foundation for studying many other topics learned in the middle grades.

How Are the Lessons Formatted?

Each lesson follows a similar format as outlined below.

Correlations

Each lesson is correlated to the Common Core State Standards and the NCTM standards. These correlations are listed in each lesson as well as in quick-reference tables at the front of the resource. Each lesson is also correlated to four of the leading middle school mathematics programs.

Lesson Introduction and Teacher Suggestions

Of significant importance to improving instruction, each lesson features carefully detailed teacher notes. The teacher notes section states the goals for the lesson and establishes the focus for teaching the lesson. An introduction to the lesson provides teachers with suggestions on how to begin the lesson and introduces essential vocabulary to students. The student engagement section offers suggestions for what the teacher should be doing while students are working on the lesson. This section also includes three types of questions to ask students as they progress through the lesson: questions for struggling students, questions for students on task, and questions to extend student thinking (See more details about the question sections below.). The teacher notes end with a summary section that provides suggestions for bringing together any strategies and representations that the students used to make sense of the mathematics in the lesson.

It is important as you prepare to teach the lesson, that you first complete the lesson yourself, and read the teacher notes. This will enhance the understanding of the teaching notes offered within the lesson.

Materials and Vocabulary

Each lesson lists any materials needed to complete the lesson, as well as suggests key vocabulary words. Note that the mathematical vocabulary may vary depending on the placement of the lesson during the course of your curriculum.

Student Engagement

Questions

The student engagement section of the teacher notes includes three types of questions to ask students as they progress through the lesson.

Questioning is a very important component of teaching—it is key to helping teachers assess their students's understanding of the mathematics. I might have the best-planned lesson, but if my students do not truly understand the mathematics, the lesson itself is meaningless. In my earlier teaching years I would delude myself that my students understood the mathematics when in fact they did not. I remember having great lessons and then giving a test only to have my students not do well. This is a painful lesson that I think many young teachers experience. In time I learned I could not afford to wait until I assessed my students formally to find out if they understood the mathematics. I resolved to start assessing daily through questioning. As I became skilled at assessing through questioning, I recognized the need to have primarily three types of questions ready for each lesson I taught: questions for struggling students, questions for students on task, and questions for students to extend their thinking about the mathematics. This resource provides questions in each category to help you begin the questioning process. The questions provided are just a starting point for the many questions you can and should ask students to verify their understanding, get them started, or pique their interest to think deeper about the mathematics concepts.

> The student engagement section of the teacher notes includes three types of questions to ask students as they progress through the lesson.
> - Questions for Struggling Students
> - Questions for Students on Task
> - Questions to Extend Student Thinking

Questions for Struggling Students

As a teacher, I used to assume, as students began a task, that they knew what they should do to solve the problem. The lack of initial questions from students often gave me the false impression that students would all get started right away on the task at hand; you can understand my surprise when they wouldn't. Sometimes it's a lack of motivation, but sometimes it's a student's uncertainly on how to enter into the task.

When I go up to a student or group of students who have not begun work on the assignment, I don't want to ask them, "Why aren't you working?" Instead I want to ask them questions that they are going to be able to answer in order to begin their thinking process. Often students shy away from my questions because they have not been successful in mathematics. I want them to feel success and be able to answer the questions I pose to them. Some teachers might say that the questions in this category are too simplistic. These questions are intentionally simple so that all students can answer them and gain motivation in getting started. The questions help the slow-to-begin student feel successful with a challenging concept. My hope is to move students into the next level of questioning as their thinking progresses.

Questions for Students on Task

Frequently we ask questions when we feel students are thinking incorrectly. It follows that students automatically think they are doing something wrong whenever we ask questions. We need to break this mold and ask questions of all students all the time. Through questioning while students are on task, teachers gain insight into a student's thinking and the connections the student is making. The types of questions in this category will help teachers form their summaries for the lesson. How are students solving the problem? What strategies are they using? How can I use their thinking to help other students make sense of the mathematics?

Other questions will come up depending on the student responses. These questions are provided to help teachers start the questioning process. They are not necessarily in sequential order, nor do they all have to be asked of every student. The questions should serve as a guide to foster a climate of always asking questions in class.

Questions to Extend Student Thinking

When students are set to task, whether they are working independently or in groups, they often finish at different times. While others are continuing to work, how do we keep students that have finished engaged? What kinds of questions can I ask students to push their thinking? If a group has finished before others, this indicates that those students are ready to think deeper about the mathematics in the situation. Instead of assigning homework or more practice problems, raise the bar in the current task to press students to delve deeper and make more connections within the mathematical problem. What questions can we ask to encourage students to continue to investigate the mathematics? The questions in this category are meant to have students working beyond the learning expectation of the lesson. Taking the mathematics to another level depends on knowing your students well enough to be able to push their thinking. These questions do not have to be asked of all students. However, we do need to validate the time students spend answering these questions. How do we add this information to the summary and honor their work? The information can be posed as extensions or examples for the rest of the class to think about. Not all students need to fully understand these ideas, rather the ideas can serve as a catalyst for students to think about as they continue to learn mathematics.

In my classroom, asking questions is a two-way street; whenever I ask questions to check for understanding my students may ask a question in response. When students ask questions, we need to make sure their questions get considered, whether through answering with a question or by listening to their peers' thoughts and explanations.

Lesson Summary

The summary section of the lesson often is the most crucial part of the lesson. Teachers need to devote time to planning the summary, yet still have flexibility to modify it when students need additional help. During the summary teachers are encouraging students to make sense of the variety of methods and strategies used. They need to determine how to guide discussions, what needs to be generalized and what connections can be made among the mathematical topics. Teachers need to keep focus on the mathematical goal(s) of the current lesson yet still think about groundwork for future lessons.

It is during the summary that students should exhibit understanding of the topic. As the summary progresses student strategies emerge and teachers perceive how they are interpreting the mathematics. During the summary, students should be asked to share thoughts, question, explain, describe, listen, observe differences and similarities, analyze, reason, revise, make connections, and develop rules and generalizations.

Suggestions are given in the Lesson Summary for accomplishing the elements named above. The goal of the summary is to bring some closure to the mathematics learned that day. Not every question needs to be answered; not everything needs to be written down by students; not every thought heard needs to be correct; not every answer needs to come from the teacher, and not every topic needs to be taught in isolation. A lesson summary is a learning experience that involves the whole class and is facilitated by the teacher to help students understand the mathematics. I think of the summary as the "heart" of the lesson.

Student Recording Page

Each lesson contains student work pages. These pages provide the problems students will solve. The work page starts with an engaging scenario and ends with questions the students need to answer. Teachers should work through the lessons before using them with students, specifically thinking about ways their students might solve the problems.

Student Recording Page Solutions

Each lesson also contains an answer key. The answer keys offer sample solutions and possible strategies students might use to solve the problem. Most of the responses provided in the answer keys stem from actual student responses that I've encountered in my classrooms. Teachers should expect students to model a variety of strategies that mirror how they reason proportionally, thus encouraging students to take ownership of their own proportional reasoning and make connections to prior learning.

Correlations to Mathematics Common Core State Standards and NCTM's *Principles and Standards*

Chapter 1	Number and Operation
Lesson 1 Equivalence: Many Names for Fractions	**Common Core State Standards** Ratios and Proportional Relationships 4.RP Understand ratio concepts and use ratio reasoning to solve problems. 1. Understand the concept of a ratio and use ratio language to describe a ratio relationship between two quantities. For example, "The ratio of wings to beaks in the bird house at the zoo was 2:1, because for every 2 wings there was 1 beak." "For every vote candidate A received, candidate B received nearly 3 votes." **NCTM *Principles and Standards*** Number and Operation Standard Understanding numbers, ways of representing numbers, relationships among numbers, and number systems. *Work flexibly with fractions, decimals, and percents to solve problems.* Understand meanings of operations and how they relate to one another. *Understand the meanings and effect of arithmetic operations with fractions, decimals, and integers.*
Lesson 2 Sale, Sale, Sale!	**Common Core State Standards** Ratios and Proportional Relationships 6.RP Understand ratio concepts and use ratio reasoning to solve problems. 3. Use ratio and rate reasoning to solve real-world and mathematical problems, e.g., by reasoning about tables of equivalent ratios, tape diagrams, double number line diagrams, or equations. c. Find a percent of a quantity as a rate per 100 (e.g., 30% of a quantity means 30/100 times the quantity); solve problems involving finding the whole, given a part and the percent. Ratios and Proportional Relationships 7.RP Analyze proportional relationships and use them to solve real-world and mathematical problems. 3. Use proportional relationships to solve multistep ratio and percent problems. Examples: simple interest, tax, markups and markdowns, gratuities and commissions, fees, percent increase and decrease, percent error. **NCTM *Principles and Standards*** Number and Operation Standard Understand numbers, ways of representing numbers, relationships among numbers, and number systems. *Work flexibly with fractions, decimals, and percents to solve problems.* Understand and use ratios and proportions to represent quantitative relationships.

Lesson 3 Dividing Fractions	**Common Core State Standards** The Number System 6.NS 　Apply and extend previous understandings of multiplication and division to divide fractions by fractions. 　1. Interpret and compute quotients of fractions, and solve word problems involving division of fractions by fractions, e.g., by using visual fraction models and equations to represent the problem. For example, create a story context for $2/3 \div 3/4$ and use a visual fraction model to show the quotient; use the relationship between multiplication and division to explain that $2/3 \div 3/4 = 8/9$ because $3/4$ of $8/9$ is $2/3$. (In general, $a/b \div c/d = ad/bc$.) How much chocolate will each person get if 3 people share $1/2$ lb of chocolate equally? How many $3/4$-cup servings are in $2/3$ of a cup of yogurt? How wide is a rectangular strip of land with length $3/4$ mi and area $1/2$ square mi? **NCTM** *Principles and Standards* Number and Operation Standard 　Understanding numbers, ways of representing numbers, relationships among numbers, and number systems. 　　*Understand and use ratios and proportions to represent quantitative relationships.* 　Understand meanings of operations and how they relate to one another. 　　*Understand the meanings and effect of arithmetic operations with fractions, decimals, and integers.* 　Compute fluently and make reasonable estimates. 　　*Select appropriate methods and tools for computing with fractions, and decimals from among mental computation, estimation, calculators and computer, and paper in pencil, depending on the situation and apply the selected methods.* 　Develop and analyze algorithms for computing with fractions, decimals, and integers and develop fluency in their use.
Lesson 4 Cookie Recipe	**Common Core State Standards** Ratios and Proportional Relationships 6.RP 　Understand ratio concepts and use ratio reasoning to solve problems. 　3. Use ratio and rate reasoning to solve real-world and mathematical problems, e.g., by reasoning about tables of equivalent ratios, tape diagrams, double number line diagrams, or equations. 　　d. Use ratio reasoning to convert measurement units; manipulate and transform units appropriately when multiplying or dividing quantities. Ratios and Proportional Relationships 7.RP 　Analyze proportional relationships and us them to solve real-world and mathematical problems. 　3. Use proportional relationships to solve multistep ratio and percent problems. Examples: simple interest, tax, markups and markdowns, gratuities and commissions, fees, percent increase and decrease, percent error. **NCTM** *Principles and Standards* Number and Operation Standard 　Understanding numbers, ways of representing numbers, relationships among numbers, and number systems. 　　*Work flexibly with fractions, decimals, and percents to solve problems.* 　　*Understand and use ratios and proportions to represent quantitative relationships.* 　Compute fluently and make reasonable estimates. 　　*Develop, analyze, and explain methods for solving problems involving proportions, such as scaling and finding equivalent ratios.*

Lesson 5 The State Fair	**Common Core State Standards** Ratios and Proportional Relationships 6.RP 　Understand ratio concepts and use ratio reasoning to solve problems. 　2. Understand the concept of a unit rate a/b associated with a ratio a:b 　　with b ≠ 0, and use rate language in the context of a ratio relationship. 　3. Use ratio and rate reasoning to solve real-world and mathematical 　　problems, 　　　a. Make tables of equivalent ratios relating quantities with whole- 　　　　number measurements, find missing values in the tables, and plot the 　　　　pairs of values on the coordinate plane. Use tables to compare ratios. 　　　b. Solve unit rate problems including those involving unit pricing and 　　　　constant speed. For example, if it took 7 hours to mow 4 lawns, then 　　　　at that rate, how many lawns could be mowed in 35 hours? At what 　　　　rate were lawns being mowed? Ratios and Proportional Relationships 7.RP 　Analyze proportional relationships and use them to solve real-world and 　mathematical problems. 　2. Recognize and represent proportional relationships between quantities. **NCTM** *Principles and Standards* Number and Operation Standard 　Compute fluently and make reasonable estimates. 　　*Select appropriate methods and tools for computing with fractions, and decimals* 　　*from among mental computation, estimation, calculators and computer, and* 　　*paper and pencil, depending on the situation and apply the selected methods.* 　　*Develop, analyze, and explain methods for solving problems involving* 　　*proportions, such as scaling and finding equivalent rations.* Algebra 　Understand patters, relations, and functions. 　　*Represent, analyze, and generalize a variety of patterns with tables, graphs,* 　　*words, and when possible, symbolic rules.*

Chapter 2　Algebraic Reasoning

Lesson 1 Walking Trip	**Common Core State Standards** Expressions and Equations 6.EE 　Reason about and solve one-variable equations and inequalities. 　5. Understand solving an equation or inequality as a process of answer a 　　question. Use substitution to determine whether a given number in a 　　specified set makes an equation or inequality true. 　7. Solve real-world and mathematical problems by writing and solving 　　equations of the form $x + p = q$ and $px = q$ for cases in which p, q, and x 　　are all nonnegative rational numbers. 　Represent and analyze quantitative relationships between dependent and 　independent variables. 　9. Use variables to represent two quantities in a real-world problem that 　　change in relationship to one another; write an equation to express one 　　quantity. Analyze the relationship between the dependent and 　　independent variables using graphs and tables, and relate these to the 　　equation. **NCTM** *Principles and Standards* Algebra 　Understand patterns, relations, and functions. 　　*Represent, analyze, and generalize a variety of patterns with tables, graphs,* 　　*words, and when possible symbolic rules.* 　Represent and analyze mathematical situations and structures using 　algebraic symbols. 　　*Use symbolic algebra to represent situations and to solve problems, especially* 　　*those that involve linear relationships.*

Lesson 2
Zapping Zombies
	Common Core State Standards
	Expressions and Equations 7.EE
	  Solve real-life and mathematical problems using numerical and algebraic
	  expressions and equations.
	  4. Use variables to represent quantities in a real-world or mathematical
	     problem, and construct simple equations and inequalities to solve
	     problems by reasoning about the quantities.
	
	NCTM *Principles and Standards*
	Numbers and Operations
	  Compute fluently and make reasonable estimates.
	    Develop, analyze, and explain methods for solving problems involving
	    proportions, such as scaling and finding equivalent ratios.
	Algebra
	  Use mathematical models to represent and understand quantitative
	  relationships.
	    Model and solve contextualized problems using various representations, such as
	    graphs, tables, and equations.
	  Analyze change in various contexts.
	    Use graphs to analyze the nature of changes in quantities in linear relationships.

Lesson 3
Downloading Music
	Common Core State Standards
	Expressions and Equations 8.EE
	  Analyze and solve linear equations and pairs of simultaneous linear
	  equations.
	  a. Understand that solutions to a system of two linear equations in two
	     variables correspond to points of intersection of their graphs, because
	     points of intersection satisfy both equations simultaneously.
	
	NCTM *Principles and Standards*
	Algebra
	  Represent and analyze mathematical situations and structures using
	  algebraic symbols.
	    Explore relationships between symbolic expressions and graphs of lines, paying
	    particular attention to the meaning of intercept and slope.
	    Use symbolic algebra to represent situations and to solve problems, especially
	    those that involve linear relationships.
	  Use mathematical models to represent and understand quantitative
	  relationships.
	    Model and solve contextualized problems using various representations, such as
	    graphs, tables, and equations.
	  Analyze change in various contexts.
	    Use graphs to analyze the nature of changes in quantities in linear relationships.

Chapter 3   Geometry

Lesson 1
What's My Size?
	Common Core State Standards
	Geometry 7.G
	  Draw, construct, and describe geometrical figures and describe the
	  relationships between them.
	  1. Solve problems involving scale drawings of geometric figures, including
	     computing actual lengths and areas from scale drawings and
	     reproducing a scale drawing at a different scale.
	
	NCTM *Principles and Standards*
	Geometry
	  Analyze characteristics and properties of two- and three-dimensional
	  geometric shapes and develop mathematical arguments about geometric
	  relationships.
	    Understand relationships among the angles, side lengths, perimeters, areas,
	    and volumes of similar objects.

Lesson 2
Candy Boxes
	Common Core State Standards
	Geometry 7.RP
	  Analyze proportional relationships and use them to solve real-world and mathematical problems.
	   2. Recognize and represent proportional relationships between quantities.
	     a. Decide whether two quantities are in a proportional relationship, e.g., by testing for equivalent ratios in tables or graphing on a coordinate plane and observing whether the graph is a straight line through the origin.
	Geometry 7.G
	  Draw, construct, and describe geometrical figures and describe the relationships between them.
	   6. Solve real-world and mathematical problems involving area, volume, and surface area of two- and three-dimensional objects composed of triangles, quadrilaterals, polygons, cubes, and right prisms.
	
	NCTM *Principles and Standards*
	Geometry
	  Analyze characteristics and properties of two- and three-dimensional geometric shapes and develop mathematical arguments about geometric relationships.
	    Understand relationships among the angles, side lengths, perimeters, areas, and volumes of similar objects.
	  Use visualization, spatial reasoning, and geometric modeling to solve problems.
	    Use two-dimensional representations of three-dimensional objects to visualize and solve problems such as those involving surface area and volume.

Lesson 3
Designing Figures
	Common Core State Standards
	Geometry 8.G
	  Understand congruence and similarity using physical models, transparencies, or geometry software.
	   3. Describe the effect of dilations, translations, rotations, and reflections on two-dimensional figures using coordinates.
	
	NCTM *Principles and Standards*
	Geometry
	  Apply transformations and use symmetry to analyze mathematical situations.
	    Describe sizes, positions, and orientations of shapes under informal transformations such as flips, turns, slides, and scaling.

Chapter 4   Measurement

Lesson 1
Centimeters to Inches
	Common Core State Standards
	Ratios and Proportional Relationships 6.RP
	Use ratio concepts and use ratio reasoning to solve problems.
	3. Understand ratio and rate reasoning to solve real-world and mathematical problems, e.g., by reasoning about tables of equivalent ratios, tape diagrams, double number line diagrams, or equations.
	   d. Use ratio reasoning to convert measurement units; manipulate and transform units appropriately when multiplying or dividing quantities.
	Ratios and Proportional Relationships 7.RP
	Analyze proportional relationships and use them to solve real-world and mathematical problems.
	2. Recognize and represent proportional relationships between quantities.
	   a. Decide whether two quantities are in a proportional relationship, e.g., by testing for equivalent ratios in a table or graphing on a coordinate plane and observing whether the graph is a straight line through the origin.
	   b. Identify the constant of proportionality (unit rate) in tables, graphs, equations, diagrams, and verbal descriptions of proportional reasoning.
	
	NCTM *Principles and Standards*
	Measurement
	Understand measurable attributes of objects and units, systems, and processes of measurement.
	Understand both metric and customary systems of measurement.

Lesson 2 How Tall?	**Common Core State Standards** Geometry 7.G Draw, construct, and describe geometric figures and describe the relationships between them. 1. Solve problems involving scale drawings of geometric figures including computing actual lengths and areas from a scale drawing and reproducing a scale drawing at a different scale. **NCTM** *Principles and Standards* Geometry Use visualization, spatial reasoning, and geometric modeling to solve problems. *Recognize and apply geometric ideas and relationships in areas outside the mathematics classroom, such as art, science, and everyday life.* Measurement Understand measurable attributes of objects and the units, systems, and processes of measurements. *Understand both metric and customary systems of measurement.* Apply appropriate techniques, tools, and formulas to determine measurements. *Select and apply techniques and tools to accurately find length, area, volume, and angle measures to appropriate levels of precision.*

Lesson 3
Park
	Common Core State Standards
	Ratios and Proportional Relationships 7.RP
	  Analyze proportional relationships and use them to solve real-world and mathematical problems.
	  2. Recognize and represent proportional relationships between quantities.
	Geometry 7.G
	  Draw, construct, and describe geometrical figures and describe the relationships between them.
	  1. Solve problems involving scale drawings of geometric figures, including computing actual lengths and areas from a scale drawing and reproducing a scale drawing at a different scale.
	  6. Solve real-world and mathematical problems involving area, volume, and surface area of two- and three-dimensional objects composed of triangles, quadrilaterals, polygons, cubes, and right prisms.
	
	NCTM *Principles and Standards*
	Geometry
	  Use visualization, spatial reasoning, and geometric modeling to solve problems.
	    Draw geometric objects with specified properties, such as side lengths or angle measures.
	Measurement
	  Apply appropriate techniques, tools, and formulas to determine measurements.
	    Select and apply techniques and tools to accurately find length, area, volume, and angle measures to appropriate levels of precision.
	    Solve problems involving scale factors, using ratio and proportion.

Chapter 5 Probability and Statistics

Lesson 1
Winner Every Time
	Common Core State Standards
	Statistics and Probability 7.SP
	  Investigate chance processes and develop, use, and evaluate probability models.
	  6. Approximate the probability of a chance event by collecting data on the chance process that produces it and observing its long-run relative frequency, and predict the approximate relative frequency given the probability. For example, when rolling a number cube 600 times, predict that a 3 or 6 would be rolled roughly 200 times, but probability not exactly 200 times.
	
	NCTM *Principles and Standards*
	Data Analysis and Probability
	  Understand and apply basic concepts of probability.
	    Use proportionality and a basic understanding of probability to make and test conjectures about the results of experiments and simulations.
	    Compute probabilities for simple, compound events, using such methods as organized lists, tree diagrams, and area models.

Lesson 2 Fair or Not?	**Common Core State Standards** Statistics and Probability 7.SP Investigate chance processes and develop, use, and evaluate probability models. 7. Develop a probability model and use it to find probabilities of events. Compare probabilities from a model to observed frequencies; if the agreement is not good, explain possible sources of the discrepancy. b. Develop a probability model (which may not be uniform) by observing frequencies in data generated from a chance process. For example, find the approximate probability that a spinning penny will land hands up or that a tossed paper cut will land open-end down. Do the outcomes for the spinning penny appear to be equally likely based on the observed frequencies? **NCTM** *Principles and Standards* Data Analysis and Probability Understand and apply basic concepts of probability. *Use proportionality and a basic understanding of probability to make and test conjectures about the results of experiments and simulations.* *Compute probabilities for simple compound events, using such methods as organized lists, tree diagrams, and area models.*
Lesson 3 Typical Me	**Common Core State Standards** Statistics and Probability 7.SP Use random sampling to draw inferences about a population. 1. Understand that statistics can be used to gain information about a population by examining a sample of that population; generalizations about a population from a sample are valid only if the sample is representative of that population. Understand that random sampling tends to produce representative samples and support valid inferences. **NCTM** *Principles and Standards* Data Analysis and Probability Formulate questions that can be addressed with data and collect, organize, and display relevant data to answer them. *Formulate questions, design studies, and collect data about a characteristic shared by two populations or different characteristics within one population.*
Lesson 4 Arms and Feet	**Common Core State Standards** Statistics and Probability 8.SP Investigate patterns of associate in bivariate data. 1. Construct and interpret scatter plots for bivariate measurement data to investigate patterns of association between two quantities. Describe patterns such as clustering, outliers, positive or negative association, linear association, and nonlinear association. **NCTM** *Principles and Standards* Data Analysis and Probability Select and use appropriate statistical methods to analyze data. *Discuss and understand the correspondence between data sets and their graphical representations, especially histograms, stem-and-leaf plots, box plots, and scatter plots.*

Correlations to Curricula

The lessons in *It's All Connected!* are herein directly correlated to four of the leading middle school mathematics programs

- Pearson: Connected Mathematics 2
- Glencoe/McGraw-Hill: Math Connects: Concepts, Skills and Problem Solving Courses 1, 2, 3
- Prentice Hall: Mathematics Courses 1, 2, 3
- Holt McDougal: Mathematics Courses 1, 2, 3

Use these tables to further facilitate the use of these lessons with your curricula.

Correlation to Pearson: Connected Mathematics 2				
It's All Connected: The Power of Proportional Reasoning to Understand Mathematics Concepts		Grade 6	Grade 7	Grade 8
Chapter 1 Number and Operation	Lesson 1: Equivalence: Many Names for Fractions	Bits and Pieces I: Investigation 2		
	Lesson 2: Sale, Sale, Sale!	Bits and Pieces III: Investigation 4	Comparing and Scaling: Investigation 2	
	Lesson 3: Dividing Fractions	Bits and Pieces II: Investigation 4		
	Lesson 4: Cookie Recipe	Bits and Pieces II: Investigation 2	Comparing and Scaling: Investigation 2	
	Lesson 5: The State Fair	Bits and Pieces III: Investigation 2		
Chapter 2 Algebraic Reasoning	Lesson 1: Walking Trip		Moving Straight Ahead: Investigation 1	Thinking with Mathematical Models: Investigation 2
	Lesson 2: Zapping Zombies		Comparing and Scaling: Investigation 3	Thinking with Mathematical Models: Investigation 2

Correlation to Pearson: Connected Mathematics 2			
It's All Connected: The Power of Proportional Reasoning to Understand Mathematics Concepts	Grade 6	Grade 7	Grade 8
Chapter 2 Algebraic Reasoning — Lesson 3: Downloading Music		Comparing and Scaling: Investigation 3	Thinking with Mathematical Models: Investigation 2
Chapter 3 Geometry — Lesson 1: What's My Size?	Covering and Surrounding: Investigation 4	Stretching and Shrinking: Investigation 2	
Chapter 3 Geometry — Lesson 2: Candy Boxes	Covering and Surrounding: Investigation 4	Filling and Wrapping: Investigation 2	Thinking with Mathematical Models: Investigation 1
Chapter 3 Geometry — Lesson 3: Designing Figures			Kaleidoscope, Hubcaps, and Mirrors: Investigation 5
Chapter 4 Measurement — Lesson 1: Centimeters to Inches	Covering and Surrounding: Investigation 2	Comparing and Scaling: Investigation 4	
Chapter 4 Measurement — Lesson 2: How Tall?	Covering and Surrounding: Investigation 4	Stretching and Shrinking: Investigation 5	Looking for Pythagoras: Investigation 4
Chapter 4 Measurement — Lesson 3: Park		Stretching and Shrinking: Investigation 3	
Chapter 5 Probability and Statistics — Lesson 1: Winner Every Time	How Likely Is It?: Investigation 4	What Do You Expect?: Investigation 1	
Chapter 5 Probability and Statistics — Lesson 2: Fair or Not?		What Do You Expect?: Investigation 1	
Chapter 5 Probability and Statistics — Lesson 3: Typical Me	Data About Us: Investigation 3	Data Distributions: Investigation 3	Samples and Populations: Investigation 2
Chapter 5 Probability and Statistics — Lesson 4: Arms and Feet			Samples and Populations: Investigation 4

Correlation to Glencoe/McGraw-Hill: Math Connects: Concepts, Skills and Problem Solving Courses 1, 2, and 3				
It's All Connected: The Power of Proportional Reasoning to Understand Mathematics Concepts		Math Connects: Course 1 Grade 6	Math Connects: Course 2 Grade 7	Math Connects: Course 3 Grade 8
Chapter 1 Number and Operation	Lesson 1: Equivalence: Many Names for Fractions	Chapter 4: Fractions and Decimals	Chapter 4: Fractions, Decimals, and Percents	
	Lesson 2: Sale, Sale, Sale!	Chapter 5: Operation with Fractions	Chapter 5: Applying Fractions	
	Lesson 3: Dividing Fractions	Chapter 5: Operations with Fractions	Chapter 5: Applying Fractions	
	Lesson 4: Cookie Recipe	Chapter 6: Ratio, Proportion and Functions	Chapter 6: Ratio and Proportions	Chapter 4: Proportions and Similarity
	Lesson 5: The State Fair	Chapter 6: Ratio, Proportion and Functions	Chapter 6: Ratio and Proportions	Chapter 4: Proportions and Similarity
Chapter 2 Algebraic Reasoning	Lesson 1: Walking Trip	Chapter 1: Algebra: Number Patterns and Functions	Chapter 1: Introduction to Algebra and Functions	Chapter 1: Algebra
	Lesson 2: Zapping Zombies	Chapter 6: Ratio, Proportion and Functions	Chapter 6: Ratio and Proportions	Chapter 4: Proportions and Similarity
	Lesson 3: Downloading Music	Chapter 12: Algebra: Properties and Equations	Chapter 3: Algebra Linear Equations and Functions	Chapter 9: Algebra: Linear Functions

Correlation to Glencoe/McGraw-Hill: Math Connects: Concepts, Skills and Problem Solving Courses 1, 2, and 3			
It's All Connected: The Power of Proportional Reasoning to Understand Mathematics Concepts	Math Connects: Course 1 Grade 6	Math Connects: Course 2 Grade 7	Math Connects: Course 3 Grade 8
Chapter 3 Geometry — Lesson 1: What's My Size?		Chapter 10: Geometry: Polygons	Chapter 4: Proportions and Similarity
Chapter 3 Geometry — Lesson 2: Candy Boxes	Chapter 12: Algebra: Properties and Equations	Chapter 6: Ratio and Proportions	
Chapter 3 Geometry — Lesson 3: Designing Figures		Chapter 10: Geometry: Polygons	Chapter 4: Proportions and Similarity
Chapter 4 Measurement — Lesson 1: Centimeters to Inches	Chapter 8: Systems of Measurements	Chapter 6: Ratio and Proportions	Chapter 6: Geometry and Spatial Reasoning
Chapter 4 Measurement — Lesson 2: How Tall?		Chapter 6: Ratio and Proportions	Chapter 6: Geometry and Spatial Reasoning
Chapter 4 Measurement — Lesson 3: Park		Chapter 12: Geometry and Measurement	Chapter 6: Geometry and Spatial Reasoning
Chapter 5 Probability and Statistics — Lesson 1: Winner Every Time	Chapter 7: Percent and Probability	Chapter 9: Probability	Chapter 12: Probability
Chapter 5 Probability and Statistics — Lesson 2: Fair or Not?	Chapter 7: Percent and Probability	Chapter 9: Probability	Chapter 12: Probability
Chapter 5 Probability and Statistics — Lesson 3: Typical Me	Chapter 6: Ratio, Proportion and Functions	Chapter 8: Statistics: Analyzing Data	Chapter 11: Statistics
Chapter 5 Probability and Statistics — Lesson 4: Arms and Feet		Chapter 8: Statistics: Analyzing Data	Chapter 9: Algebra: Linear Functions

Correlation to Prentice Hall: Mathematics Courses 1, 2, and 3			
It's All Connected: The Power of Proportional Reasoning to Understand Mathematics Concepts		Mathematics Course 1 Grade 6	Mathematics Course 2 Grade 7	Mathematics Course 3 Grade 8
Chapter 1 Number and Operation	Lesson 1: Equivalence: Many Names for Fractions	Chapter 4: Number Theory and Fractions	Chapter 2: Exponents, Factors, and Fractions	Chapter 2: Rational Numbers
	Lesson 2: Sale, Sale, Sale!	Chapter 7: Ratio, Proportions, and Percents	Chapter 5: Ratios, Rates, and Proportions	Chapter 5: Application of Percent
	Lesson 3: Dividing Fractions	Chapter 6: Multiplying and Dividing Fractions	Chapter 3: Operations with Fractions	Chapter 2: Rational Numbers
	Lesson 4: Cookie Recipe	Chapter 7: Ratio, Proportions, and Percents	Chapter 5: Ratios, Rates, and Proportions	Chapter 4: Application of Proportions
	Lesson 5: The State Fair	Chapter 1: Whole Numbers and Decimals	Chapter 1: Decimals and Integers	Chapter 2: Rational Numbers
Chapter 2 Algebraic Reasoning	Lesson 1: Walking Trip	Chapter 11: Integers	Chapter 4 Equations and Inequalities	Chapter 6: Equations and Inequalities
	Lesson 2: Zapping Zombies	Chapter 11: Integers	Chapter 4 Equations and Inequalities	Chapter 4: Application of Proportions
	Lesson 3: Downloading Music	Chapter 11: Integers	Chapter 4 Equations and Inequalities	Chapter 6: Equations and Inequalities

Correlation to Prentice Hall: Mathematics Courses 1, 2, and 3				
It's All Connected: The Power of Proportional Reasoning to Understand Mathematics Concepts		Mathematics Course 1 Grade 6	Mathematics Course 2 Grade 7	Mathematics Course 3 Grade 8
Chapter 3 Geometry	Lesson 1: What's My Size?	Chapter 8: Tools of Geometry	Chapter 7: Geometry	Chapter 4: Application of Proportions
	Lesson 2: Candy Boxes	Chapter 9: Geometry and Measurement	Chapter 8: Measurement	Chapter 8: Measurement
	Lesson 3: Designing Figures			Chapter 4: Application of Proportions
Chapter 4 Measurement	Lesson 1: Centimeters to Inches	Chapter 9: Geometry and Measurement	Chapter 9: Patterns and Rules	Chapter 8: Measurement
	Lesson 2: How Tall?		Chapter 5: Ratios, Rates, and Proportions	Chapter 4: Application of Proportions
	Lesson 3: Park		Chapter 5: Ratios, Rates, and Proportions	Chapter 4: Application of Proportions
Chapter 5 Probability and Statistics	Lesson 1: Winner Every Time	Chapter 10: Exploring Probability	Chapter 12: Using Probability	Chapter 10: Probability
	Lesson 2: Fair or Not?	Chapter 10: Exploring Probability	Chapter 12: Using Probability	Chapter 10: Probability
	Lesson 3: Typical Me	Chapter 10: Exploring Probability	Chapter 11: Displaying and Analyzing Data	Chapter 9: Using Graphs to Analyze Data
	Lesson 4: Arms and Feet		Chapter 11: Displaying and Analyzing Data	Chapter 9: Using Graphs to Analyze Data

Correlation to Holt McDougal: Mathematics Courses 1, 2, and 3				
It's All Connected: The Power of Proportional Reasoning to Understand Mathematics Concepts		**Mathematics Course 1 Grade 6**	**Mathematics Course 2 Grade 7**	**Mathematics Course 3 Grade 8**
Chapter 1 Number and Operation	Lesson 1: Equivalence: Many Names for Fractions	Chapter 4: Number Theory and Fractions		
	Lesson 2: Sale, Sale, Sale!	Chapter 7: Proportional Relationships	Chapter 4: Proportional Relationships	Chapter 2: Rational Numbers
	Lesson 3: Dividing Fractions	Chapter 5: Fraction Operations	Chapter 3: Applying Rational Numbers	Chapter 2: Rational Numbers
	Lesson 4: Cookie Recipe	Chapter 7: Proportional Relationships	Chapter 8: Percents	
	Lesson 5: The State Fair	Chapter 7: Proportional Relationships	Chapter 4: Proportional Relationships	Chapter 5: Ratios, Proportions, and Similarity
Chapter 2 Algebraic Reasoning	Lesson 1: Walking Trip	Chapter 13: Functions, Equations, and Inequalities	Chapter 5: Graphs and Functions	Chapter 3: Graphs and Functions
	Lesson 2: Zapping Zombies	Chapter 13: Functions, Equations, and Inequalities	Chapter 5: Graphs and Functions	Chapter 5: Ratios, Proportions, and Similarity
	Lesson 3: Downloading Music		Chapter 5: Graphs and Functions	Chapter 5: Graphs and Functions

Correlation to Holt McDougal: Mathematics Courses 1, 2, and 3			
It's All Connected: The Power of Proportional Reasoning to Understand Mathematics Concepts	**Mathematics Course 1 Grade 6**	**Mathematics Course 2 Grade 7**	**Mathematics Course 3 Grade 8**
Chapter 3 Geometry	Lesson 1: What's My Size?		Chapter 4: Proportional Relationships	Chapter 7: Foundations of Geometry
	Lesson 2: Candy Boxes	Chapter 10: Measurement: Area and Volume	Chapter 8: Geometric Figures	Chapter 8: Perimeter, Area, and Volume
	Lesson 3: Designing Figures			Chapter 5: Ratios, Proportions, and Similarity
Chapter 4 Measurement	Lesson 1: Centimeters to Inches	Chapter 9: Measurement and Geometry	Chapter 4: Proportional Relationships	
	Lesson 2: How Tall?		Chapter 8: Geometric figures	Chapter 7: Foundations of Geometry
	Lesson 3: Park		Chapter 9: Measurement: Two-Dimensional Figures	Chapter 7: Foundations of Geometry
Chapter 5 Probability and Statistics	Lesson 1: Winner Every Time	Chapter 12: Probability	Chapter 11: Probability	Chapter 10: Probability
	Lesson 2: Fair or Not?	Chapter 12: Probability	Chapter 11: Probability	Chapter 10: Probability
	Lesson 3: Typical Me	Chapter 6: Collecting and Displaying Data	Chapter 7: Collecting, Displaying, and Analyzing Data	Chapter 9: Data and Statistics
	Lesson 4: Arms and Feet			Chapter 9: Data and Statistics

CHAPTER 1 — NUMBER AND OPERATIONS

LESSON 1

EQUIVALENCE: MANY NAMES FOR FRACTIONS

Common Core State Standards
Ratios and Proportional
Relationships 4.RP

Understand ratio concepts
and use ratio reasoning to
solve problems.

1. Understand the
   concept of a ratio and use
   ratio language to describe
   a ratio relationship
   between two quantities.
   For example, "The ratio of
   wings to beaks in the bird
   house at the zoo was 2:1,
   because for every 2 wings
   there was 1 beak." "For
   every vote candidate A
   received, candidate B
   received nearly 3 votes."

NCTM Correlation
Number and Operation Standard
Understanding numbers,
ways of representing
numbers, relationships
among numbers, and
number systems.
*Work flexibly with
fractions, decimals, and
percents to solve
problems.*
Understand meanings of
operations and how they
relate to one another.
*Understand the
meanings and effect of
arithmetic operations
with fractions, decimals,
and integers.*

LESSON GOALS

- To identify the numerator and denominator of a fraction and how each relates to the part and the whole.
- Develop strategies for finding equivalent fractions.
- Simplify a fraction.

LESSON INTRODUCTION

In this lesson, students will develop strategies to find equivalent fractions. Some students might suggest, "If you multiply the numerator and the denominator by the same number, you get an equivalent fraction." Students will use a model to make sense of why this works.

> **Equivalents fractions** have the same value, but they look different. Multiply or divide the numerator and denominator of a fraction by 1, written as a fraction, to produce an equivalent fraction.

Take students through a review to remind them what the numerator and what the denominator tells them. Students may discuss that two fractions may name the same part of the whole; for example, $\frac{1}{2}$ and $\frac{3}{6}$.

The role of proportional reasoning helps students develop strategies for making sense of equivalent fractions.

Discuss with students the role of 1 when writing equivalent fractions.

TEACHING SUGGESTIONS

Within the bulleted text below are suggestions on how to begin the lesson, introduce essential vocabulary, and question students so that they are prepared to complete the Student Recording Page on their own or with minimal assistance.

- What happens when a number is multiplied by one?
    Any number n multiplied by 1 equals n.
    Any number n × 1 = n.
    $24 \times 1 = 24 \quad 1,000 \times 1 = 1,000 \quad 1,697 \times 1 = 1,697$

- What happens when a number is divided by one?
    Any number n divided by 1 = n.
    $32 \div 1 = 32 \quad 2,500 \div 1 = 2,500 \quad 876 \div 1 = 876$

- What happens if you multiply or divide a fraction by 1?

    $\frac{2}{3} \times 1 = \frac{2}{3}$ $\qquad\qquad$ $\frac{3}{5} \div 1 = \frac{3}{5}$

    $\frac{3}{4} \times 1 = \frac{3}{4}$ $\qquad\qquad$ $\frac{7}{8} \div 1 = \frac{7}{8}$

Because 1 can be written as $\frac{n}{n}$, you can multiply or divide any fraction by $\frac{n}{n}$ to get an equivalent fraction.

$$\frac{3}{4} \times \boxed{\frac{4}{4}} = \frac{12}{16} \qquad\qquad \frac{12}{16} \div \boxed{\frac{4}{4}} = \frac{3}{4}$$

In the illustration above, $\frac{3}{4}$ is in simplest form, but $\frac{12}{16}$ is not.

> A fraction written in **simplest form** means that its numerator and denominator have no common whole number factors. To **simplify** a fraction is to write the fraction in simplest form.

Draw the figure below on the board. Work with students to answer the following questions:

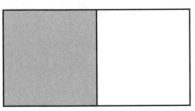

- If this represented a sheet of wrapping paper that was about to be cut, what fraction of the sheet would be cut? $\frac{1}{2}$

- If this whole was cut into 6 equal parts , what would the $\frac{1}{2}$ now represent? $\frac{3}{6}$

- If the whole was cut into 12 equal parts, what would the $\frac{1}{2}$ now represent? $\frac{6}{12}$

- Suppose the whole was cut into 50 equal parts, what would the $\frac{1}{2}$ now represent? $\frac{25}{50}$

- What is another name that could describe this shaded part?
  Possible answer: $\frac{50}{100}$

- Why does the same shaded area have multiple fraction names?
  The shaded amount does not change, but the number and size of parts can increase or decrease. This results in multiple names to describe the shaded amount.

- What can be said about these fractions? *The fractions are equivalent.*

STUDENT ENGAGEMENT

Instruct students that their challenge is to find a strategy to generate multiple fraction names that describe the same shaded area or quantity. Have students work in groups to complete Student Recording Page 1.1. As students work, ask questions to check for understanding.

QUESTIONS FOR STRUGGLING STUDENTS

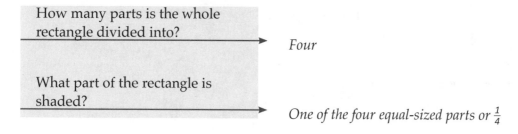

How many parts is the whole rectangle divided into?

→ *Four*

What part of the rectangle is shaded?

→ *One of the four equal-sized parts or $\frac{1}{4}$*

What does the numerator of a fraction represent?

→ *the number of equal-sized parts you are considering*

What does the denominator of a fraction represent?

→ *the number of equal-sized parts into which the whole has been divided*

If you divide only the shaded area of the rectangle, would you be able to name the fraction?

→ *No, because the whole rectangle will not be cut into equal-sized parts*

As you divide the whole into more parts, what happens to the size of the parts? What happens to the denominator of the fraction that describes the part/whole relationship?

→ *The equal-sized parts get smaller and the denominator becomes greater.*

Why is $\frac{1}{2}$ equivalent to $\frac{6}{12}$?

→ *If the original fraction was $\frac{1}{2}$ that means the whole was cut up into two equal-size parts and those parts are considered. A denominator of 12 means each of the original 2 parts have 6 equal-sized parts. So, there are 12 parts in all. To keep the fraction equivalent the 1 in my numerator has to be cut into 6 equal-sized parts so that $\frac{1}{2} = \frac{6}{12}$.*

Draw a number line. Where are $\frac{1}{2}$ and $\frac{6}{12}$ (or any two equivalent fractions) located on a number line?

→ *in the same location*

What does the picture above Question 1 represent?

→ *a rectangle divided into 4 equal-sized parts with one of those parts shaded, or $\frac{1}{4}$ shaded*

What happens to the fraction as you cut the whole into more parts?

→ *The denominator becomes greater, and the fraction representing the shaded region is renamed.*

What do you know about the first two fractions?

→ *They are equivalent to each other.*

How can you find another fraction name to represent this shaded region?

→ *Find another equivalent fraction; you can multiply the fraction by 1 in the form of $\frac{5}{5}$ to get $\frac{5}{20}$.*

Can you find a fraction with a denominator of 36 that would represent the same amount?

→ *Find the $\frac{9}{9}$ multiple of the numerator and denominator that will name the new fraction; $\frac{9}{36}$.*

What strategy did you use to find an equivalent fraction?

→ *Multiply or divide by different forms of 1; for example $\frac{2}{2}$, $\frac{5}{5}$, and $\frac{6}{6}$.*

In the first task, you dealt with the fractions $\frac{1}{4}$, $\frac{2}{8}$, and $\frac{4}{16}$. Draw and locate these numbers on a number line. Which fraction is closest to 0?

→ *Students should realize these are equivalent fractions are represented by the same location on a number line.*

Why do fractions have different names for the same amount?

> *It depends on the number of parts into which the whole was divided.*

If you have the fraction $\frac{2}{3}$ and you want to find an equivalent fraction with a numerator of 8, what form of 1 do you need? What operation do you use? What will be the denominator?

> *Multiply by $\frac{4}{4}$. The denominator will be 12.*

Is $\frac{2}{7}$ another name used to describe $\frac{14}{35}$? Explain why or why not.

> *No, because you need to multiply $\frac{2}{7}$ by 1 in the form of $\frac{7}{7}$ to get a numerator of 14, but the denominator would be 49, not 35.*

What is another fraction name for $\frac{2}{7}$?

> *Another fraction name for $\frac{2}{7}$ is $\frac{14}{49}$.*

What operation do you use to rename a fraction using fewer parts?

> *division*

If you have two equivalent fractions, what happens to the fraction model as the numerator and denominator get larger?

> *The whole is divided into smaller parts. It takes more of the smaller parts to be equivalent to the original fraction.*

What role do factors and multiples play when working with equivalent fractions?

When you have equivalent fractions, both numerators and denominators of the fractions can be either factors of each other or multiples of each other. For example, $\frac{2}{3} = \frac{6}{9}$, 6 is a multiple of 2 and 9 is a multiple of 3. For $\frac{8}{20} = \frac{2}{5}$, 2 is a factor of 8 and 5 is a factor of 20.

What makes two or more fractions easy to compare?

Fractions with the same denominators means the whole is partitioned into the same number of parts. You can compare how many of those parts you have by comparing the numerators. Fractions with the same numerators means comparing the same number of parts but a different number of total parts. The greater the number in the denominator, the smaller the parts.

Using what you know about equivalent fractions, tell how you can find three factions between $\frac{4}{5}$ and $\frac{5}{4}$?

Rename the fractions to $\frac{16}{20}$ and $\frac{25}{20}$, then name any fraction between these two fractions.

How can you prove $\frac{4}{6} + \frac{2}{9} = \frac{8}{9}$?

$\frac{4}{6}$ simplifies to $\frac{2}{3}$; rename $\frac{2}{3}$ to $\frac{6}{9}$; $\frac{6}{9} + \frac{2}{9} = \frac{8}{9}$.

LESSON SUMMARY

As you summarize the Student Recording Pages ask students questions about generalizing strategies for finding equivalent fractions. Students should connect their strategies of multiplying by a form of one to the model. Proportional reasoning comes into play when students see that if the total number of parts are doubled, tripled, etc, then the number of shaded parts will double, triple, etc, as well.

Students connect this to the mathematical representation of the numerator and denominator being operated on by the same multiple (i.e. if the new numerator is 5 times greater than the old numerator, then the new denominator must be 5 times greater as well). If students see equivalent fractions as keeping things proportionally balanced, they begin to see the role of proportional reasoning in finding equivalent fractions.

This becomes an opportunity to view fraction parts as increasing or decreasing by the same rate to represent the same amount of the whole.

Addition and subtraction of fractions have connections to equivalence. When students understand equivalence, they use this knowledge to make sense of finding common denominators, which leads to the algorithms for addition and subtraction of fractions.

CHECK FOR SUCCESS

☐ Have students write about the strategies used in this lesson to help them cement their thinking about each situation.

☐ Have students write two fractions with different denominators. Then, students can rewrite the fractions as equivalent fractions so the new fractions have common denominators.

Student _____ Class _____ Date _____

LESSON 1

EQUIVALENCE: MANY NAMES FOR FRACTIONS

Use the rectangle below for Questions 1 – 3.

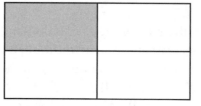

1. Name the part of the rectangle that is shaded. Divide each of the parts of the
    rectangle into two equal-sized parts. Write another fraction name that
    represents the shaded part of the rectangle.

2. Redraw your new rectangle. Divide each of the parts into two equal-sized
    parts. Write another fraction name that represents the shaded part of the
    rectangle.

3. Write the fraction names for the shaded parts of the three rectangles. What is
    the relationship among the fractions? Use mathematics to justify the
    relationship.

From *It's All Connected: The Power of Proportional Reasoning to Understand Mathematics Concepts, Grades 6–8* by Carmen Whitman. © 2011 Scholastic Inc. Permission granted to photocopy for nonprofit use in a classroom or similar place dedicated to face-to-face educational instruction.

4. Write three equivalent fractions for each fraction.

   a. $\frac{2}{3}$

   b. $\frac{3}{5}$

   c. $\frac{6}{8}$

   d.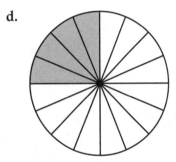

5. Use the equivalent fractions for $\frac{2}{3}$ to draw models that prove the fractions are equivalent.

6. A fraction written in simplest form means that its numerator and denominator have no common whole number factors. In Question 4, are all your answers fractions in the simplest form? Which of fractions were given in simplest form? Write the simplest form for each fraction in Question 4.

7. Write $\frac{16}{40}$ in simplest form. Justify your answer.

8. Write a strategy for finding any equivalent fraction.

9. Write each fraction in simplest form.

   a. $\frac{6}{8}$ **b.** $\frac{5}{15}$

   c. $\frac{36}{42}$ **d.** $\frac{7}{21}$

   e. $7\frac{6}{9}$ **f.** $\frac{15}{40}$

   g. $\frac{9}{27}$ **h.** $5\frac{3}{33}$

10. Taylor said that the fractions $\frac{2}{6}$ and $\frac{5}{15}$ are equivalent. Do you agree? Explain.

From *It's All Connected: The Power of Proportional Reasoning to Understand Mathematics Concepts, Grades 6–8* by Carmen Whitman. © 2011 Scholastic Inc. Permission granted to photocopy for nonprofit use in a classroom or similar place dedicated to face-to-face educational instruction.

1. $\frac{1}{4}$; 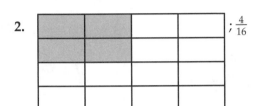 ; Another fraction name is $\frac{2}{8}$.

2. 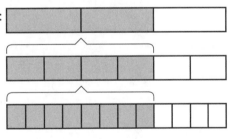 ; $\frac{4}{16}$

3. $\frac{1}{4}$, $\frac{2}{8}$, and $\frac{4}{16}$ are equivalent fractions;

$$\frac{1}{4} \times \frac{2}{2} = \frac{2}{8} \qquad \frac{2}{8} \times \frac{2}{2} = \frac{4}{16} \qquad \frac{1}{4} \times \frac{4}{4} = \frac{4}{16} \qquad \text{So, } \frac{1}{4} = \frac{2}{8} = \frac{4}{16}$$

4. Sample answers:
   a. $\frac{4}{6}, \frac{6}{9}, \frac{8}{12}$ b. $\frac{6}{10}, \frac{9}{15}, \frac{12}{20}$ c. $\frac{12}{16}, \frac{18}{24}, \frac{24}{32}$ d. $\frac{1}{4}, \frac{2}{8}, \frac{8}{32}$

5. Answers will vary; Sample answer:

$$\frac{2}{3} = \frac{4}{6} = \frac{8}{12}$$

6. No; parts a and b, $\frac{2}{3}$ and $\frac{3}{5}$, are in simplest form. The simplest form of $\frac{6}{8}$ is $\frac{3}{4}$. The simplest form of $\frac{4}{16}$ is $\frac{1}{4}$.

7. $\frac{2}{5}$; Justifications may vary; $\dfrac{16}{40} \div \dfrac{8}{8} = \dfrac{2}{5}$

8. Some suggested strategies:

   - To find equivalent fractions, multiply or divide by 1 in the form of $\frac{n}{n}$.

   - To find equivalent fractions, multiply or divide the numerator and denominator by the same factor.

9. a. $\frac{6}{8} = \frac{3}{4}$

    b. $\frac{5}{15} = \frac{1}{3}$

    c. $\frac{36}{42} = \frac{6}{7}$

    d. $\frac{7}{21} = \frac{1}{3}$

    e. $7\frac{6}{9} = 7\frac{2}{3}$

    f. $\frac{15}{40} = \frac{3}{8}$

    g. $\frac{9}{27} = \frac{1}{3}$

    h. $5\frac{3}{33} = 5\frac{1}{11}$

10. Yes, $\frac{2}{6}$ simplifies to $\frac{1}{3}$ by dividing by 1 in the form of $\frac{2}{2}$; $\frac{5}{15}$ also simplifies to $\frac{1}{3}$ by dividing by 1 in the form of $\frac{5}{5}$.

Common Core State Standards

Ratios and Proportional Relationships 6.RP

Understand ratio concepts and use ratio reasoning to solve problems.

3. Use ratio and rate reasoning to solve real-world and mathematical problems, e.g., by reasoning about tables of equivalent ratios, tape diagrams, double number line diagrams, or equations.

   c. Find a percent of a quantity as a rate per 100 (e.g., 30% of a quantity means 30/100 times the quantity); solve problems involving finding the whole, given a part and the percent.

Ratios and Proportional Relationships 7.RP

Analyze proportional relationships and use them to solve real-world and mathematical problems.

3. Use proportional relationships to solve multistep ratio and percent problems. Examples: simple interest, tax, markups and markdowns, gratuities and commissions, fees, percent increase and decrease, percent error.

LESSON GOALS

- Introduce percents and percent bars (i.e. double number line diagram) as a visual representation of a part-whole relationship out of 100.
- Make connections between characteristics of proportional relationships to percent situations.
- Use partitioning and benchmarks to make sense of percents.

LESSON INTRODUCTION

To begin the lesson, arrange students into two groups to play a minute challenge game. Each group tosses paper balls into a wastebasket. At the end of the minute, discuss with students how to decide which group won the challenge. Example: Group 1 made 15 out of 20 shots and Group 2 made 13 out of 18 shots.

- How can we find out which group won?
  Find a percentage.

Encourage students that while they work on the lesson and learn new vocabulary terms to consider how to find which group won the challenge. After instructing students on the lesson, return the discussion to the one-minute challenge and determine which group had the best percentage to win the challenge.

> **Percent** means per one hundred; out of 100. A misconception students have about percents is the total must be 100.

Students can use their understanding of proportional relationships to make sense of percents.

TEACHING SUGGESTIONS

Within the bulleted text below are suggestions on how to begin the lesson, introduce essential vocabulary, and question students so that they are prepared to complete the Student Recording Page on their own or with minimal assistance.

- In what type of situations do you hear the word *percent* used? What are some real-life examples that involve percent?
  Answers will vary, but will likely include test scores.

- Explain the meaning of percent.

Explain that 20 out of 50 is 40%. Instruct students to think, if you answered 20 out of 50 questions correct, how many questions out of 100 would you answer correctly if you performed with the same accuracy?
50 doubled is 100, so you have to double 20 to get 40.

Another example is 5 out of 10 is 50%. You have to multiply 10 by 10 to get 100; so multiply 5 by 10 to get 50.

The following equation, or formula, can help students understand the relationships of original price and a discount.

percent discount + percent paid = 100% original price

- Introduce a percent bar (i.e. double number line diagram) to students. Use 1-in. × $8\frac{1}{2}$ in. strips of paper that can be affixed to larger paper or have the students draw a bar on their papers. The strips are optimal as students can fold strips into equal parts to determine their benchmarks. Tell students to use what they know about fractions or decimals to help create a percent bar diagram.

A **percent bar diagram** is a visual method of showing 100% and comparing percents. Percent bars are available in the educational manipulatives market or handmade percent bars can be made using strips of paper.

NCTM Correlation
Number and Operation Standard
   Understand numbers, ways of representing numbers, relationships among numbers, and number systems.
      Work flexibly with fractions, decimals, and percents to solve problems.
   Understand and use ratios and proportions to represent quantitative relationships.

Materials
   Student Recording Page 1.2
   Paper balls
   Waste paper basket
   Straightedge
Optional:
   Paper strips 1-by-$8\frac{1}{2}$ inch
   Tape
   Glue

Vocabulary
   Percent
   Percent discount
   Percent bar diagrams

Percent discount means the percentage is subtracted from the original amount.

- When using Fraction Bars, what does one bar represent? *It represents a whole, or 1.*

- What do you think the whole represents in a percent bar? *100%*

Draw and label the diagram shown below.

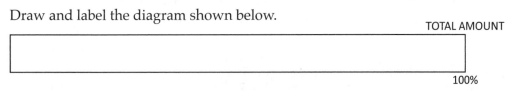

TOTAL AMOUNT

100%

- When the bar is folded in half into 2 equal parts, what fraction can you use to name the fold in the center? $\frac{1}{2}$

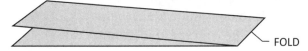

FOLD

- What do you think we can name that fold in our percent bar? *50%*

Draw and label the diagram shown below.

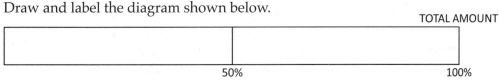

TOTAL AMOUNT

50%   100%

- What other benchmarks could we find and label on the percent bar?
  Answers may include 10%, 25%, and 75%

- If 100% represents 60, how can that be shown on the percent bar?
  Write 60 at the end where 100% is, but write it above the bar.

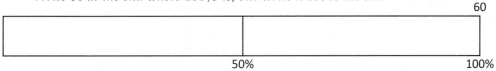

60

50%   100%

- When the whole is 60, what number is represented by the 50% mark? *30*

- What other benchmarks can you find and label?
  Students should find and label at least 25% and 75%.

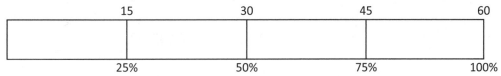

15   30   45   60

25%   50%   75%   100%

- Can the 100% represent any whole amount? *Yes*

- Today's problem involves determining the sale prices. Instead of finding the percentage of problems correct on a test, you will be finding a percent of a dollar amount.

- Have students make a percent bar that represents $80.00 as the 100% and have them find 10%, 20%, 30%, 40%, 50%, 60%, 70%, 80%, and 90%.

STUDENT ENGAGEMENT

Have students work with a partner. Students should read the problem on Student Recording Page 1.2 and restate the problem using their own words to their partners. Explain to students their challenge is to determine which store offers the better buy. Make sure students understand the concept of discount.

Let the groups discuss Question 1 briefly. Then have them write their conjectures for Question 1. You want students to think generally about the situation and have an opinion on what they think is the better deal before they solve the problem. Direct the students to complete the rest of the Student Recording Page with their partners to determine if their predictions are correct. As students work, pose questions that clarify that they understand the specifics of each sale and questions to check for understanding.

QUESTIONS FOR STRUGGLING STUDENTS

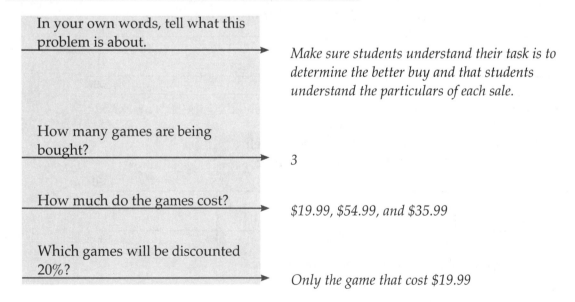

In your own words, tell what this problem is about.

Make sure students understand their task is to determine the better buy and that students understand the particulars of each sale.

How many games are being bought?

3

How much do the games cost?

$19.99, $54.99, and $35.99

Which games will be discounted 20%?

Only the game that cost $19.99

Which games will be discounted 30%?

→ *the games that cost $54.99 and $34.99*

Does this problem require that exact prices be used or can you estimate?

→ *I should use exact prices, but I probably can do some rounding.*

What is the deal at *Games For You*?

→ *20% discount if the game costs $30.00 or less and 30% discount if the game costs more than $30.00. Then include another $\frac{1}{4}$-off discount.*

Does the coupon apply to the original price or the discounted sale price?

→ *the discounted sale price*

What amounts represent the 100%?

→ *Answers may vary depending on the way students handle the games; they may have worked with each game separately, in groups, or as one group.*

How are percents related to fractions?

→ *Percents can represent fractions as they both represent a part of a whole.*

What is 50% of $19.99?

→ *about $10.00*

How can knowing 10% help you find 20%? 30%?

→ *If I find 10%, then I can double that number to find 20%; triple it to find 30%.*

QUESTIONS FOR STUDENTS ON TASK

If you know 50%, how can you find 10%?

→ *If I know 50%, I can divide that amount by 5 to get 10%.*

Do all the games get the same discount? Explain.

→ *No, it depends on the sale at each store.*

If the discount is 20% off, what percent do you end up paying?

→ *80% of the original price*

Is a 20% discount followed with an additional 25% discount different from a 45% discount?

→ *In the first situation, you apply the 20% discount to the original price, thus you pay only 80% of the original price. The manufacturer's coupon is applied to the sale price, which is only 80% of the original value. Therefore, the coupon would deduct 25% from only a portion (i.e. 80%) of the original price. The amount of this discount is less than deducting 25% from the original price. The second scenario deducts the entire 45% from the original price.*

QUESTIONS TO EXTEND STUDENT THINKING

At *Games For You*, does it make a difference if you apply the manufacturer's coupon first and then the store discount? Explain your reasoning.

→ *No, taking 25% then 30% is the same as taking 30% and then 25%. For example if the total is $10.00, 25% off equals $2.50, which makes the price $7.50; 30% off of $7.50 equals $2.25 making the final cost $5.25. If you take 30% off $10.00, you get $10 − $3.00, or $7.00; then 25% off is $1.75, which makes the final cost $5.25.*

Is taking 25% off, then 30% off the same as taking 55% off?

No, taking 55% off makes the final cost $4.50.

Suppose you bought a game at Games For You and paid $14.99 before tax, what was the original price of the game? Explain your answer and illustrate the work.

$25.00. Working backwards, the amount paid was $14.99. The game was discounted 20% with an additional 25%. This means that $14.99 is 75% of the first discounted price and then 80% of that amount is the amount it originally cost. If 75% of the discounted price is $14.99, the amount is about $20.00. Use a percent bar to show this. Then use another percent bar to show that 80% is $20.00. You would need to find 100% to find the original price of the game, about $25.00.

Game Price = $14.99

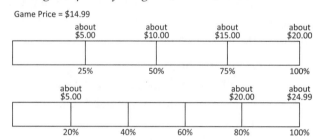

If 25% of 100 is 25, then what can be said about 25% of 50?

50 is $\frac{1}{2}$ of 100 , so $\frac{1}{2}$ of 25% is $12\frac{1}{2}$%.

How can you use 10% to find 1% of a number?

If you know 10%, then divide that amount by 10 to get 1%

How can you use 1% to find any percent of a number (e.g. 8%, 23%)?

If you know 1%, then you can find 8% by multiplying that amount by 8. If you need 23%, you multiply the 1% amount by 23.

Name another proportional
relationship that deals with
percents.

$\longrightarrow$ *Answers will vary.*

LESSON SUMMARY

Before students share their models and their answers, have them share their conjectures about the better deal they predicted in Question 1. You wanted students to think generally about the situation and have an opinion on what they thought was the better deal before they solved the problem. After they have solved the problems, have students go back and revisit their initial thoughts.

Have students share their models for finding the cost of the games. Did students all use the same percent benchmarks to find the cost of the games? This lesson helps students see the use of proportional relationships to find percents. As students advance their understanding, they will use more efficient models, but the models used in this lesson will help you gauge their understanding of percents.

Some students might divide the bar into 10%, where others will divide the bar into 20% or 50%, and then estimate smaller amounts. Ask students if it matters what benchmark percents were used. Discuss with students how they found different percents.

Before ending the summary have students revisit their predictions about the better deal in Question 1. Question if students had the correct answer and if their reasoning was accurate. Ask if anyone thinks differently after having solved the problem.

☐ Have students explain how if they know 10% of a price, they can use that to find 5%, 15% or 20%.

☐ Have students explain how to find 33% of a number.

☐ Ask students to explore and explain how to find 1% of a number.

☐ Discuss with students the difference between a 20% discount and then a 25% discount as opposed to a 45% discount. Have students try examples using simple numbers so they look at relationships and do not get lost in the computations.

☐ Ask students if percent bars can help them find the winner of the minute challenge from the beginning of the lesson. If time permits ask students to find the winner of the minute challenge. If not, it may be assigned as homework.

LESSON 2   SALE, SALE, SALE!

Use the sale signs posted at two different stores to answer the questions.

Ella and Mike want to buy three video games. The prices of the games are $19.99, $54.99, and $35.99.

Games For You is having a sale on video games to clear their shelves for next year's editions. The store offers a discount of 20% if the game costs $30.00 or less and a 30% discount if the game costs more than $30.00. The store will also accept a manufacturer's coupon that gives buyers an additional $\frac{1}{4}$-off the already-reduced prices of the games.

Gametown is having a clearance sale, which offers a 50% discount on all games.

1. When you first looked at the sale advertisements, which store did you think was offering the best deal? Explain your prediction.

2. Draw a diagram to illustrate how much each of the three games will cost at *Games For You*. Draw a diagram to illustrate how much each of the three games will cost at *Gametown*. Which store offers a better deal? Explain your answer.

3. While shopping at a third store, Ella found another game she decided to purchase, which was discounted 25%. Ella was charged $18.00 before taxes for the game. What was the original price of the game? Use a diagram to justify your answer.

1. Answers will vary. Possible answer: Games For You will have a better deal because two of the games have prices greater than $30.00, which means buyers get 30% off and then an additional 25% off because the manufacturer's coupon gives an additional $\frac{1}{4}$ off; 25% = $\frac{1}{4}$.

2. Models will vary depending on benchmarks used.

   Games for You Cost

   Game 1 $19.99   20% discount

   Game 2 $54.99
   Game 3   +$35.99   Add prices of games that get 30% off.

   $90.98   30% discount

   Game 1   Find 20% of about $20.00.

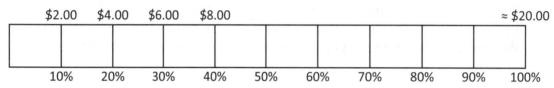

   20% of $20.00 ≈ $4.00; So, the cost of Game 1 is $19.99 − $4.00 = $15.99.

   Games 2 and 3   Find 30% of $90.98.

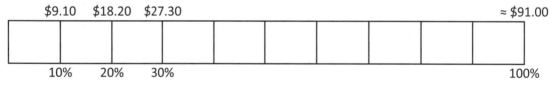

   30% of $91.00 ≈ $27.30; So, the cost of Games 2 and 3 is $90.98 − $27.30 = $63.68

   After the first discount games cost $15.99 + $63.68 = $79.67.

   Find the additional $\frac{1}{4}$ off or 25% discount of $79.67.

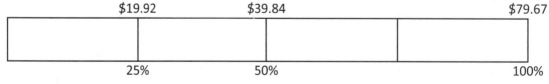

   Additional 25% off ≈ $19.92; so $79.67 − $19.92 = $59.75. Before tax, the cost of the three games is $59.75.

Gametown

Cost of Games 1, 2, and 3: $19.99 + $54.99 + $35.99 = $110.97

Find 50% of $110.97.

Before tax, the cost of the three games is $55.49.

The better deal is *Gametown*.

3. The cost was $18.00. This was 25% off, which means it was 75% of the total price.

$18.00 is $\frac{3}{4}$ cost of the whole. $\frac{1}{4}$ or 25% is $6.00. 50% is $12.00. The original cost will be $24.00.

Students may also use a table.

PERCENT	0	25	50	75	100
COST	$0	$6.00	$12.00	$18.00	$24.00

Common Core State Standards
The Number System 6.NS
  Apply and extend previous understandings of multiplication and division to divide fractions by fractions.
  1. Interpret and compute quotients of fractions, and solve word problems involving division of fractions by fractions, e.g., by using visual fraction models and equations to represent the problem. For example, create a story context for 2/3 ÷ 3/4 and use a visual fraction model to show the quotient; use the relationship between multiplication and division to explain that 2/3 ÷ 3/4 = 8/9 because 3/4 of 8/9 is 2/3. (In general, a/b ÷ c/d = ad/bc.) How much chocolate will each person get if 3 people share 1/2 lb of chocolate equally? How many 3/4-cup servings are in 2/3 of a cup of yogurt? How wide is a rectangular strip of land with length 3/4 mi and area 1/2 square mi?

NCTM Correlation
Number and Operation Standard
  Understanding numbers, ways of representing numbers, relationships among numbers, and number systems.
    Understand and use ratios and proportions to represent quantitative relationships.

LESSON GOALS

- Use models to represent division of a whole number by a fraction and link the actions performed to the model to the steps of the algorithm.
- Understand the meaning of division when dividing by a fraction and estimate the size of the quotient relative to its dividend.
- Develop strategies for dividing a whole number by a fraction.

LESSON INTRODUCTION

This lesson focuses on division of a whole number by a fraction. Students will use models to make sense of the situation. Students will need a solid understanding of division of a whole number by a whole number to succeed on this lesson.

- What does it mean to divide?

- Does this meaning change if division is by a fraction?

To create a model for division, students will use their sense of proportional reasoning and partitioning.

Explain to students that using their sense of proportional reasoning will help them understand the concept of division of fractions.

TEACHING SUGGESTIONS

Within the bulleted text below are suggestions on how to begin the lesson, introduce essential vocabulary, and question students so that they are prepared to complete the Student Recording Page on their own or with minimal assistance.

Write the expression $4 \div \frac{1}{2}$ on the board.

- **What does this expression mean?**
  There are 4 wholes and you want to see how many groups of a $\frac{1}{2}$ you can make.

- Is the quotient more or less than 4? *more*

- **What does a quotient of 8 tell you?** *The quotient 8 means there are 8 groups of $\frac{1}{2}$ in the 4 wholes.*

Discuss with students the meaning of division in this situation.

- **What does the dividend represent?** *the whole*

- **What does the divisor represent?** *the size of the groups*

- **What does the quotient represent?** *the number of groups*

- **What do you know about the size of the quotient?** *In this case, the dividend is 4, the divisor is less than one ($\frac{1}{2}$), so the quotient will be greater than 4.*

Clarify any questions students may have about the divisor, dividend, or quotient. Explain to students that dividing with fractions is still finding how many of a certain-sized group (divisor) there are within the original group (dividend), and that the answer is the quotient. An algorithm will help them find the quotient.

Instruct students that they need to write number sentences that relate to the models they create. It is important that there is a connection between the model and the number sentence. The number sentence should help clarify the model. Making this connection helps solidify their understanding of the process.

Students should use proportional reasoning to make their models. Students should be able to explain how they decided the model to draw and what has to be true for a model to fit a situation.

NCTM Correlation (continued)
Understand meanings of operations and how they relate to one another.
Understand the meanings and effect of arithmetic operations with fractions, decimals, and integers.
Compute fluently and make reasonable estimates.
Select appropriate methods and tools for computing with fractions, and decimals from among mental computation, estimation, calculators and computer, and paper in pencil, depending on the situation and apply the selected methods.
Develop and analyze algorithms for computing with fractions, decimals, and integers and develop fluency in their use.

Materials
Student Recording Page 1.3
Chart Paper
Markers

Vocabulary
Algorithm

An **algorithm** is a set of well-defined steps for a process that is the same each time you perform it. The steps of division are an algorithm.

STUDENT ENGAGEMENT

Have students read the situation presented on Student Recording Page 1.3. Tell groups their task is to discover a method to divide a whole number by a fraction amount and subsequently write an algorithm for the process. Inform students that they will need to be prepared to explain their models and connect the actions taken in the models to their written algorithms. Students may work in small groups and each group needs to show their work on chart paper. Clarify that each size tabletop takes a different amount of paint and that there are 6 gallons of paint to use.

Instruct students to show their work on chart paper for Questions 1 – 3. As students complete their work for these questions, ask them to post their chart work on the wall. The first group will post it at a designated spot. The next group has to decide if the strategies used are similar to a group's work already posted. If yes, then they post their work next to it; if they used a different strategy, they post it in a different location of the room. The next group then has to decide where to post their work: with the first group or the second group. If they used yet another strategy they post it somewhere else. This allows students to think about the different strategies used and how some strategies might look a bit different, but still are the same strategy or how different strategies can be used to answer the same problem. This process also allows the students to look critically at similarities and differences in student work. Summarize Questions 1 – 3 before all students proceed.

After posting their work, students should continue to answer the rest of the questions. As students work, ask questions to check for understanding. Make sure they write a number sentence that relates to the models they have created. It is important that there is a connection between the model and the number sentence. The number sentence should help clarify the model. Making this connection helps solidify their understanding of the process. Be sure students are thinking and using proportional reasoning to make their models. As students draw their models, be sure they know what has to be true for a model to fit a situation.

QUESTIONS FOR STRUGGLING STUDENTS

How many gallons of paint were donated? How can you model that?

6; draw six shapes to represent 6 whole units.

How much paint is needed to paint the small-sized tables? Medium-sized tables? Large-sized tables? How can you model that?

→ *$\frac{1}{5}$, $\frac{1}{4}$, $\frac{1}{3}$. Divide each whole into groups.*

What are you trying to find out in the first situation?

→ *How many groups of $\frac{1}{5}$ there are in 6.*

What picture can you draw to help solve the problem?

→ *Draw whole shapes divided into groups.*

What does your whole represent?

→ *a gallon of paint*

Why did you choose to divide your whole into that many parts?

→ *The parts tell how much paint it takes to paint a table.*

What does the dividend tell you?

→ *How much paint it takes to paint a table.*

What will the quotient tell you?

→ *How many tables can be painted with the 6 gallons of paint.*

What do you know about dividing a whole by a fractional part?

→ *If the whole was divided into $\frac{1}{5}$s, then the whole should be divided into 5 equal-sized pieces.*

What does the denominator of the fraction describe?

→ *The denominator tells the number of equal-sized pieces the whole has been divided into.*

What does the numerator of the fraction describe?

→ *The number of pieces you are considering from the whole group.*

How does dividing a whole number by a unit fraction (e.g. $\frac{1}{6}$) compare to dividing the same whole number by a non-unit fraction (e.g. $\frac{5}{6}$)? How do the quotients compare?

When you divide a whole number by a unit fraction, you can multiply the whole number by the denominator to get the quotient. When the dividend has the same denominator, but a different numerator, the numerator in the dividend increases, and the quotient decreases.

What will the solution to $6 \div \frac{1}{5}$ tell you?

the number groups of $\frac{1}{5}$ in the 6 whole groups you have

What do you know about the size of the quotient?

Since the divisor is less than one, I will get 6 groups.

What would be a reasonable estimate of $4 \div \frac{5}{6}$? Give a reasonable estimate for your quotient and explain your reasoning.

A bit more than 4; I am making groups of $\frac{5}{6}$, which is almost 1, so I will have at least 4, not quite 5.

Another group recorded $6 = \frac{30}{5}$, can you explain why this makes sense?

If you divide 6 wholes into $\frac{1}{5}$s, you get 30 of those $\frac{1}{5}$s, which is equal to $\frac{30}{5}$. If you divide a whole into fifths, you have 5 fifths in each whole. If you divide 5 wholes into fifths, that makes 30 fifths, which can be expressed at $\frac{30}{5}$.

Suppose you had 3 gallons of paint and needed $\frac{2}{5}$ of a gallon to paint a tabletop, (i.e. $3 \div \frac{2}{5}$). This scenario involves a remainder. If you used all the paint, how many tables could you paint?

Your quotient to the problem is $7\frac{1}{2}$. You could paint 7 tables, would but have one section, $\frac{1}{5}$ left. It took 2 of these sections to make a whole, so you have $\frac{1}{2}$ of a group remaining, which means you can paint 7 tables and $\frac{1}{2}$ of another.

Give a real-world situation that can be represented as $8 \div \frac{3}{4}$.

Javier has 8 gallons of ice cream. It takes $\frac{3}{4}$ of a gallon to make his super special banana splits. How many banana splits can he make?

Explain how the quotients for $12 \div \frac{1}{5}$, $12 \div \frac{2}{5}$, and $12 \div \frac{4}{5}$ are related?

The quotient for $12 \div \frac{1}{5}$ is 60. In the second expression, there are still 60 fifths in all but every group consists of two of these fifths. This means that it takes twice as many fifths to make a group resulting in half the number of groups. Instead of 60 groups of one-fifths there are 30 groups of two-fifths. In $12 \div \frac{4}{5}$, there are still 60 fifths in all, but now every group consists of 4 of these fifths. It will take four times as many to make a group resulting in a fourth of the original groups. Instead of 60 groups of one-fifth, there are 15 groups of four-fifths.

LESSON SUMMARY

Summarize Questions 1 – 3 before all students proceed. As students post their work on the walls, note the different strategies used.

- How many different strategies do you think the class used to solve these problems?

  Select a strategy and have the students explain their work. For example if the students show the following work:

$6 \div \frac{1}{5} = 30$

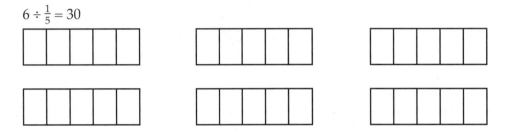

They might suggest: First 6 rectangles were drawn to represent the 6 gallons. Each gallon was divided into $\frac{1}{5}$s to find out how many $\frac{1}{5}$s are in 6. So when you divided the 6 into $\frac{1}{5}$s, what did you get? How many $\frac{1}{5}$s? $\frac{30}{5}$

Important: Record this on the poster if students do not have it, as it will play a role in the upcoming algorithm discussion. Say: So you changed, or renamed, the 6 wholes to/as $\frac{30}{5}$. Then what did you do? We found out how many $\frac{1}{5}$s we could make. Write "$\frac{30}{5}$ divided into $\frac{1}{5}$-sized groups made 30 groups." Then write the equation $\frac{30}{5} \div \frac{1}{5} = \frac{30}{1} = 30$ tables. What other groups used this strategy? Review other work that used the same strategy. Summarize the discussion for Questions 1 – 3 (division by unit fraction) by writing the equations (number sentences) for each of the situations.

$\frac{30}{5} \div \frac{1}{5} = \frac{30}{1} = 30$ small-sized tables

$\frac{24}{4} \div \frac{1}{4} = \frac{24}{1} = 24$ medium-sized tables

$\frac{18}{3} \div \frac{1}{3} = \frac{18}{1} = 18$ large-sized tables

Students usually notice common denominators and division of the numerators and the denominators. Test this pattern by using different problems involving a whole number divided by a unit fraction to see if their conjectures hold true. The purpose here is to develop a strategy for dividing fractions. This is a developing process and is the first step is to ensure students can make sense of dividing a whole number by a unit fraction.

Next share and discuss a different strategy students applied. Another strategy students often use is multiplication. Students realize that the denominator tells how many equal parts you will divide the whole into. Students see that each of the six gallons consists of five-fifths; therefore, 6 × 5 would tell you how many small tables you could paint. To clarify this strategy, write the equations for each of the situations as shown below:

$6 \div \frac{1}{5} = 30$ small-sized tables

$6 \div \frac{1}{4} = 24$ medium-sized tables

$6 \div \frac{1}{3} = 18$ large-sized tables

Do you notice any patterns? You can multiply the whole number and the denominator to get the number of tables that can be painted. Test to see if this pattern holds true by using different problems involving a whole number divided by a unit fraction. Does this strategy hold true for any whole number divided by a unit fraction?

Direct students to Question 4. This question asks students to write an algorithm for dividing a whole number by a fraction.

Will your algorithm work to answer Question 5a and 5b? Students find the algorithm using common denominators will work, but the one using multiplication does not. *Why does the multiplication algorithm not work? What is different about these problems?* Questions 1 – 3 used division by unit fractions and these do not. *How can we adjust our multiplication algorithm so that it works? What are we trying to find in 5a?* How many groups of $\frac{2}{3}$s there are in 6. *How can we use 6 × 3 to help answer how many groups of $\frac{2}{3}$s there are in 6?* We still have 18 parts but now it takes two of those parts to make a group. So how many groups can we make if we put two parts in each group? How is this grouping action shown in the number sentence? Dividing our whole in to groups with two parts in each group can be recorded by dividing by two. Our picture shows we can form nine groups (or tables) if we divide all the parts into groups of two; thus we can paint nine tables in this situation. Pose similar problems involving dividing a whole number by any fraction (non-unit fraction including those greater than 1) to see if this conjecture holds true.

Students have explored two different algorithms for dividing a whole number by a fraction. It is not as important for students to fully understand both ways at this time; however, students should leave this problem being able to make sense of and replicate at least one of the strategies.

Students should now have the use of models, proportional reasoning, partitioning and grouping, and algorithms to make sense of and verify answers. As they progress through division of fractions, continue to check for understanding of the situation and explanations of why the process works. Students will need more opportunities to explore various situations and to recognize forming equal-sized groups is necessary to the solution. In doing so, students will continue to use their knowledge of partitioning and equivalence to make equal-sized groups and their understanding of division applications will strengthen, thus solidifying the division algorithm.

CHECK FOR SUCCESS

☐ Write the following problems on the board. Ask students to solve the problems and write some statements about what they notice. Ask, How will the models differ? How will the solutions differ? Which quotient would you expect to be the smallest and why?

$3 \div \frac{1}{3}$

$3 \div \frac{2}{3}$

$3 \div \frac{3}{3}$

Students should mention:

The dividend or the number they are dividing into stays the same so the three wholes will all be divided into 3 parts for a total of 9 parts.

As the divisor or the group size they are making increases, the fewer groups they can make. In other words, as the dividend increases, the quotient decreases.

In the second problem since $\frac{2}{3}$ is double the size of $\frac{1}{3}$ expect the quotient to be half the size.

☐ Before leaving the lesson, have a discussion about remainders using Questions 7e and 7f.

Use a model to help explain remainders.

Eight whole groups divided into $\frac{1}{6}$s. For the situation, it takes five of these $\frac{1}{6}$s to make a group. We can make nine groups. We have three parts of the five parts needed to make another group. So, the remainder is $\frac{3}{5}$.

We can paint $9\frac{3}{5}$ tables.

Why isn't the remainder 3 out of 6, or $\frac{3}{6}$, because the wholes are divided into sixths? Discuss that when dividing by a fraction, the number of parts that it takes to make a group is determined by the fraction. In essence, the unit has changed. Instead of parts of a gallon, the situation is talking about parts of a table, and you need to paint the whole table. The unit size has been redefined, so it takes a different amount of the whole to create a group. The remainder should also be described using the new unit size.

LESSON 3 · DIVIDING FRACTIONS

Avery's father donated 6 gallons of paint to her school. The teachers at Avery's school have decided to paint tabletops with the paint. It will take $\frac{1}{5}$ of a gallon of paint to cover a small-sized table. It will take $\frac{1}{4}$ of a gallon of paint to cover a medium-sized table, and $\frac{1}{3}$ of a gallon of paint for a large-sized table.

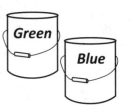

1. How many small-sized tables can the teachers paint if they use all of the paint? Show a model and write a number sentence that relates to your model.

2. How many medium-sized tables can the teachers paint if they use all of the paint? Show a model and write a number sentence that relates to your model.

3. How many large-sized tables can the teachers paint if they use all of the paint? Show a model and write a number sentence that relates to your model.

4. Based on your observations, write an algorithm that makes sense for dividing any whole number by any unit fraction.

From *It's All Connected: The Power of Proportional Reasoning to Understand Mathematics Concepts, Grades 6–8* by Carmen Whitman. © 2011 Scholastic Inc. Permission granted to photocopy for nonprofit use in a classroom or similar place dedicated to face-to-face educational instruction.

Student _____ Class _____ Date _____

5. Avery found some green tables and blue tables that needed painting in the cafeteria. Her father agreed to donate 6 more gallons of paint. It will take $\frac{2}{3}$ of a gallon to repaint the green tables and $\frac{4}{5}$ of a gallon to repaint the blue tables.

    a. If the teachers uses all of the paint, how many green tables can they paint? Use a model and write a number sentence that relates to the model.

    b. If the teachers uses all of the paint, how many blue tables can they paint? Use a model and write a number sentence that relates to the model.

6. In Question 4, you described an algorithm for dividing fractions. Does your algorithm work for the situations in Question 5? If needed, revise your algorithm so that it does work.

7. Use your algorithm to solve the following problems. What do you notice about your answers?

    a. $4 \div \frac{1}{12}$ b. $4 \div \frac{2}{12}$ c. $4 \div \frac{4}{12}$

8. Based on this relationships, can you predict the answer to $4 \div \frac{8}{12}$? Solve the problem, was your prediction correct?

1. A small-sized table uses $\frac{1}{5}$ gallon of paint.

Represents a
gallon of paint

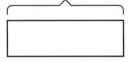

| $\frac{1}{5}$ | $\frac{1}{5}$ | $\frac{1}{5}$ | $\frac{1}{5}$ | $\frac{1}{5}$ | $= \frac{5}{5}$ | $= \frac{5}{5}$ | $= \frac{5}{5}$ |

 $= \frac{5}{5}$ $= \frac{5}{5}$ $= \frac{5}{5}$

Six gallons changed to fifths: $\frac{30}{5} \div \frac{1}{5} = \frac{30}{1} = 30$ small-sized tables painted.

Another approach: One gallon of paint covers 5 tables.

Represents a
gallon of paint

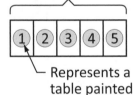

Represents a
table painted

Each gallon covers 5 small-sized tables: 6 gallons × 5 tables = 30 tables.
So, $6 \div \frac{1}{5}$ is equal to 6 × 5.

2. A medium-sized table uses $\frac{1}{4}$ gallon of paint.

Represents a
gallon of paint

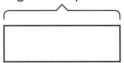

| $\frac{1}{4}$ | $\frac{1}{4}$ | $\frac{1}{4}$ | $\frac{1}{4}$ | $= \frac{4}{4}$ | $= \frac{4}{4}$ | $= \frac{4}{4}$ |

 $= \frac{4}{4}$ $= \frac{4}{4}$ $= \frac{4}{4}$

Six gallons changed to fourths: $\frac{24}{4} \div \frac{1}{4} = \frac{24}{1} = 24$ medium-sized tables painted

Another approach: One gallon of paint covers 4 tables.

Represents a
gallon of paint

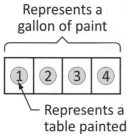

Represents a
table painted

Each gallon covers 4 medium-sized tables: 6 gallons × 4 tables = 24 tables.
So, $6 \div \frac{1}{4}$ is equal to 6 × 4.

3. A large-sized table uses $\frac{1}{3}$ gallon of paint.

Represents a
gallon of paint

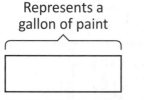

Six gallons changed to thirds: $\frac{18}{3} \div \frac{1}{3} = \frac{18}{1} = 18$ large-sized tables painted

Another approach: One gallon of paint covers 3 tables.

Represents a
gallon of paint

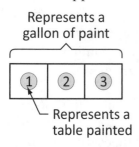

Represents a
table painted

Each gallon paints 3 large-sized tables: 6 gallons × 3 tables = 18 tables.
So, $6 \div \frac{1}{3}$ is equal to 6 × 3.

4. One student might suggest: Find common denominators. Then, divide numerators
and divide denominators.

5. a.

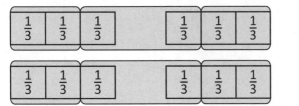

I divided the 6 gallons into thirds and got $\frac{18}{3}$. It took 2 of these $\frac{1}{3}$s to paint a table. So, then I grouped them by two. I found 9 groups.

$\frac{18}{3} \div \frac{2}{3} = \frac{9}{1} = 9$ tables.

Another picture might show a number grouping such as

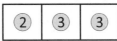

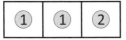

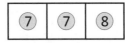

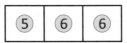

b.

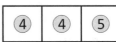

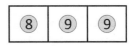

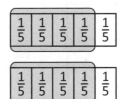

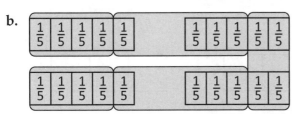

I divided the 6 gallons into fifths and got $\frac{30}{5}$. It took $\frac{4}{5}$ of a gallon to paint a table. I found 7 groups. With 2 parts left over. I need 4 parts of make a group. So, I have $\frac{2}{4}$ of another group. 7 groups and $\frac{2}{4}$ of another group equals $7\frac{1}{2}$ groups.

$\frac{30}{5} \div \frac{4}{5} = \frac{\frac{30}{4}}{1} = \frac{7\frac{2}{4}}{1} = 7\frac{1}{2}$ I can paint $7\frac{1}{2}$ tables.

6. Using common denominators still works for these problems; if students multiplied the whole number and the denominator, they have to adjust for using non-unit fractions. They might say: multiply the whole number and the denominator of the fraction then divide that number by the numerator to find your answer.

7. a. 48; **b.** 24; **c.** 12; When using the same denominator, I noticed that as the numerator gets greater the number of groups I can make is less. The answer was 48 but in *b* the answer was only half of that, 24, because it took 2 times the amount to make a group.

8. I predict the answer should be half of 12, because $4 \div \frac{4}{12}$ and finding groups of $\frac{8}{12}$ requires double the amount. The answer is 6.

$4 \div \frac{8}{12} = \frac{48}{12} \div \frac{8}{12} = \frac{6}{1} = 6$

LESSON 4 — COOKIE RECIPE

Common Core State Standards

Ratios and Proportional
Relationships 6.RP

Understand ratio concepts
and use ratio reasoning to
solve problems.

3. Use ratio and rate
reasoning to solve
real-world and
mathematical problems,
e.g., by reasoning about
tables of equivalent ratios,
tape diagrams, double
number line diagrams, or
equations.

d. Use ratio reasoning
to convert
measurement units;
manipulate and
transform units
appropriately when
multiplying or dividing
quantities.

Ratios and Proportional
Relationships 7.RP

Analyze proportional
relationships and use them to
solve real-world and
mathematical problems.

3. Use proportional
relationships to solve
multistep ratio and percent
problems. Examples: simple
interest, tax, markups and
markdowns, gratuities
and commissions, fees,
percent increase and
decrease, percent error.

LESSON GOALS

- Use operations to solve problems and justify a solution involving proportional relationships.

LESSON INTRODUCTION

In this lesson, students are challenged with problem situations in which making decisions are based on comparisons. These problems ask students to take a recipe and compare and determine equivalent recipes. Students are also asked to scale a recipe. If students rely on their knowledge that the recipe needs to increase or decrease proportionally, there are several approaches to solving the problem. A variety of possible strategies are modeled in the Student Recording Page Solutions.

Students can think of the situations as an additive reasoning or as a multiplicative reasoning. If they think of it as an additive process, guide students so that by the end of the lesson, they can make the connection to the multiplicative process.

To introduce the lesson, ask the following:
If one pizza feeds four people, how many pizzas would feed 18 people?

- What do you need to know?

- How can you find the number of pizzas needed?

If you travel 55 miles per hour, what does that mean?

- What other information can be obtained from *55 miles per hour*?

- How is the 55 mi/h related to the pizza scenario?

TEACHING SUGGESTIONS

Within the bulleted text below are suggestions on how to begin the lesson, introduce essential vocabulary, and question students so that they are prepared to complete the Student Recording Page on their own or with minimal assistance.

- Introduce the problem by talking about the cookie recipe.

- Have students read the scenarios and discuss what they know about the problems. Review the facts about the problem, but do not discuss how to answer the problem.

- Review the meaning of ratio.

> A **ratio** is a comparison of two quantities. A ratio can be written in three formats: $\frac{1}{4}$, 1:4, and 1 to 4.

- Remind students that a proportion has two ratios set equal to each other.

> A **proportion** is an equation that states two ratios are equal.

- Ask students where they may have encountered a scale factor before. Some students in the class will be able to relate scale factors to model building, while others may mention road maps.

> **Scaling** is the process used to increase or decrease a quantity using multiplication by a factor. **Scale factor** is a number used as a multiplier when scaling a quantity.

- Explain to students that when scaling, you can be increasing an amount, or decreasing an amount. A factor greater than 1 increases the result and a factor less than 1 decreases the result.

NCTM Correlation
Number and Operation Standard
Understanding numbers, ways of representing numbers, relationships among numbers, and number systems.
Work flexibly with fractions, decimals, and percents to solve problems.
Understand and use ratios and proportions to represent quantitative relationships.
Compute fluently and make reasonable estimates.
Develop, analyze, and explain methods for solving problems involving proportions, such as scaling and finding equivalent ratios.

Materials
Student Recording Page 1.4

Vocabulary
Ratio
Proportion
Scaling
Scale factor

Your introduction should leave the problem open allowing students to use their own ideas to solve the problem. In other words, do not model or dictate how students should solve these problems, as that will eliminate the need for students to reason proportionally through these situations.

Student Engagement

Students can work in pairs to complete Student Recording Page 1.4. As students work on solving the cookie recipe problems, continue to ask questions about relationships between the related variables to check for understanding.

Questions for Struggling Students

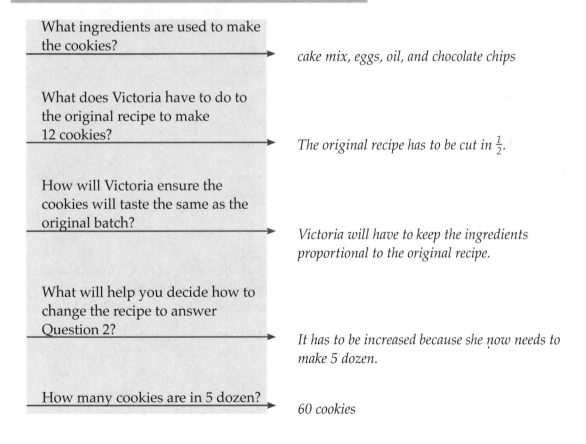

What ingredients are used to make the cookies?

> *cake mix, eggs, oil, and chocolate chips*

What does Victoria have to do to the original recipe to make 12 cookies?

> *The original recipe has to be cut in $\frac{1}{2}$.*

How will Victoria ensure the cookies will taste the same as the original batch?

> *Victoria will have to keep the ingredients proportional to the original recipe.*

What will help you decide how to change the recipe to answer Question 2?

> *It has to be increased because she now needs to make 5 dozen.*

How many cookies are in 5 dozen?

> *60 cookies*

If Victoria makes 5 times the recipe, how many people at the reunion would get a cookie?

→ *Each recipe makes 24 cookies. Victoria would have only 120 cookies. So, 120 people would get one cookie or 60 people would get 2 cookies.*

How can the fundraiser cookie recipe amounts help you determine the amount of the ingredients needed for the family reunion recipe?

→ *Because the fundraiser recipe makes 60 cookies. Victoria could triple it to make the 180 cookies needed for the family reunion.*

How can you find out how many cookies Victoria needs for the reunion?

→ *180 guests times 2, because she wants everyone to get 2 cookies.*

How can you find out the number of dozens Victoria needs?

→ *Divide the number of cookies by 12.*

QUESTIONS FOR STUDENTS ON TASK

How is the cookie recipe related to the pizza scenario and the 55 miles per hour discussion?

→ *You are finding a rate in each. This is how much per person in the pizza scenario or how much per hour in the miles per hour scenario.*

Tell how the original recipe is going to change each time Victoria needs to make cookies.

→ *The first time the recipe will decrease and the other times the recipe will increase.*

If Victoria needs to increase the recipe 5 times, how many eggs would she need?

→ *Each recipe calls for 2 eggs, so increasing the recipe 5 times means Victoria needs 5 times as many eggs. Victoria needs 10 eggs.*

If Victoria increases the recipe $1\frac{1}{2}$ times, how does she find the amount of each ingredient needed?

→ *Multiply the amount of each ingredient by $1\frac{1}{2}$.*

Two recipes make how many dozen cookies?

→ *4 dozen*

How can you be certain that the new recipes produce cookies that taste exactly the same as the original recipe?

→ *Keep the amounts of ingredients proportional to the original recipe.*

QUESTIONS TO EXTEND STUDENT THINKING

In a different recipe, 15 batches serve 100 people. How many recipes would serve 75 people?

→ *75:100 is a 3:4 relationship, so $\frac{3}{4}$ of 15 recipes; $11\frac{1}{4}$ recipes would serve 75 people.*

If Victorias use 3 cups of chocolate chips, how many cups of vegetable oil is needed to keep the recipe proportional?

→ *If 3 cups of chocolate chips were used then Victoria made 4 times the original recipe. So, she will need 4 times the amount of vegetable oil in the original recipe. Each recipe calls for $\frac{1}{2}$ cup. Victoria needs 4 one-half cups, or 2 cups.*

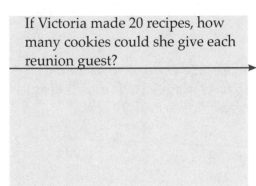

If Victoria made 20 recipes, how many cookies could she give each reunion guest?

20 recipes makes 480 cookies and there are 180 guests. $\frac{480}{180} = 2\frac{2}{3}$ cookies. Another response might suggest: 15 batches + 5 more batches. 5 batches makes 24 × 5 = 120 cookies, which when shared equally gives everyone $\frac{120}{180}$ths of a cookie or $\frac{2}{3}$. So, 2 + $\frac{2}{3}$ = $2\frac{2}{3}$ cookies.

LESSON SUMMARY

As students present their methods and solutions, highlight different strategies that students used to solve the problems. Some students may use equivalence, rate tables, scale factor, or set up proportions to solve the problems. Students may use a combination of both additive and multiplicative reasoning in solving problems. (See sample answers.)

Take these opportunities to compare and contrast additive versus multiplicative reasoning. Students should start reasoning proportionally. Post a list of the different strategies students used to solve the problems.

CHECK FOR SUCCESS

☐ Have students identify different ratios used to solve the problems. (Examples are cookies per recipe, ingredients per recipe, or cookies per guest.)

☐ Ask students what different strategies have in common. Students must realize that no matter what strategy used, the relationship between ingredients had to remain proportional in each of the new recipes. Therefore any amount of cookies could be made using this recipe.

☐ Have students explain how the cookie recipe is related to the pizza problem and the 55 miles per hour conversation from the introduction of the lesson.

☐ Have students identify other examples that are similar and tell why these examples are similar.

Student _____ Class _____ Date _____

LESSON 4 ▸ COOKIE RECIPE

Victoria has found a recipe for Chocolate Delight cookies.
Use the recipe for Questions 1 – 5.

Chocolate Delight Cookies
Ingredients
1 package Devil's Food cake mix
2 eggs
$\frac{1}{2}$ cup vegetable oil
$\frac{3}{4}$ cup semi-sweet chocolate chips
Makes 24 cookies

1. Victoria wants to try the recipe, but only needs to make 12 cookies. How much of each ingredient does she need? Show and explain your work.

2. Victoria decides she likes the cookies and decides to make them for a fundraiser at her school. She needs to make 5 dozen cookies. How can she adjust her recipe? Show and explain your work.

3. The cookies were a success at the fundraiser, so Victoria plans to make them for a family reunion. They expect 180 people to attend the reunion. She wants to make two cookies for each person. How should she adjust her recipe? Show and explain your work.

4. Victoria decides that adding pecans would make the cookies even better. She decided the original recipe needed one cup of chopped pecans. How many cups of chopped pecans will she need to make the cookies for the reunion?

5. Victoria found pecans that cost $6.85 per pound. There are 4 cups of pecans in one pound. How much will Victoria spend to add pecans to the cookies for the reunion?

1. The original recipe makes 24 cookies and Victoria only needs 12, so she needs $\frac{1}{2}$ the recipe. I multiplied the amount of each ingredient by $\frac{1}{2}$ to find the amount for half the recipe.

Ingredients	Original recipe for 24 cookies	Process ($\frac{1}{2}$ of each ingredient)	Recipe for 12 cookies
Cake mix	1 package of cake mix	$\frac{1}{2} \times 1$	$\frac{1}{2}$ package of cake mix
Eggs	2 eggs	$\frac{1}{2} \times 2$	1 egg
Vegetable oil	$\frac{1}{2}$ cup	$\frac{1}{2} \times \frac{1}{2}$	$\frac{1}{4}$ cup
Chocolate chips	$\frac{3}{4}$ cup	$\frac{1}{2} \times \frac{3}{4}$	$\frac{3}{8}$ cup

2. Students may suggest: Victoria needs 5-dozen cookies. Each dozen has 12 cookies, so she needs $5 \times 12 = 60$ cookies. One recipe makes 24 cookies. She needs $24 + 24 + 12$, or $2\frac{1}{2}$ batches. Multiply the amount of each ingredient by $2\frac{1}{2}$.

Ingredients	Original recipe for 24 cookies	Process ($2\frac{1}{2}$ of each ingredient)	Recipe for 60 cookies
Cake mix	1 package of cake mix	$2\frac{1}{2} \times 1$	$2\frac{1}{2}$ package of cake mix
Eggs	2 eggs	$2\frac{1}{2} \times 2$	5 eggs
Vegetable oil	$\frac{1}{2}$ cup	$2\frac{1}{2} \times \frac{1}{2}$	$1\frac{1}{4}$ cups
Chocolate chips	$\frac{3}{4}$ cup	$2\frac{1}{2} \times \frac{3}{4}$	$1\frac{7}{8}$ cups

3. Victoria will need to make $180 \times 2 = 360$ cookies. One recipe makes 24 cookies.

   Think: if Victoria needs 360 cookies, how many of the original recipe is needed?

   $$\frac{1 \text{ recipe}}{24 \text{ cookies}} = \frac{x \text{ recipes}}{360 \text{ cookies}} \rightarrow \frac{1}{24} \times \frac{15}{15} = \frac{15}{360}$$

   Use a scale factor of 15 to find out how much of each ingredient Victoria needs.

Ingredients	Original recipe for 24 cookies	Process (15 times original recipe)	Recipe for 360 cookies
Cake mix	1 package of cake mix	15×1	15 package of cake mix
Eggs	2 eggs	15×2	30 eggs
Vegetable oil	$\frac{1}{2}$ cup	$15 \times \frac{1}{2}$	$7\frac{1}{2}$ cups
Chocolate chips	$\frac{3}{4}$ cup	$15 \times \frac{3}{4}$	$11\frac{1}{4}$ cups

4.

Ingredients	Original recipe for 24 cookies	Process (15 times original recipe)	Recipe for 360 cookies
Pecans	1 cup	15×1	15 cups

5. Victoria needs 15 cups of pecans: There are 4 cups of pecans in 1 pound. How many pounds does 15 cups make? There is a 1:4 relationship, which means the following relationships are also true 2:8, 3:12, and 4:16. Victoria needs less than 4 pounds because 4 pounds equals 16 cups and Victoria only needs 15 cups. Another method is to find an equivalent fraction to $\frac{1}{4}$ with 15 as a denominator.

   $$\frac{1}{4} = \frac{x}{15} \rightarrow \frac{1}{4} \times \frac{3\frac{3}{4}}{3\frac{3}{4}} = \frac{3\frac{3}{4}}{15}$$

   Victoria needs $3\frac{3}{4}$ lb of pecans.

   Each pound of pecans costs $6.85. Multiply.
       cost per pound × number of pounds needed
       $\$6.85 \times 3\frac{3}{4} = \$6.85 \times 3.75 \approx \$25.69$

   The pecans will cost Victoria $25.69 before tax.

LESSON 5 — THE STATE FAIR

Common Core State Standards

Ratios and Proportional Relationships 6.RP

Understand ratio concepts and use ratio reasoning to solve problems.

2. Understand the concept of a unit rate a/b associated with a ratio a:b with b ≠ 0, and use rate language in the context of a ratio relationship.

3. Use ratio and rate reasoning to solve real-world and mathematical problems,

   a. Make tables of equivalent ratios relating quantities with whole-number measurements, find missing values in the tables, and plot the pairs of values on the coordinate plane. Use tables to compare ratios.

   b. Solve unit rate problems including those involving unit pricing and constant speed. For example, if it took 7 hours to mow 4 lawns, then at that rate, how many lawns could be mowed in 35 hours? At what rate were lawns being mowed?

Ratios and Proportional Relationships 7.RP

Analyze proportional relationships and use them to solve real-world and mathematical problems.

2. Recognize and represent proportional relationships between quantities.

LESSON GOALS

- Use multiplication and division to solve problems including situations involving equivalent ratios and rates.
- Use tables to represent and describe proportional relationships.
- Apply different strategies for explaining comparisons between quantities.

LESSON INTRODUCTION

Write 2:3, 5 to 7, and $\frac{3}{5}$ on the board. Ask students to tell what they know about these statements. Students might suggest: They are ratios; They are rates; They are numbers comparing two quantities; They are comparisons of part-to-part relationships; They are comparisons of part-to-whole relationships. Discuss each of the statements made by students.

This lesson helps students investigate how ratios are formed and how to find equivalent ratios to make comparisons.

Students need to understand that the form they use to represent the ratios is a choice (preference), but it does not change the relationship of what is being compared.

When a quantity of x is proportional to another quantity y by a factor of k, the relationship can be written as $x = ky$ or $k = \frac{x}{y}$. A **constant of proportionality** cannot equal 0.

In this lesson, students will investigate constant ratios. Using the variables x and y, they will look at the definition of constant of proportionality. Constants of proportionality are often used when solving problems related to the price of one item and the price of multiple items. When studying relationships that have a constant of proportionality, students will discover that as one variable increases, the other variables changes proportionally.

Introduce the state fair scenario to students. Make sure they understand that stores are selling discounted tickets and that rides and food booths only accept tickets, not cash for payment.

TEACHING SUGGESTIONS

Within the bulleted text below are suggestions on how to begin the lesson, introduce essential vocabulary, and question students so that they are prepared to complete the Student Recording Page on their own or with minimal assistance.

- What could the relationships 2:3, 5 to 7, and $\frac{3}{5}$ represent?

- Can you give an example where 5 to 7 represents a part-to-whole relationship? *There are 7 students and 5 of them are girls.*

- How can the same ratio represent a part-to-part relationship? *There are 5 girls to every 7 boys in the class.*

NCTM Correlation

Number and Operation Standard
Compute fluently and make reasonable estimates.
Select appropriate methods and tools for computing with fractions, and decimals from among mental computation, estimation, calculators and computer, and paper and pencil, depending on the situation and apply the selected methods.
Develop, analyze, and explain methods for solving problems involving proportions, such as scaling and finding equivalent rations.

Algebra
Understand patterns, relations, and functions.
Represent, analyze, and generalize a variety of patterns with tables, graphs, words, and when possible, symbolic rules.

Materials
Student Recording Page 1.5

Vocabulary
Constant of proportionality
Rate
Ratio
Unit rate

- Be sure that the students have an understanding of both rate and ratio. A rate can be thought of as a direct comparison of two sets.

- Ask what is the difference between a ratio and a rate.

- What is the difference between a rate and a unit rate?

STUDENT ENGAGEMENT

As students begin working to complete Student Recording Page 1.5, check the strategies being used. Watch for students who still think that making comparisons means only finding the differences. Ask students questions about comparisons being made and ratios being used to check for understanding.

A **ratio** is a comparison of two quantities. A ratio can be written in three formats: 1/4, 1:4, and 1 to 4.

Often expressed as a fraction, equivalent decimals or percents, a **rate** is a comparison of quantities measured in two different units.

A **unit rate** is a comparison of two quantities where one of the quantities is 1. It describes how many units of one quantity corresponds to one unit of a second quantity.

QUESTIONS FOR STRUGGLING STUDENTS

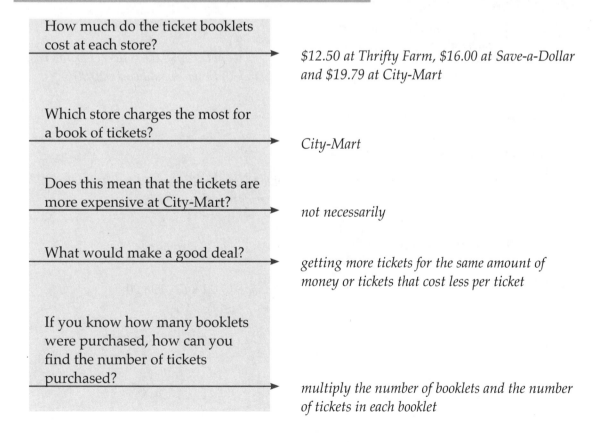

How much do the ticket booklets cost at each store?

→ *$12.50 at Thrifty Farm, $16.00 at Save-a-Dollar and $19.79 at City-Mart*

Which store charges the most for a book of tickets?

→ *City-Mart*

Does this mean that the tickets are more expensive at City-Mart?

→ *not necessarily*

What would make a good deal?

→ *getting more tickets for the same amount of money or tickets that cost less per ticket*

If you know how many booklets were purchased, how can you find the number of tickets purchased?

→ *multiply the number of booklets and the number of tickets in each booklet*

What makes it hard to determine which store has the best deal?

They offer different amounts of tickets for different prices.

What would need to change so that it is easier to see which store has the best deal on tickets?

It would be easier to compare if either the cost or the amount of tickets in a booklet offered were the same at each store.

What math do you need to perform in order to make it easier to compare ticket prices?

Find the unit price per ticket.

What could the ratio 20:16 represent in this problem?

20 tickets cost $16.00

At that rate, how much would only 10 tickets cost? 5 tickets? 25 tickets?

10 tickets would cost $8.00, 5 tickets would cost $4.00, and 25 tickets would cost $20.00.

Suppose Thrifty Farm store agreed to sell individual tickets. How can you determine the price per ticket?

Divide the cost of the book of tickets by the number of tickets in a book.

How many booklets of tickets can a customer purchase at Save-a-Dollar if he or she wants to spend $100.00?

6 because $16.00 × 6 = $96.00

Explain why the better buy cannot be determined readily from the prices given.

→ *because they are all sold using different rates*

What would make it easier to determine the better buy?

→ *knowing the unit rate of the ticket at each store*

What ratio represents the cost of the tickets at Save-a-Dollar?

→ *20:16, 20 to 16, or 20/16; all of these ratios represent 20 tickets for $16.00.*

Is there another way to write the same relationship?

→ *16:20, 16 to 20, or $\frac{16}{20}$; all of these represent 16 tickets for $20.00.*

How can you compare different rates?

→ *You could find a unit rate for each and compare those.*

How does the rate of 1 ticket for $2.50 compare to the rate of 2 tickets for $5.00?

→ *The rates are equivalent.*

If you are given a part-to-part ratio, such as 2:3, what else can you deduce from that ratio?

→ *If I know that 2:3 is a part-to-part relationship then I could say that the part-to-whole relationship is 2:5*

How are these problems related to finding equivalent fractions?

The value of the numbers are not changing. We are just making groups look the same so that we can compare quantities. This is similar to finding equivalent fractions; the part of the whole is not changing. We are just renaming so that we have equal-sized pieces.

Which is better to know, a part-to-part relationship or a part-to-whole relationship?

One is not better to know than the other; each tells some information about a relationship.

Suppose you own a store and decide to sell tickets to the State Fair as well. You decided to keep the ticket book prices competitive with the other stores in town. What price would you charge for a ticket book and how many tickets per book would you sell?

Answers will vary.

Karen's school collected exactly 300 tickets from these stores as a donation for the students. List the number of booklets each store could have donated if all stores donated at least one booklet.

One possibility:
Thrifty Farms — 4 booklets
Save-a-Dollar — 7 booklets
City-Mart — 4 booklets

Ask students to present their strategies used to solve Question 1. Have students tell why their strategies make sense to use. Bring out all successful strategies used and make a list.

Examples might include:

- Find unit rates.
- Find same amount of tickets, then compare cost.
- Find the same dollar amount and then compare number of tickets.
- Think about them as fractions and find common denominators.
- Make a table.

Students should have a variety of ways to reason through these types of situations. Making the connections to fraction work helps students reason through these situations. For example, when setting up proportions students often use their knowledge of equivalent fractions to reason through the proportion.

When summarizing the rest of the lesson ask students to explain other comparisons made. Be sure students are thinking proportionally. Some students may use rate tables to help them answer questions. Double one of the entries in the table. Ask students to provide the corresponding value. Have students identify the constant of proportionality, unit rate in the table.

CHECK FOR SUCCESS

☐ Ask students to write a strategy used by another student that they understood. Have students try out the new strategy by solving the following problem:

Two more stores decide to offer deals.

| Romans | 30 tickets for $24.50 |
| Save Time | 12 tickets for $9.50 |

Between these two stores, which one offers the better deal?

From *It's All Connected: The Power of Proportional Reasoning to Understand Mathematics Concepts, Grades 6–8* by Carmen Whitman. © 2011 Scholastic Inc. Permission granted to photocopy for nonprofit use in a classroom or similar place dedicated to face-to-face educational instruction.

Student _____ Class _____ Date _____

LESSON 5 THE STATE FAIR

A group of students are spending the day at their state fair. There are many carnival rides and a variety of food items that can be purchased. Stores around the area are offering discounted carnival ride tickets sold in booklets. The stores' ticket prices are shown below.

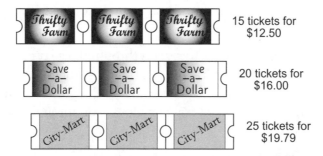

Thrifty Farm — 15 tickets for $12.50

Save -a- Dollar — 20 tickets for $16.00

City-Mart — 25 tickets for $19.79

1. Which store offers the best deal? Justify your choice.

2. It takes 4 tickets to ride the *Hurricane*. If Emma bought two ticket books from Save-a-Dollar and invited 4 friends, how many times can each person ride on the *Hurricane* using Emma's tickets?

3. The Math Club decides to go to the State Fair and buys 6 ticket books at City-Mart. The club has 8 members. Each member buys a drink that uses 1 ticket. Their favorite ride is the *Twister* and it takes 5 tickets to ride. If each member rides the same number of times, how many times can they ride? Explain your answer.

4. Karen and 4 friends used 175 tickets. They each rode the *Storm* 5 times and used all of the tickets. How many tickets did it take to ride the *Storm*? At this rate, how many tickets will it take for Karen to ride the *Storm* 5 more times?

1. Sample 1: Find the unit rate at each store.

   Thrifty Farms: 15 tickets costs $12.50, so $\frac{\$12.50}{15 \text{ tickets}} = \$0.83$ per ticket

   Save-a-Dollar: 20 tickets costs $16.00, so $\frac{\$16.00}{20 \text{ tickets}} = \$0.80$ per ticket

   City-Mart: 25 tickets costs $19.79, so $\frac{\$19.79}{25 \text{ tickets}} = \$0.79$ per ticket

   City-Mart has the best deal.

   Sample 2: Consider Thrifty Farms and Save-a-Dollar and find out how much 60 tickets would cost. Thrifty Farms rates are 15:12.50; the same as 30:25, which is also the same as 60:50. Save-a-Dollar rates are 20:16 which is the same as 60:48. Compare tickets to dollars. Save-a-Dollar is the best deal so far. Now compare Save-a-Dollar and City-Mart.

   $$\frac{\text{Save-a-Dollar 20 tickets}}{\$16.00} = \frac{5 \text{ tickets}}{\$4.00}$$

   $$\frac{\text{City-Mart 25 tickets}}{\$19.75} = \frac{5 \text{ tickets}}{\$3.95}$$

   At Save-a-Dollar 5 tickets would cost $4.00, while at City-Mart 5 tickets would cost $3.95. So the best deal would be at City-Mart.

2. Emma and her friends would have 2 × 20 = 40 tickets to use. Each person would be able to ride the *Hurricane* two times each.

   $$\frac{1 \text{ person}}{4 \text{ tickets}} = \frac{5 \text{ people}}{20 \text{ tickets}}$$

   One person requires 4 tickets to ride the *Hurricane*. If 5 people ride, they need 20 tickets.

   $$\frac{1 \text{ ride for 5 people}}{20 \text{ tickets}} = \frac{2 \text{ rides for 5 people}}{40 \text{ tickets}}$$

   One ride for 5 people will use 20 tickets. Two rides for 5 people will use 40 tickets.

3. Make sure students can explain how each number was determined or if they use a table, you might want to suggest a process column. Here are some examples of tables that students may use:

Example 1:

Number of rides per person	Number of tickets for rides	Number of tickets for drinks	Number of tickets needed in all
1	40	8	48
2	80	8	88
3	120	8	128
4	160	8	168

Example 2:

Number of Rides	1	2	3	4
Number of drink tickets + (number of rides × number of tickets × number of people)	8 + 40	8 + 80	8 + 120	8 + 160
Total cost of tickets	48	88	128	168

Six booklets of tickets at City-Mart cost 150 tickets. Each person can ride the *Twister* 3 times.

4. Information known: The group had 175 tickets. There were 5 riders.

$\dfrac{1 \text{ person}}{5 \text{ rides}} = \dfrac{5 \text{ people}}{25 \text{ rides}}$ If 1 person rode 5 times, then 5 people rode 25 times.

$\dfrac{25 \text{ rides}}{175 \text{ tickets}} = \dfrac{1 \text{ ride}}{7 \text{ tickets}}$ 25 rides uses 175 tickets. 50 rides uses 7 tickets.

$\dfrac{1 \text{ ride} \times 5}{7 \text{ tickets} \times 5} = \dfrac{5 \text{ rides}}{35 \text{ tickets}}$ Each ride uses 7 tickets. 5 rides would use 35 tickets.

Karen would need 35 tickets to ride the *Storm* 5 more times.

CHAPTER 2 ALGEBRAIC REASONING

LESSON 1 — WALKING TRIP

Common Core State Standards
Expressions and Equations 6.EE
Reason about and solve
one-variable equations and
inequalities.
5. Understand solving an
   equation or inequality as a
   process of answering a
   question. Use substitution
   to determine whether a
   given number in a specified
   set makes an equation or
   inequality true.
7. Solve real-world and
   mathematical problems by
   writing and solving
   equations of the form
   $x + p = q$ and $px = q$ for
   cases in which p, q, and x
   are all nonnegative rational
   numbers.
Represent and analyze
quantitative relationships
between dependent and
independent variables.
9. Use variables to represent
   two quantities in a real-
   world problem that change
   in relationship to one
   another; write an equation
   to express one quantity.
   Analyze the relationship
   between the dependent
   and independent variables
   using graphs and tables,
   and relate those to the
   equation.

LESSON GOALS

- Introduce patterns of change between variables.

LESSON INTRODUCTION

This lesson is about rate. Ask students to give examples of rates and make a list on the board of the rates they share. In this lesson, students may use tables, graphs, or equations to solve the problems.

> A **rate** is a ratio of two measurements.

For students to get a complete understanding of rates and the proportional relationship involved, it is important to make connections between the different representations used by students.

For one question in the Student Recording Page, students are asked to find their own walking rate. Upon completion of the lesson, you can have students share their strategies for finding how long it would take them to walk 2 miles. Once again students can approach this situation using a variety of different rates and a variety of different strategies. Discuss with students the use of proportional reasoning in all of the strategies.

Students should realize as they progress through this lesson that a proportional relationship is graphed as a straight line that passes through the origin.

TEACHING SUGGESTIONS

Within the bulleted text below are suggestions on how to begin the lesson, introduce essential vocabulary, and question students so that they are prepared to complete the Student Recording Page on their own or with minimal assistance.

- If I told you my walking rate was 0.75, would that be enough information to predict how far I could walk in 1 hour?

- What additional information would you need?

- Discuss walking rates. What is a walking rate?

- How could you find a walking rate? What two variables do you need to find a walking rate?

- How are walking rates recorded?

Have a discussion about how some rates are reported.

- In this lesson, you will be asked to find your own walking rate. What do you think you will need to find your walking rate?

Discuss students' ideas briefly. Leave the discussion open enough to allow students to decide how they will collect and record their walking rates.

Introduce the problem to students.

- Does Yvonne and Lisa's walking rate seem reasonable?

- When students use rates in the Student Recording Page, instruct them to always include labels.

- Instruct students to pay attention to the scales used when graphing so the data does not get distorted.

NCTM Correlation

Algebra

Understand patterns, relations, and functions.

Represent, analyze, and generalize a variety of patterns with tables, graphs, words, and when possible, symbolic rules.

Represent and analyze mathematical situations and structures using algebraic symbols.

Use symbolic algebra to represent situations and to solve problems, especially those that involve linear relationships.

Materials
Student Recording Page 2.1

Vocabulary
Rate

Students are to complete Student Recording Page 2.1. When students begin work on Question 7, have them work in groups of three or four. They are finding their own walking rates and will need access to a hallway or breezeway to collect their times and distances data.

As students work on this lesson, ask questions to check for understanding. Ask questions about the relationships they are using. If students are using rates, ask them to define the rates using labels.

QUESTIONS FOR STRUGGLING STUDENTS

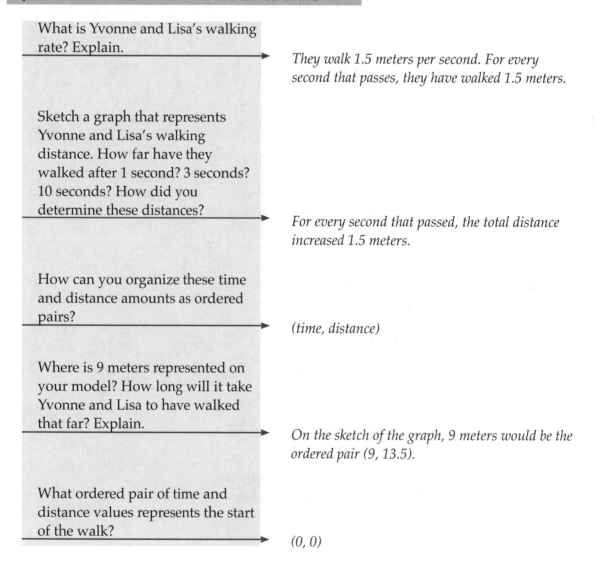

What is Yvonne and Lisa's walking rate? Explain.

They walk 1.5 meters per second. For every second that passes, they have walked 1.5 meters.

Sketch a graph that represents Yvonne and Lisa's walking distance. How far have they walked after 1 second? 3 seconds? 10 seconds? How did you determine these distances?

For every second that passed, the total distance increased 1.5 meters.

How can you organize these time and distance amounts as ordered pairs?

(time, distance)

Where is 9 meters represented on your model? How long will it take Yvonne and Lisa to have walked that far? Explain.

On the sketch of the graph, 9 meters would be the ordered pair (9, 13.5).

What ordered pair of time and distance values represents the start of the walk?

(0, 0)

What does it mean when the problem states, "they walk at a constant rate of 1.5 meters per second?"

→ *They walk at a steady rate in a proportional relationship.*

What does their walking rate mean?

→ *the distance a person travels in a given amount of time*

What units are used in their walking rate?

→ *meters and seconds*

If you know how far they walk in a second, how can you find out how far they walk in a minute? Hour?

→ *Multiply the distance by 60 because there are 60 seconds in a minute. Multiply that answer by 60 because there are 60 minutes in an hour.*

How do you think Lisa determined the constant walking rate?

→ *She walked for a certain amount of time and found how far she had walked.*

If you had a timer and a tape measure, how could you determine your walking rate?

→ *Measure a distance on the floor and time how long it takes to walk that distance.*

How long do you think it will take you to walk from here to there (e.g. one end of chalk board to the other) walking at your usual pace? How can you check your prediction?

→ *about 1 second; find the walking rate*

How far do you think you should walk to establish an accurate walking rate?

→ *Possible response: Walk for at least 10 seconds or 10 meters.*

What units will you use to find your walking rate?

→ *meters/second or seconds/meter*

QUESTIONS FOR STUDENTS ON TASK

Name two unit rates in this problem.

→ *1.5 meters per second, 1,600 meters in a mile*

How does knowing how many meters are in a $\frac{1}{2}$ mile help you?

→ *The information could be used to find the number of meters in a mile.*

How many seconds are in an hour?

→ *3,600*

If you know meters per hour, how can you find meters per minute?

→ *Divide the number of meters by 60, because there are 60 minutes in 1 hour.*

What are some rates that might help you answer the questions?

→ *seconds/minute, minutes/hour, meters/hour, miles/hour*

What are the variables in this situation?

→ *time and distance*

Which variable is the independent variable and why?

→ *time, because distance is dependent on time*

What patterns of change do you see?

Students may suggest: The longer (time) you walk, the longer distance travelled. For every hour that passes, Yvonne and Lisa walk 5,400 meters.

How does the distance for 3 hours compare to the distance at 6 hours? 9 hours?

The distance at 6 hours is double the distance at 3 hours, and the distance at 9 hours is triple the distance at 3 hours.

Is the walking rate data proportional? How do you know?

Yes, for every second that passes they walk 1.5 meters.

Will all time/distance relationships always be proportional?

Only if the rate traveled is kept constant; in reality, it would be almost impossible for a person to walk/run/drive/bike/fly for a relatively long distance at a constant rate without slowing down or speeding up.

If a walking rate is 2 meters per second, how does the table of values differ from Yvonne's table of data?

Sample answer: The rate would be 7,200 meters per hour, and the table of values would increase by 7,200 every hour.

If a walking rate is 2 meters per second, how does the graph compare to Yvonne and Lisa's graph? What would be the same? What would be different?

The graph is still proportional, but would have a steeper rate of change (slope).

QUESTIONS FOR STUDENTS ON TASK (CONTINUED)

If a walking rate were 2 meters/second, what distance can be walked in 40 seconds?

→ *80 meters*

How far would Yvonne and Lisa have traveled in the same amount of time?

→ *60 meters*

QUESTIONS TO EXTEND STUDENT THINKING

What would the graph for Yvonne and Lisa's walking rate look like?

→ *It would start on (0,0) and be a linear relationship.*

If a walking rate was 1 meter/1.5 seconds, how could you find out how fast a person was walking per second?

→ *Set up a proportional relationship between 1 meter/1.5 seconds and $\frac{x}{1}$ second. The rate is $\frac{2}{3}$ meter/second or 0.67 meter/second.*

How would increasing your walking rate affect the values in the table? The graph? The equation?

→ *In the table you will see the constant rate of change increase. In the graph the slope or steepness of the graph will increase. In the equation the value of r will increase.*

How would a slower walking rate affect the values in the table? the graph? the equation?

→ *A table showing a slower walking rate would increase less each hour, the graph would not be as steep, and the value of r would be less.*

Lesson Summary

Begin by looking at some of the sketches students created for Question 1. Compare the graphs and what affected their appearances. Discuss that graphs should all show proportional relationships but some graphs will be steeper than others, depending on the walking rates and scales used when graphing. Students may have several approaches to answering the questions. Some students use one rate to solve the problems; others will look at relationships that grow. For example in Question 2, some students use the ratio 3,600 seconds/1 hour; others will use 60 seconds/1 minute and then 60 minutes/1 hour. Have students show how these rates are equivalent. Discuss the equivalency of the rates. Ask students to share the rates they used and compare them to other rates used.

Ask a student to share the equation found for Question 5. As a class, decide on the variables used and what the different parts of the equation represent. Students should be able to identify where the rate appears in the equation. Have some students share how they used their equations to solve Question 6.

Check for Success

☐ Have students describe the effect on the graph if Yvonne decided to jog to her friend's house. Then students can tell how jogging changes the table and an equation.

☐ To reinforce their learning, have students explain patterns of change and where they are found in different representations.

☐ Have students write a description of how they found their own walking rates. Students should also be able to represent their rate in a table and a graph. Students need to be able to explain the pattern of change represented in the table, graph, and equation and state if that change is proportional.

☐ To verify that they understand the concept, have students give another example of a situation that involves another proportional relationship. Students should name the variables involved, describe what a table of values for the relationship will look like, and explain how the graph will look. Students should then write an equation for the relationship.

LESSON 1   WALKING TRIP

In the evenings Yvonne and Lisa enjoy taking walks. Lisa says they walk at a constant rate of 1.5 meters per second. One day they decide they want to walk to a friend's house 10 miles away. Yvonne remembers that 800 meters is about one-half mile. She says it will take them all day to walk. Answer the following questions to decide if the walk to the friend's home will take all day.

1. Sketch a graph showing Yvonne and Lisa's walking rate.

2. How far will Yvonne and Lisa have walked in 1 hour?

3. Make a table showing a distance walked, in meters, in 6 hours. What kind of relationship is shown in the table? What does the graph look like?

4. How long will it take Yvonne and Lisa to walk 2 miles?

5. How long will it take Yvonne and Lisa to walk 10 miles? Write an equation for how long it will take Yvonne and Lisa to walk any number of miles.

6. Using your equation from Question 5, how long will it take Yvonne and Lisa to walk 20 miles? 4 miles?

7. Find the rate at which you walk.

8. Define the variables you used to determine your walking rate assuming you can continue to walk at this constant rate. Describe the relationships between the variables.

9. If you and Yvonne both left at the same time to walk 2 miles to a friend's house, who would get there first?

1.

Yvonne & Lisa's Walking Rate

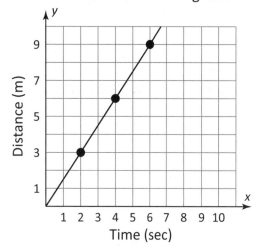

2. Example 1:

$$\frac{1.5\ m}{1\ sec} = \frac{m}{60\ sec}$$

Example 2: $\frac{1.5\ m}{1\ sec} = \frac{90\ m}{60\ sec}$

$y = 90x$, where y represents min and x represents distance

$$\frac{1.5\ m}{1\ sec} \times \frac{60}{60} = \frac{90\ m}{60\ sec}$$

$y = 90(60)$
$y = 5,400$
5,400 meters per 60 minutes

$$\frac{90\ m}{1\ min} \times \frac{60}{60} = \frac{5,400\ m}{60\ min}$$

3.

Hours	Meters Walked
1	5,400
2	10,800
3	16,200
4	21,600
5	27,000
6	32,400

Students should notice that the relationship is proportional. The graph shows a linear relationship that passes through the origin.

4. d = distance walked = 2 miles; r = walking rate; t = time
If $\frac{1}{2}$ mile ≈ 800 meters then 1 mile ≈ 1,600 meters and 2 miles ≈ 3,200 meters.
If in 60 minutes, the distance is 5,400 meters, then 5,400 ÷ 60 gives the rate for 1 minute. Rate for 1 minute is 90 meters/min. Now use $d = rt$.

4. (continued)

$3{,}200 = 90r$

$35.6 \approx r$ It will take about $35\frac{1}{2}$ minutes to walk 2 miles.

Another method students can use to answer this question:

$$\frac{1{,}600 \text{ m}}{1 \text{ mi}} = \frac{?}{2 \text{ mi}} \qquad \frac{1{,}600 \text{ m}}{1 \text{ mi}} \times \frac{2}{2} = \frac{3{,}200 \text{ m}}{2 \text{ mi}}$$

From the table, I see that they walk a rate of 5,400m/1 h. I set up a proportion.

$$\frac{5{,}400}{1 \text{ h}} = \frac{3{,}200}{?}$$

$3{,}200 \div 5{,}400 \approx 0.593$

$$\frac{5{,}400 \text{ m}}{60 \text{ min}} \times \frac{0.593}{0.593} = \frac{3{,}200 \text{ m}}{35.5 \text{ min}}$$

5. Example 1:

$$\frac{2 \text{ mi}}{35\frac{1}{2} \text{ min}} = \frac{10 \text{ mi}}{X}$$

$$\frac{2 \text{ mi}}{35\frac{1}{2} \text{ min}} \times \frac{5}{5} = \frac{10 \text{ mi}}{177\frac{1}{2} \text{ min}}$$

$\frac{60 \text{ min}}{1 \text{ hr}}$ $177.5 \div 60 = 2.96$ hrs
It will take them about
3 h to walk 10 miles.

$$\frac{2 \text{ mi}}{35\frac{1}{2} \text{ min}} = \frac{1 \text{ m}}{17.75 \text{ min}}$$ So, $y = 17.75x$

Example 2:

x (min)	y (min)
1	17.75
2	35.5
3	53.25
4	71
5	88.75
6	106.5
x	17.75(x)

$y = 17.75x$
$y = 17.75(10) = 177.5$
It will take 177.5 min or 2 h 57.5 min

6. When $x = 20$ miles, it will take about 355 minutes or 5 hours 55 minutes
When $x = 4$ miles, it will take about 71 minutes or 1 hour 11 minutes

7. Answers will vary. Walking rates should be in the 2 meters/second range.

8. The variables are time and distance. The relationship is proportional. As the time increases by 1 hour, the distance they walk increases 5,400 meters. The relationship is also linear. If I graph the relationship, I get points that lie on a straight line.

9. Answers will vary; I know it takes Yvonne $35\frac{1}{2}$ minutes to walk 2 miles.

Common Core State Standards
Expressions and Equations 7.EE
  Solve real-life and
  mathematical problems using
  numerical and algebraic
  expressions and equations.
  4. Use variables to represent
    quantities in a real-world
    or mathematical problem,
    and construct simple
    equations and inequalities
    to solve problems by
    reasoning about the
    quantities.

NCTM Correlation
Numbers and Operations
  Compute fluently and make
  reasonable estimates.
    *Develop, analyze, and
    explain methods for solving
    problems involving
    proportions, such as scaling
    and finding equivalent
    ratios.*
Algebra
  Use mathematical models to
  represent and understand
  quantitative relationships.
    *Model and solve
    contextualized problems
    using various
    representations, such as
    graphs, tables, and
    equations.*
  Analyze change in various
  contexts.
    *Use graphs to analyze the
    nature of changes in
    quantities in linear
    relationships.*

LESSON GOALS

- Represent relationships in tabular, verbal, graphical, and symbolic form.
- Compare tabular and graphic representations of the same data and connect to the symbolic representation.
- Identify and understand how unit rate is represented in an equation, table, and graph.

LESSON INTRODUCTION

In this lesson students translate among representations so that their understanding can advance from words to tables to graphs to equations. The concepts are covered in the context of playing a video game where zombies are zapped to score points and players advance through levels in the game. Introduce to students the background about the video game. The main goal of the game is to earn points by zapping zombies. Have a brief conversation about game levels and points earned. As students work through this lesson, keep them focused on the relationship between the different parts of the table.

The understanding of proportional relationships in this problem helps students make the connections between the different representations.

TEACHING SUGGESTIONS

Within the bulleted text below are suggestions on how to begin the lesson, introduce essential vocabulary, and question students so that they are prepared to complete the Student Recording Page on their own or with minimal assistance.

- Make sure students can read the table by reviewing the information known and ask questions about the information needed to complete the table. Leave the discussion open enough to allow students to decide on a method for finding the missing values.

- To help struggling students, suggest students write a verbal description of the situation.

- Before discussing rates, review the definition of ratio.

  > A **ratio** is a comparison of two quantities. Ratios can be written using three formats. 2 to 3; 2:3, and $\frac{2}{3}$

- Use guiding questions to help students understand the significance of what a unit rate is and what role it plays in generalizing the pattern. They then can translate their rule to symbolic form using variables.

  > A **rate** is a ratio of two measurements. A **unit rate** is a rate where one of the measurements is 1. Sample unit rates are: 12 inches: 1 foot, $25 per ticket, 4 hours:1 room.

- Have a discussion to review the components of a graph in preparation for students graphing relationships in this lesson. Include in the review the concept of slope.

  > **Slope** is the **constant rate of change** of a linear relationship. When the equation of a line is given in a form $y = mx + b$, the **coefficient** of the x-term, m, is the slope.

Materials
Student Recording Page 2.2
Optional:
Graph Paper
Graphing Calculator

Vocabulary
Ratio
Rate
Unit Rate
Slope
Constant Rate
Coefficient
Independent Variable
Dependent Variable

- Instruct students on how to distinguish between the independent and dependent variables in a relationship.

- Explain the equations also show how variables are related to each other, just like tables and graphs.

- Encourage students to share their strategies for completing the table.

- For students that use a repeated addition process to fill in parts of the table, ask questions that will focus them on the multiplicative nature of the values.

- As the level numbers tripled from 2 to 6, how did the number of zombies change? How did the number of points change?

- How would you determine the number of zombies you zapped if you reached level 5? level 20?

> An **independent variable** in a relationship, or ordered pair, is the variable that stands alone and is not affected or changed by the relationship. A **dependent variable** in a relationship, or ordered pair, is the variable affected by the independent variable. The value of the independent variable changes the value of the dependent variable.

STUDENT ENGAGEMENT

Students need to complete Student Recording Page 2.2. As students begin working, ask them to estimate the values that belong in the table and explain why their estimates make sense. As students begin graphing, be sure they have identified the independent and dependent variables correctly and have selected an appropriate scale. As students work on this recording page, continue to ask questions about the relationships between variables of the situations to check for understanding.

What variables are involved?

Levels, Zombies, and Points

What information can you gather from the table?

Possible answers include: When you reach Level 6 you have zapped 210 zombies and earned 23,100 points. You earned 7,700 points for Level 2. To exit Level 8 you need 30,800 points.

What information in the table helps you find the number of zombies needed to advance?

The number of zombies increased from 140 to 210 between Levels 4 and 6. The number of zombies needed to complete two levels is 70.

What rate helps you complete the table?

210 zombies zapped to 23,100 points earned

How are the level numbers changing in the table?

by 2 each time

How are the numbers of zombies zapped changing in the table?

by 70 for every 2 levels

How do the numbers of points earned change in the table?

by 7,700 every 2 levels

Identify a ratio found in the table.

The ratio between the level and the number of zombies zapped; the ratio between the numbers of zombies zapped to the number of points earned; or the level to the number of points earned

You know the number of zombies zapped for every two levels. Use that information to find how many zombies need to be zapped at every level. This is the unit rate. What other unit rates can you find?

→ *For every level you need to zap 35 zombies. 1 zombie gets 110 points; every level earns 3,850 points.*

What do you know about Level 10? Given that, what can you determine about Level 5?

→ *The number of zombies zapped; 350 zombies zapped, 38,500 points earned; Level 5 should be half of each of the values.*

What is the relationship between the levels earned and the numbers of zombies zapped?

→ *For every two levels, the number of zombies zapped increases by 70.*

What labels do you use for the graphs?

→ *Levels and Zombies, Zombies and Points, or Levels and Points*

For each variable, name the minimum and maximum values you need to include on your *x*- and *y*-axes. What is a reasonable scale to use for the axes? (e.g. What would be an effective way to skip-count, if your range went from 0 to nearly 50,000?)

→ *For Levels, a scale of 1 with a minimum of 0 and a maximum of 15; for zombies, a scale of 35 with a minimum of 0 and a maximum of 500; for Points, a scale of 5,000 with a minimum of 0 and a maximum of 50,000*

Describe how to find the missing values to complete the table. Show examples to explain your thinking.

Use the values you know to help find the missing values. Find out how the table changes from one value to the next both horizontally and vertically.

What patterns do you see in the table? Ask students questions about any patterns that are not mentioned.

Students may suggest: As levels increase by 2, the number of zombies increases by 70. As levels increase by 1, the number of zombies increases by 35. As levels increase by 1, the number of points increases by 3,850.

If the pattern shows that the number of zombies zapped increases by 70 zombies for every two levels, how many zombies need to be zapped per level?

35

Describe the relationships between the variables. Encourage students to be as specific as possible. Students may suggest the following: As the levels increase, the other variables increase. Suggest students be more specific by asking "By how much?"

For every two levels you advance, the number of zombies zapped increases by 70. For every 70 zombies, a player scores 7,700 points. For every level increased, a player zaps 35 zombies. For every level increased, a player earns 3,850 points.

Questions for Students on Task (continued)

What are the attributes of a proportional relationship?

→ *As the independent variable increases by one unit, the dependent variable increases at a constant rate. If you look at a graph, you see a linear relationship that passes through the origin.*

What relationships can be graphed? What do you predict the graphs to look like?

→ *Levels and Number of Zombies Zapped; Levels and Number of Points earned; and Zombies Zapped and Number of Points earned; The graphs will be linear.*

How can you tell if a relationship is proportional using a graph?

→ *The graph is linear and passes through the origin.*

Questions to Extend Student Thinking

Suppose Leo purchased a newer version of Zapping Zombies. In this version, the number of zombies zapped at each level increases from 35 to 50 zombies. How would this affect the original table of values? How would this affect the original graph? How would this affect the original equation?

→ *In the table, the values would increase more rapidly; in the graph, the trend line would be steeper; and in the equation, the coefficient of x would be 50, not 35.*

What would the values be if you extended the table to level 13?

→ *The number of zombies zapped would reach 455; the number of points earned would be 50,050.*

After playing for many hours, Leo had a total of 92,400 points. What level did he complete? Show how to use the table, graph, and equation to justify your solution.

He would be on level 24. Each level was worth 3,850 points, so divide 92,400 by 3,850 to get a quotient of 24. Follow the trend on the graph to estimate the level and use the equation $p = 3850l$, to solve for l, where l is the level and p = 92,400.

Leo's little brother said he beat the level and zapped a total of 990 zombies. Leo didn't believe him. Mathematically justify which brother is correct.

Level 24 would only zap 840 zombies; $24 \cdot 35 = 840$ zombies zapped. Leo's little bother is correct.

If during the bonus round, scores triple points for every zombie zapped, and you earn 16,500 points in that round, how many zombies did you zap? Explain.

You normally earn 110 points per zombie. If points are tripled, then you earn 330 points per zombie. $16,500 \div 330 = 50$ zombies

What benefits does the table, graph, or equation give you in understanding the specific relationships?

The table shows you specific data points. The graph shows you the relationship holistically, such as what is happening with the relationships. The equations tell you about the specific rates in the relationships.

Students experienced identifying patterns involving a constant rate of change, completing a table, creating graphs, and writing equations. Students should recognize that all of these representations show that the relationships are proportional. They all increase with a constant rate of change as the other variable increases by 1. The relationships are all based on the proportional relationship between the levels, zombies, and points. Have students go back to the fact that all of these relationships are balanced the same way in each representation, so all share a constant of proportionality among the compared variables.

Continue to focus students on the patterns of change (i.e. unit rate) in each equation. Discuss the connection between the coefficient of the variable in the equation, which is also the slope of the line, and the rate in the table. As students move through the topic of algebraic reasoning, it would be helpful for students to recognize how the different representations are related and how each representation is equally valuable.

Students should be able to tell you the information readily seen from a table is the exact values of the ordered pairs. Information readily seen from a graph is the general pattern of the relationship. From the equation, they can find the solution.

For each relationship, students should identify the constant of proportionality. Generate a list of all patterns observed (horizontally and vertically) in the table. Have students share their strategies for finding the missing values in the table. Record these strategies and have students record at least one strategy they fully understand. Focus students on the multiplicative relationships.

Have students share their graphs. As a class compare and contrast the graphs. Discuss the following: all relationships are linear; all graphs of the line pass through the origin; and proportional relationships are linear, but can have different rates. Include in the discussion questions so students can verbalize what they notice in the graphs and what they have learned.

CHECK FOR SUCCESS

☐ Have students generate a list of all possible unit rates and explain the information that can be gathered from a unit rate.

☐ Have students summarize and explain the equations they used in the lessons. Instruct students the summary should include the process they used to write the equation, including if they wrote the rule in words before they wrote the equation.

☐ Have students solve the following problem.

Leo purchased Beyond Zapping Zombies. When looking at the game codes on line, Leo found the table of data given below. Have students predict how the tables, graphs, and equations will differ for this game.

Level	3	6	9	12	15	18
Maximum Number of Zombies Zapped	180		540		900	
Points Earned		27,000		54,000		81,000

From *It's All Connected: The Power of Proportional Reasoning to Understand Mathematics Concepts, Grades 6–8* by Carmen Whitman. Permission granted to photocopy for nonprofit use in a classroom or similar place dedicated to face-to-face educational instruction. © 2011 Scholastic Inc.

LESSON 2 ZAPPING ZOMBIES

Leo likes playing a video game where he has to zap zombies and turn them into statues before they invade a town. In the game, zombies hide everywhere. Leo's goal is to clear all the zombies to make the town safe again.

To advance to the next level a player has to zap all the zombies in that level. Each level has the same number of zombies and the same number of points are earned for each zapped Zombie. As players move through the levels, the zombies get harder to zap.

Leo made the table below to show a relationship between the total number of zombies zapped and accumulated points earned.

Level	2	4	6	8	10	12
Total Number of Zombies Zapped		140	210		350	
Accumulated Points Earned	7,700		23,100	30,800		

1. Complete the table above. Look for relationships and patterns in the table. Describe at least three patterns.

2. Describe the ratios between the levels and the maximum number of zombies zapped. How are these ratios related?

3. What are the ratios of the number of zombies zapped to the number of points earned? How are these ratios related?

4. Name at least two different rates you can find in this game.

5. List the unit rates in this problem. How do you know the rates are unit rates?

6. Graph each rate. How does this support your findings from Question 5?

7. Write an equation for each relationship described below.
   a. the level in the game and the number of zombies zapped

   b. the number of zombies zapped and the points earned

   c. the level in the game and the points earned

8. How did you use a unit rate to write each equation?

1.

Level	2	4	6	8	10	12
Total Number of Zombies Zapped	70	140	210	280	350	420
Accumulated Points Earned	7,700	15,400	23,100	30,800	38,500	46,200

Levels increase by 2. Zombies zapped increases by 70 for every 2 levels. Points earned increases by 7,700 for every 70 zombies zapped. Each level you earn 3,850 for every 35 zombies zapped. You can earn 3,850 points in every level for zapping zombies.

2. Answers may include: There is a ratio of 2 levels: 70 zapped zombies. There is a ratio of 6 levels: 210 zapped zombies. There is a ratio of 12 levels: 420 zapped zombies. There is a ratio of 1 level: 35 zapped zombies. There are 35 zombies per level. All ratios are equivalent: $\frac{2}{70} = \frac{6}{210} = \frac{12}{420} = \frac{1}{35}$.

3. Answers may include: There is a ratio of 70 zombies zapped: 7,700 points earned There is a ratio of 210 zombies zapped: 23,100 points earned. There is a ratio of 420 zombies zapped: 46,200 points earned. There is a ratio of 35 zombies zapped: 3,850 points earned. There is a ratio of 1 Zombie zapped: 110 points earned. For each level, the ratio of the number of zombies zapped compared to the number of points earned is equivalent. Each zapped zombie is worth 110 points.

4. Answers may include: There is a rate between the levels and zombies zapped. There is a rate between zombies zapped and points earned. There is a rate between levels and points earned.

5. Answers may include: All the rates in the table are constant. All numbers are increasing by a constant factor. As the levels increase by two, the number of zombies zapped increases by 70, and the number of points increases by 7,700.

Levels to Zombies: $\dfrac{2 \text{ Levels} \times \frac{1}{2}}{70 \text{ Levels} \times \frac{1}{2}} = \dfrac{1 \text{ Level}}{35 \text{ Zombies}} = \dfrac{2}{70} = \dfrac{1}{35}$

Zombies to Points: $\dfrac{70 \text{ Zombies} \times \frac{1}{70}}{7,700 \text{ Points} \times \frac{1}{70}} = \dfrac{1 \text{ Zombie}}{110 \text{ Points}} = \dfrac{70}{7,700} = \dfrac{1}{110}$

Levels to Points: $\dfrac{2 \text{ Levels} \times \frac{1}{2}}{7,700 \text{ Points} \times \frac{1}{2}} = \dfrac{1 \text{ Level}}{3,850 \text{ Points}} = \dfrac{2}{7,700} = \dfrac{1}{3,850}$

These rates can also be described as follows: for every level a player has to zap 35 zombies; for every zombie zapped, a player scores 110 points; and for every level completed, a player scores 3,850 points.

6.

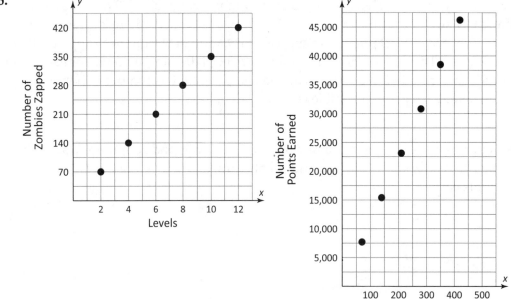

6. (continued)

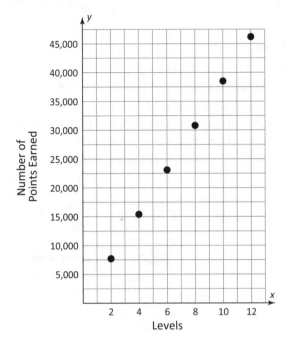

The rates found in Question in each situation become the constant rat of change in each graph, which makes the graph linear.

7. a. $z = 35l$

   b. $p = 110z$

   c. $p = 3,850l$

8. Answers may include: From the table, I found the unit rate in each relationship and used it as the slope of the equation. From the graph, I found the slope (the amount of vertical change for every one unit of horizontal change) and write the equation $y = mx$.

Common Core State Standards

Expressions and Equations 8.EE

Analyze and solve linear equations and pairs of simultaneous linear equations.

a. Understand that solutions to a system of two linear equations in two variables correspond to points of intersection of their graphs, because points of intersection satisfy both equations simultaneously.

NCTM Correlation

Algebra

Represent and analyze mathematical situations and structures using algebraic symbols.

Explore relationships between symbolic expressions and graphs of lines, paying particular attention to the meaning of intercept and slope.

Use symbolic algebra to represent situations and to solve problems, especially those that involve linear relationships.

Use mathematical models to represent and understand quantitative relationships.

Model and solve contextualized problems using various representations, such as graphs, tables, and equations.

Analyze change in various contexts.

Use graphs to analyze the nature of changes in quantities in linear relationships.

LESSON GOALS

- Explore linear relationships.
- Use tables, graphs, and equations that represent relationships to solve problems.
- Compare and contrast proportional and non-proportional relationships using multiple representations.
- Describe patterns of change between variables.

LESSON INTRODUCTION

Review with students that a linear equation or a linear graph is related to a straight line.

Display the graph below.

Linear is an adjective that means a straight line. A linear equation has a **constant rate of change**, which is shown in a graph as a constant increase or a constant decrease.

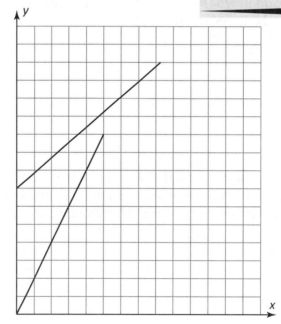

One graph shows a linear relationship that is proportional and another that is non-proportional.

Ask students, what they notice about the graphs. Discuss differences in the graphs, by referencing the points on the graphs, the slopes, and where the graphs begin and end. Ask students to think of a scenario that could be represented by the graphs and ask the following question that can be answered using the graphs.

- If these graphs represented the time and distance during a race, what could you tell about each person's progress?

Some graphs in this lesson will be graphed on the same coordinate plane and students will be able to identify where the graphs intersect. The ordered pair of that point will have special meaning in regard to the situation being graphed.

TEACHING SUGGESTIONS

Within the bulleted text below are suggestions on how to begin the lesson, introduce essential vocabulary, and question students so that they are prepared to complete the Student Recording Page on their own or with minimal assistance.

Introduce the scenarios of the music lesson to the students.

- Have students make some conjectures about the different plans. Discuss some reasons that might convince students that they have the best plan.

- Make a list of these so that you can revisit them in the summary. Have a brief discussion about any different representations. For example, how do you see rate of change in the table, graph, or equation? What information can you get from a table that you might not get from an equation?

Materials
Student Recording Page 2.3
Graph Paper
Colored Pencils
Optional:
Graphing Calculator

Vocabulary
Linear
Constant rate of change
Proportional relationships
Non-proportional relationships
y-intercept
Point of intersection

A graph that shows a **proportional relationship** is one that is the graph of a line that passes through the origin, (0, 0). The graph of a proportional relationship has a **y-intercept** whose ordered pair is (0, 0).

A graph that shows a **non-proportional relationship** is one that may or may not be a linear graph, but if linear it does not pass through the point (0, 0). This means that the ordered pair for the **y-intercept** of a non-proportional relationship is (0, y).

- Explain to students that they will be graphing lines in the lesson. Make some general statements about how scale affects graphs.

- In general, discuss with students that rate paid for each song will determine how steep the line is in the graph. Ask students to predict if a greater rate per song will result in a steeper graph or a less steep graph.

- Direct students attention to the plan that has an initial cost. Ask how much will be paid before any song is downloaded? What ordered pair will represent this situation? The graph will start at (0, 6).

- When you graph two plans on the same coordinate grid, the lines intersect at a point that is common to both lines. What does that point represent?
  The point of intersection is the number of songs and the amount paid where both plans are equal.

> The **point of intersection** of two lines is the point where the lines cross each other. The ordered pair names a point that is on both lines.

STUDENT ENGAGEMENT

As students begin working on the problems, continue to ask questions about the relationships they are using. Have students discuss the variables they select in each representation and identify which is the independent variable and which is the dependent variable.

If students struggle to write equations you can suggest they write rules using words then change those words into equations. Have them think about which representation they find most helpful and why that is the case.

Initially have students begin work on the Student Recording Page 2.3 problems individually to develop their own strategies; then move students into small groups to share ideas and complete the task.

> An **independent variable** in a relationship, or ordered pair, is the variable that stands alone and is not affected or changed by the relationship.
> A **dependent variable** in a relationship, or ordered pair, is the variable affected by the independent variable. The value of the independent variable changes the value of the dependent variable.

What do know about Anna's plan?

It costs $6.00 to start plus $1.00 for every download.

What do know about Gena's plan?

There is initial cost for the plan and she pays $1.49 per download.

What are the variables in each situation? (i.e., What are the quantities that are changing in this problem?)

cost and number of songs bought

What information do you need to make a table to compare the plans?

the number of downloads, the cost of Anna's plan, the cost of Gena's plan

What two variables are you comparing?

the numbers of downloads to cost

For 1 download what will Anna pay? Gena?

$7.00, $1

For 2 downloads, what would both costs be? Explain how to find the cost of 5 songs.

For Anna if would be $6.00 + 2 = $8.00, and for Gena it would be $1.49 × 2 = $2.98. Five songs cost Anna $6.00 + 6 × 1= $12.00 and cost Gena 5 × $1.49 = $7.45.

What patterns do you observe? Explain why these patterns occur.

For Gena it is the cost of the song by the number of songs she buys, and for Anna it is $6.00 plus the number of songs times $1.49.

Questions for Struggling Students (continued)

What would be the related costs for zero downloads?	*Anna would pay $6.00; Gena would pay $0.00.*
What does proportional mean? Which download offer(s) appear to be proportional and why?	*For every 1 change in x, there is a constant rate of change in y, and the relationship passes through the origin when graphed. Anna's is non-proportional and Gena's is proportional.*
How do you know if the relationship is proportional from a table of values?	*There has to be a constant rate of change for each unit increase in x (e.g. number of songs) throughout the table, and no initial cost for zero downloads.*
What would you put on the x-axis of the graph?	*the independent variable*
What would you put on the y-axis?	*the dependent variable*
When you are setting up the scale for your graph what do you have to consider?	*the range of numbers that describes the variables in the situations; for example, the number of downloads and cost*
What is the minimum value needed on the y-axis?	*0*
What is the greatest value needed on the y-axis?	*Answers may vary.*

When writing the equation, what variables should you consider?

→ *cost and number of downloads*

How did you determine the costs for one download? Two downloads? Three downloads? Any number of downloads?

→ *The cost of 1 download is the scenario and the rest is determined by multiplying.*

How are variables in this situation related to each other?

→ *As the number of downloads increase, the cost increases.*

QUESTIONS FOR STUDENTS ON TASK

Why does the first entry in the table reflect that there is $6.00 for Anna and $0 for Gena for 0 downloads?

→ *This is the amount each has to pay before downloading any songs.*

How does the cost change as the number of downloads increases?

→ *The cost increases.*

Which table of values increases proportionally? How do you know?

→ *Gena's values increase because there is no initial cost of $6.00 like Anna's plan.*

How do you select the labels for your graphs?

→ *The variables in the situation dictate the labels. The independent variable goes on the x-axis and the dependent variable goes on the y-axis.*

As the graphs are getting closer to each other, what do you know about the price plans?

→ *In this situation as the graphs approach each other, the amount of money spent is getting closer to the same amount.*

How does the initial cost of the plan show up in the graphs?

→ *The initial cost is the y-intercept.*

How does the graph help you see a proportional relationship?

→ *The points that lie on a straight line that has a slope of 1.49, and the graph passes through the origin. The other plan is not proportional since its graph does not cross through the origin because of the initial $6 for 0 downloads.*

Describe how you would find the price of 5 downloads for Anna.

→ *Look in the table, or find the 5 on the x-axis and find the y-axis value, or use corresponding equation c = 1s + 6, and substitute 5 for s. Solve for c.*

How does the initial cost of the plans show up in the equation?

→ *In these equations it is what is being added. For example in Anna's plan, c = 1s + 6, the 6 represents the up-front fee which is represented as (0, 6), which is the y-intercept.*

In the equation, what shows you that it is a proportional situation?

→ *There is a constant rate of change, and the value of c is 0 when s is 0.*

How would you use the equation to find the price of any number of downloads?

→ *Substitute the number of downloads for s in each of the equations.*

How would you use the equation to find the number of downloads if the cost was given?

⟶ *In Gena's, you would divide the cost by $1.49. In Anna's, you would subtract $6.00 from the cost. In Aricela's, you would subtract $10.00 from the cost and divide by $0.50.*

QUESTIONS TO EXTEND STUDENT THINKING

What are the strengths and weakness of each representation?

⟶ *Students may suggest: the graph helps you quickly see how the plan changes. It shows how the plans increase as you download more songs, but it does not give exact cost. The table tells the exact cost in each plan but it may not help you see the pattern of change in the plan as readily. The equations can help you find the exact cost for any number of downloads, or vice versa, but it does not easily allow you to compare when the plans change.*

What questions would help you decide if a relationship was proportional?

⟶ *Is there a constant rate of change? Does the graph go through the origin?*

Examine the table of values for the proportional scenario. What do the related values all have in common?

⟶ *They would all be equivalent ratios.*

Suppose Anna's initial cost is reduced to $4.00.

How will this affect the table values? The graph? The equation?

⟶ *The initial cost in the table would only be $4.00, not $6.00. The graph would have a y-intercept at $(0, 4)$, and the equation would be $c = 1s + 4$.*

When will Anna's plan become less expensive than Gena's? → *When they buy 9 downloads, Anna will pay $13.00 and Gena will pay $13.41.*

Anna's plan is having a Saturday promotion that will allow you to download 2 songs for the cost of 1. How does that change her plan? → *Her plan still charges the $6.00, but for Saturday the rate for downloads is $0.50 per song.*

LESSON SUMMARY

Revisit the list made in the introduction of the lesson to discuss what makes a better plan.

- Did you use any of these as you answered the questions about the plays? Have students show the table completed in Question 1. Did all students have the same values listed? Correct any incorrect information.

- Using your table, what can you tell about each plan? Based on this information do you know who has the best plan? Will that plan remain the best plan even if you download more songs? What helps you determine that?

- Students should notice that the difference in the cost of the plans is decreasing. How is this shown in the table?

Display graphs made by students. Select graphs that use different scales. Compare and contrast these graphs. Students should be able to tell from looking at a graph which ones have faster rates and which ones increase gradually.

- Why do they look different? What do you notice? Some students will recognize that the graphs are linear. Question students to provide reasons for why the graphs are linear. Others may suggest that Gena's graph is steeper.

- Why would that be true? Her rate, the cost per song, is more than the other offer. Anna's graph starts at (0, 6). Why? Because she has an initial cost to pay. The graphs are getting closer together. Why? Because the cost difference between the plans is decreasing.

LESSON SUMMARY (CONTINUED)

- Go to a set of graphs that used a different scale. Do all your findings still hold true for this graph?

- Suppose Gena's price per download decreased. How would that affect the table? The graph?

Students should also be able to verbalize why their graphs are linear and understand the proportionality of the rate shown by the slope.

Students should have decided that Gena has the better plan if only 10 songs are downloaded. However, you should guide the discussion so that students realize this is not true if more songs are purchased.

- When would the costs be the same for the number of downloads?

One major point that students should comprehend is cost of the plans will never be the same because you cannot buy part of a song. This data is discrete data. This means it is not continuous and that nothing is happening between the points. Point out to students that they can see the plan costs are approaching each other then crossing each other when one plan becomes a better rate than the other.

- After buying 10 more songs, who has the better plan? How do you know?

Some students may use the table and others the graph to determine the better plan. Make sure you discuss how each representation allows you to decide.

Discuss the equations that students used to describe the relationships.

- How did you select the variables? Where do you find the rate of downloads in the equation? How does the y-intercept relate to the situation?

When summarizing Aricela's plan, students move from the graph to the table to the equation. Ask students to share strategies they used to complete the table and the equation. Discuss what happens if you put all the graphs on the same coordinate grid.

- What can students tell you about when the graphs cross each other? They should mention that plans become better or worse at the point where graphs cross.

Question 13 gives students an opportunity to demonstrate their understanding or using equations to answer a question. Ask questions about order or operations and substitution to check understanding. Question 14 refocuses the students on the different representation of the proportional and non-proportional relationships. Students should be able to tell if a relationship is proportional from the table, graph, and the equation. Often students rely on one representation to make sense of the situation.

LESSON SUMMARY (CONTINUED)

Have conversations to help students see the connections among the different representations and the advantages of using all types of representations.

CHECK FOR SUCCESS

☐ Have students explain how they used the information given to decide who has the better plan? Have students extend their explanations to address if the plan will remain the best plan even if more songs are downloaded.

☐ Have students write about when the graphs cross each other and the significance of that point.

☐ Have students suggest a question that can best be answered using a table, using a graph, and using an equation.

☐ Have students write the equation they used for the music download plans in this lesson. Then have them identify the variables and what they represent, and the slope and y-intercept of the line. Lastly, have students explain the meaning of the y-intercept and slope in this situation.

Student _____ Class _____ Date _____

LESSON 3   DOWNLOADING MUSIC

Anna and Gena love to listen to music. They each received an MP3 player as a gift. They want to buy some music and download the songs. Anna found a website that charges $6.00 to sign up then $1.00 for every song she downloads. Gena's website charges $1.49 per song.

1. Anna and Gena want to know who has the better plan. Make a table to show what each girl will pay for 0 to 10 songs.

2. Using grid paper, graph the music plans using the same coordinate axes. Use a different color for each website.

3. Who has the better plan for 10 songs? How do you know?

4. In this scenario, what does the point (5, 11) represent?

5. If Anna and Gena each bought 10 more songs, who would have the better plan? Extend the table and graph to show the new information. Explain your reasoning. How is the better buy represented in the table? in the graph?

6. Write an equation for each music plan. Tell what each variable and number represents in terms of the scenario.

7. What patterns do you notice in the table? in the graph?

8. Are these proportional relationships? Why or why not?

9. What happens if each girl downloads twice as many songs; does the price double also? Explain why or why not.

Student _____ Class _____ Date _____

Aricela tells Anna and Gena about her plan. She shows them the graph at the right representing her plan.

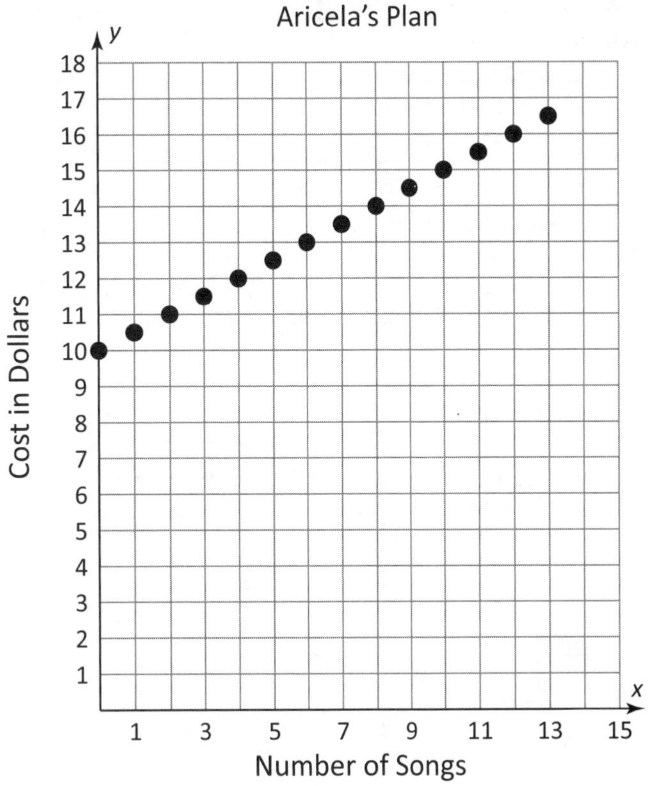

Aricela's Plan

10. Create a table and an equation that represents the relationship found in Aricela's graph.

11. Describe the relationship found in Aricela's music plan. Which plan is best now?

12. Using the equations found for all 3 plans, show the cost of buying 25 songs. Explain your strategy.

13. How do the table, graph, and equation help you see the relationships in the situation?

1.

Number of songs	0	1	2	3	4	5	6	7	8	9	10
Anna's Plan (Cost in dollars)	6	7	8	9	10	11	12	13	14	15	16
Gena's Plan (Cost in dollars)	0	1.49	2.98	4.47	5.96	7.45	8.94	10.43	11.92	13.41	14.90

2.

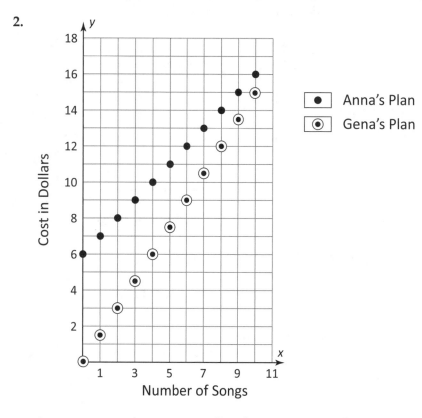

3. Answers may suggest: Gena has the better plan; she spent $14.90 on 10 songs and Anna spent $16.00 on 10 songs.

4. The point (5, 11) is a point on Anna's graph and it means for 5 songs she will pay $11.00.

5.

Number of songs	11	12	13	14	15	16	17	18	19	20
Anna's Plan (Cost in dollars)	17	18	19	20	21	22	23	24	25	26
Gena's Plan (Cost in dollars)	16.39	17.88	19.37	20.86	22.35	23.84	25.33	26.82	28.31	29.80

I extended the table. After looking at the table, I see that Gena has a better plan for 1-12 songs. After 12 songs Anna has the better plan.

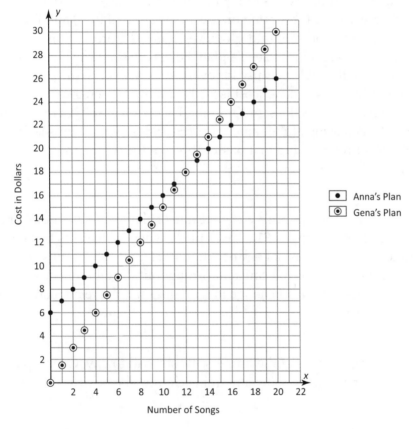

Cost in Dollars

Number of Songs

Anna's Plan
Gena's Plan

Extend the lines and see that they intersect. At 13 songs Gena's plan became more expensive.

In the table at 13 songs you see that Gena will pay more. In the graph at 13 songs you see Gena's graph crossover Anna's graph, which means Gena starts paying more.

6. Anna's plan: $c = 1.00s + 6$; The c represents the total cost. The s represents the number of songs purchased. The 1.00 represents the cost per song. The 6 represents the fee to start the plan. Gena's plan: $c = 1.49s$; The c represents the total cost. The 1.49 represents the cost per song. The s represents the number of songs purchased.

7. Anna's plan: For every song she buys, she pays $1.00. That pattern seems to be consistent throughout the table; however she must pay $6.00 to start her plan. So, if I look for a pattern, it seems that for every song Anna buys she should increase her cost by $1.00. But when she goes from 0 songs to 1 song the increase is $6.00, so it does not increase at a constant rate. Her graph started on the y-axis at point (0, 6) and is a linear relationship that increases at a constant rate. However, it is not a proportional relationship because of the start-up fee. Gena's plan: For every song she buys, she pays $1.49. You can see it in the table because for every song she buys, the price increases by $1.49. If she buys 0 songs her cost is $0.00. For every increase in the number of songs she buys she pays the same amount. Using the graph, Gena's plan starts at (0, 0) and starts increasing at the same rate of $1.49 for every song she buys. Her graph showed a linear relationship that passes through the origin; therefore it is a proportional relationship.

8. Anna pays $6.00 for 0 songs. There is not a constant rate of change. As the number of songs purchased increases, the cost is $1.00, except for when it increases from 0 to 1, the cost increase there is $6.00. This is not a proportional relationship, because the relationship between the variables is not constant throughout the table. Gena on the other hand does have a constant rate of change in her table, and the relationship starts at (0, 0). Her plan is proportional.

9. Anna's plan will not double because of the initial $6.00 she had to pay; Gena's plan will double because she is paying the same amount each time she buys a song.

10.

Number of songs	0	1	2	3	4	5	6	7	8	9	10	11	12	13
Aricela's Plan (cost in dollars)	10	10.50	11	11.50	12	12.50	13	13.50	14	14.50	15	15.50	16	16.50

Aricela's plan: $c = 0.50s + 10$; The c represents the total cost. The s represents the number of songs purchased. The 10 represents the fee to start the plan.

11. Aricela will have to pay $10.00 to start her plan, then $0.50 for every song she downloads. Aricela's initial cost is more; however, she pays less for each download. At 11 songs, Anna pays $17.00; Gena pays $16.39, but Aricela pay $15.50. Therefore, at this point Aricela has the better plan. Aricela's plan starts out more expensive but her price per song is lower, so her plan increases at a lower rate than the other two. It all depends on how many songs are bought.

12. Anna's plan: $c = 1s + 6$; Gena's plan: $c = 1.49s$; Aricela's plan: $c = 0.50s + 10$
Since s represents the number of songs downloaded, substitute 25 for s then solve for cost.
Anna's cost $\quad c = 1(25) + 6 = 25 + 6 = 31$
Gena's cost $\quad c = 1.49(25) = 37.25$
Aricela's cost $\quad c = 0.50(25) + 10 = 12.50 + 10 = 22.50$

13. Possible responses: The table helps find specific data points about the plans. If the relationship was proportional, you could use the numbers to find equivalent ratios for missing data. You can also look for patterns of change to help find missing values. The graphs show the relationships between the variables. They showed that there was a linear relationships between the number of downloads and the cost. By reading the line you can find an estimate for the missing values. If you did not have to know specific values, you could easily evaluate the graphs to tell when one music plan becomes more cost effective than another The equation allows you to find the cost for any number of downloads. The equation can also allow you to find how many downloads you can have for any given amount of money. However the equation does not allow me to see more than one point at a time. It would be difficult to determine when one plan becomes better than another.

CHAPTER 3 GEOMETRY

Common Core State Standards
Geometry 7.G
   Draw, construct, and describe geometrical figures and describe the relationships between them.
   1. Solve problems involving scale drawings of geometric figures, including computing actual lengths and areas from scale drawings and reproducing a scale drawing at a different scale.

NCTM Correlation
Geometry
   Analyze characteristics and properties of two- and three-dimensional geometric shapes and develop mathematical arguments about geometric relationships.
   Understand relationships among the angles, side lengths, perimeters, areas, and volumes of similar objects.

Similar figures are figures that have the same shape but may be different sizes. To verify two figures are similar, you must be able to show that their corresponding angles are congruent and their corresponding sides are proportional.

LESSON GOALS

- Identify the properties and characteristics of a proportional relationship.
- Create similar figures.
- Identify proportional relationships in problem situations.
- Solve problems involving proportional relationships.

LESSON INTRODUCTION

This lesson serves as a problem-solving situation for proportional relationships. Prerequisite knowledge necessary to solve this puzzle includes understanding equivalent ratios, basic knowledge of the concept of scale factor, attributes of similar figures, and an understanding of proportional growth.

Students should understand that when scaling a measurement of a figure, it will either become larger or become smaller. Explain that to scale and make a figure larger, the calculation must be multiplication by a number greater than 1. To scale and make a figure smaller, the calculation needed is multiplication by a number between 0 and 1.

A **scale factor** is a number used to proportionately change a quantity.

Students should be able to recognize when figures are similar and justify why they are similar with more evidence than just "they look the same, but are different sizes." The most basic skill of identifying similar figures is being able to pair corresponding angles and corresponding sides between the two figures.

This lesson helps students apply their knowledge of proportional growth.

TEACHING SUGGESTIONS

Within the bulleted text below are suggestions on how to begin the lesson, introduce essential vocabulary, and question students so that they are prepared to complete the Student Recording Page on their own or with minimal assistance.

Show students two scalene right triangles that are proportional. Ask students to identify which angles match up to make corresponding angles and which sides match up to make corresponding sides.

Corresponding sides of similar figures are two sides, one from each figure, that are in the same relative location in the figures. Each pair of corresponding sides in similar figures must be proportional to all pairs of sides in the figures. **Corresponding angles** of similar figures are angles that are in the same relative location in the figures. Corresponding angles in similar figures must be congruent.

- When solving problems about proportional relationships, students should be able to identify a constant of proportionality to describe the relationship.

- Discuss with students the attributes of a proportional relationship, such as a constant rate of change. Guide students to know how to recognize if an equation has a constant rate of change and if a graph shows a relationship that has constant rate of change.

- Introduce the puzzle to the students. Distribute the envelope containing the eight puzzle pieces. Explain to students that they will work in small groups to form a square using the puzzle pieces.

Materials
Student Recording Page 3.1
Envelopes
Pre-cut Puzzle Pieces
(Work Page 3.1)
Rulers
Scissors
Centimeter grid paper
Protractor or angle ruler

Vocabulary
Scale Factor
Constant of Proportionality
Similar Figures
Corresponding Sides

A **constant of proportionality** in a situation is a constant value, or unchanging value, of the ratios of proportional quantities. A constant of proportionality is often expressed as a decimal or a fraction.

STUDENT ENGAGEMENT

Review briefly the characteristics of a square. Read the list of directions provided on the Student Recording Page 3.1. Explain that students will work on the lesson as a group. However, tell them when they begin enlarging a puzzle piece, they should work independently. Students need to be given time to think independently and to select a strategy to use. Instruct students to note the strategies they use to enlarge their puzzle pieces.

Tell students their challenge involves creating a new puzzle that is mathematically similar to the original. Each group of students needs the puzzle on Work Page 3.1, pre-cut into individual pieces and placed in an envelope.

Throughout the lesson encourage students to explain the reasoning behind their strategies. Caution: Some students will erroneously proceed to add a length of 3 cm to each new side length. If this happens they should be asked to justify that their pieces are mathematically similar to the original puzzle piece. When the group tries to fit puzzle pieces that have been enlarged using this strategy, the puzzle will not fit together again.

Have students talk about the additive versus the multiplicative process. For example, consider the rectangle with the dimensions of 1 cm by 4 cm.

- If you enlarged the rectangle by adding 3 cm to each side length, what are the new dimensions? *4 cm by 7 cm*

They should focus on the shortest side length of 1 cm that was enlarged to 4 cm.

- About how much bigger is the new side length? Is it about double its original length? Triple? How many times longer is it? *4 times longer*

- Is that true for the other rectangle side length? Did the other rectangle side length quadruple, as it was enlarged from 4 cm to 7 cm?

Students may still think the figures look proportional especially if their puzzle piece is a rectangle. As students work on this problem, encourage them to use a variety of representations to support their ideas of proportional relationships and ask questions to check for understanding.

What shape did the original puzzle form? → *square*

What shape will the new puzzle form if they must be mathematically similar? → *square*

Do you think your new square will be larger or smaller than the original? Explain your reasoning. → *larger because the side length is getting larger*

What do the instructions ask you to do to each piece of the puzzle? → *Measure the pieces.*

What unit of measure do you want to use to measure? Why? → *Students often say centimeters because they don't have to estimate as much with a centimeter being a smaller-sized unit.*

What measurements can you find? → *Possible responses: length, width, area, perimeter*

How does the given clue help? → *It tells that the length of a side has grown from 4 cm to 7 cm.*

If the puzzles are mathematically similar, what must be true about the side lengths of the pieces? The angles? → *The measures of the side lengths have to be proportional, and the angle measures have to be equal.*

What measurements of the figures might help you with this problem? → *Answers may vary, but should include some of the following: length, width, height, and angle measure.*

The clue states: My length once measured 4 cm, but now it measures 7 cm. What does that mean when you are trying to create a similar figure?

That tells how the length changed. In similar figures the growth has to be proportional, so it is necessary to figure out how to proportionally change 4 cm to 7 cm.

How could you write that mathematically?

4 times what is 7?

QUESTIONS FOR STUDENTS ON TASK

What is true about the sides in similar figures? The angles?

The measures of the corresponding side lengths have to be proportional, and the corresponding angle measures have to be the same.

Compare the lengths in the given clue.

Students may suggest one is bigger than the other, one is smaller than the other, or one is just a little less than double the other.

Describe the relationship between an original length compared to a new length.

All of the same comparisons made above still should hold true.

Why not just add 3 cm to each side?

If 3 cm is added to each side, the figure would not be similar. If 3 cm is added to a length that measures 1 cm, it gets 3 times larger. If you add 3 cm to 5 cm it does not quite double, so the sides are not growing proportionally.

QUESTIONS FOR STUDENTS ON TASK (CONTINUED)

What remains the same when a figure is enlarged to create a similar figure? → *angle measurements and the shape of the figure*

How will the side lengths of similar figures compare? How will the perimeters of similar figures compare? → *Side lengths of similar figures will be proportional and so will the perimeters.*

Find at least three equivalent ratios in this task. How can you convince the class the ratios are equivalent? → *Students can give a ratio of length to width of one of the original figures and the length to width of the new figures, and they should be equivalent.*

How does knowing how to find equivalence help you with this problem? → *Equivalence helps you understand how the ratios are proportional.*

What is a ratio that will help you find the new puzzle pieces? How does it help? → $\frac{7}{4}$; *It becomes the scale factor used to find proportional lengths.*

What is the decimal equivalent of the ratio? → *1.75*

If the ratio for increasing the puzzle piece was 4 to 6, what would be the scale factor? → *1.5*

QUESTIONS FOR STUDENTS ON TASK (CONTINUED)

What is the constant of proportionality?

→ *If the length of the new puzzle piece is proportional to the length of the original puzzle piece, then the constant of proportionality in this situation is $\frac{7}{4}$.*

Is this a proportional relationship? How do you know?

→ *Yes, this is a proportional relationship. In the table, for every change in x there is a constant change in y. In the graph of the equation, there is a linear relationship that passes through the origin. In the equation, $y = \frac{7}{4}x$, $\frac{7}{4}$ is the constant of proportionality.*

Will the relationship between the original perimeters and the enlarged perimeters be proportional? Explain your thinking.

→ *Yes; They will all grow by the same scale factor.*

QUESTIONS TO EXTEND STUDENT THINKING

What if you had used a different unit of measure (e.g. inches instead of cm)? How would this have changed your scale factor?

→ *The measurement would be in inches, but the scale factor would be the same.*

Suppose you were originally given the larger square and asked to make another puzzle proportional to the original, and the clue provided stated "My length once measured 7 cm, but now it measures 4 cm." What would the constant of proportionality be?

→ *The constant of proportionality would be less than 1, because the length is being reduced. The constant of proportionality would be $\frac{4}{7}$.*

Questions to Extend Student Thinking (continued)

How does the area of a similar figure grow? How would the graph of the side length to area look? → *The area of the new figure grows by the square of the scale factor. The graph increases quickly; it is not a straight-line graph.*

How do perimeters of similar figures compare? What does the graph of side length to perimeter look like? → *The perimeter grows by the same scale factor that the side lengths grow. The graph shows a linear relationship.*

How could you make a reduction of the figure? → *Multiply the original figure by a scale factor less than 1.*

If you want to enlarge the figure 2.5 times larger than it was originally, what equation can you use to determine the lengths of the other sides? → $y = 2.5x$, *where* y = *the new length and* x = *the original length*

As you summarize this lesson you can begin by asking students about the strategies they used to enlarge the puzzle pieces. Discuss the additive process and why it did not work. Investigate the addition to the length of two puzzle pieces versus the length of one puzzle piece as seen in the diagram below.

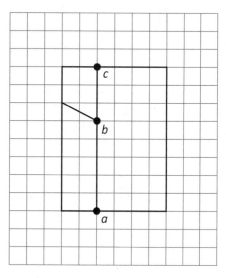

$$\overline{ab} + \overline{bc} = \overline{ac}$$

$$(\overline{ab} + 3) + (\overline{bc} + 3) \neq (\overline{ac} + 3)$$

Using examples of rectangles with measurements once again will help students reason why adding 3 cm to each side will not work.

Compare the different strategies students used to create similar puzzle pieces. Some students may have used equivalence, scale factor, set up proportions, created a table, or written equations to create corresponding sides.

- How are these strategies the same? Are there any differences?

- What also has to be true to have similar puzzle pieces? *Corresponding angles must be equivalent.*

Allow students to measure angles if they haven't already. Discuss any issues students may have with angle measurement.

Have students help you recreate the table in Question 5. Leave the process column and the last row blank for the moment. Have students correct their own tables.

- What patterns do you see? *Students should mention the proportional growth.*

- What process did you use to complete the table? *Some students might have used a scale factor of 1.75 and others, a ratio of $\frac{7}{4}$. Be sure students see the equivalence between the two values.*

- What patterns do you notice in the process column? How will this information help to find the new length for any length, *n*? How will it help to write an equation?

Define the parts of the equation.

When you believe students have an understanding about the relationships, ask the following questions.

- How could you find the scale factor if all you have are the dimensions of the original puzzle piece and the dimensions of the corresponding sides of the new puzzle pieces?

- If you know the new length of a puzzle piece and the scale factor, what would be the original length?

There is an opportunity to start exploring how area grows in similar figures. You might want your students to explore this as an extension. Have students each place the original puzzle piece and the new puzzle piece in front of them. Ask them to find the area of each piece. Make a class table with the area of the original puzzle piece and the area of the new puzzle piece. What patterns do you notice? Students should notice a growth pattern, however they may not describe it as the area increasing by the scale factor squared. You might want to explore this at a later time.

CHECK FOR SUCCESS

Have students answer the following questions.

☐ How can you determine if two figures are similar?

☐ What has to be true to create a similar, enlarged puzzle?

☐ What are attributes of a proportional relationship? (constant rate of change, equation, graph, constant of proportionality, etc.)

From *It's All Connected: The Power of Proportional Reasoning to Understand Mathematics Concepts, Grades 6–8* by Carmen Whitman. Permission granted to photocopy for nonprofit use in a classroom or similar place dedicated to face-to-face educational instruction. © 2011 Scholastic Inc.

Student _____ Class _____ Date _____

LESSON 1   WHAT'S MY SIZE?

Work in a small group. Use the eight puzzle pieces in the envelope and follow the directions below.

Clue: My length once measured 4 cm, but now it measures 7 cm.

1. As a group, use all of the puzzle pieces to create a square.
2. Then, divide the pieces among the group members.
3. Measure your puzzle piece(s) and record the dimension(s).
4. Use the clue to create new puzzle piece(s).
   Record the new dimension(s).
5. Create a new puzzle piece that is similar to the original puzzle piece.
6. After you have created your new puzzle piece(s), help others in your group.
7. When all puzzle pieces have been made, create a new square with the larger puzzle pieces.

Working with your group, answer the following questions.

1. What information does the clue provide about the relationship between the original lengths versus the new lengths?

2. What strategy did you use to create your puzzle piece(s)?

3. If an original puzzle piece had a length of 18 cm, what would be the new length? Explain your reasoning.

4. If a new puzzle piece had a length of 28 cm, what would the original length have been?

5. Complete the following table using the process you used to create the new puzzle pieces.

Original Length	Process	New Length
0		
1		
2		
3		
4		
5		
6		
12		
15		
n		

6. What patterns do you notice in the table?

7. Write an equation that will help you find the new lengths of each puzzle piece.

1. It tells that a length of 4 cm in the original puzzle is now 7 cm in the new puzzle. The puzzle is enlarged by a ratio of $\frac{7}{4}$.

2. Possible response: Some may have tried to add 3 cm to each length, but the puzzle was not fitting together right. Some set up the dimensions of the pieces as equivalent fractions. For example, using the rectangle that measures 2 cm by 5 cm, the new puzzle piece would measure 3.5 cm by 8.75 cm. Work is shown below.

   Ratio for the length of the original puzzle piece is 4 cm: 2 cm.

   Ratio for the length of the new puzzle piece is 7 cm: ?

   $$\frac{4\text{ cm}}{2\text{ cm}} \times \frac{1\frac{3}{4}}{1\frac{3}{4}} = \frac{7\text{ cm}}{3.5\text{ cm}}$$

   Ratio for the width of the original puzzle piece is 4 cm: 5 cm.

   Ratio for the width of the new puzzle piece is 7 cm: ?

   $$\frac{4\text{ cm}}{5\text{ cm}} \times \frac{1\frac{3}{4}}{1\frac{3}{4}} = \frac{7\text{ cm}}{8.75\text{ cm}}$$

   Some students might say they used a scale factor of 1.75 and multiplied each side length by the scale factor 1.75.

3. $18 \cdot 1.75 = 31.5$

   Use the clue to find the scale factor between the measurements in the clue. Then multiplied the length of 18 cm by the scale factor, which is 1.75. The new piece measures 31.5 cm.

4. Some students may suggest:

   $x \cdot 1.75 = 28$

   $x \cdot \frac{1.75}{1.75} = \frac{28}{1.75}$

   $x = 16$

   The original length would have been 16 cm.

5.

Original Length (cm)	Process	New Length (cm)
0	1.75(0)	0
1	1.75(1)	1.75
2	1.75(2)	3.5
3	1.75(3)	5.25
4	1.75(4)	7
5	1.75(5)	8.75
6	1.75(6)	10.5
12	1.75(12)	21
15	1.75(15)	26.25
n	1.75(n)	1.75n

6. As the length of the original piece increases by 1, the new length increases by 1.75.

7. $y = 1.75n$ or $y = \frac{7}{4}n$ or $n = \frac{4}{7}y$; $y =$ the measurement of the new puzzle piece and $n =$ the measurement of the original puzzle piece.

LESSON 2

CANDY BOXES

Common Core State Standards
Geometry 7.RP
  Analyze proportional
  relationships and use them to
  solve real-world and
  mathematical problems.
  2. Recognize and represent
      proportional relationships
      between quantities.
      a. Decide whether two
          quantities are in a
          proportional
          relationship, e.g., by
          testing for equivalent
          ratios in tables or
          graphing on a
          coordinate plane and
          observing whether the
          graph is a straight line
          through the origin.
Geometry 7.G
  Draw, construct, and describe
  geometrical figures and
  describe the relationships
  between them.
  6. Solve real-world and
      mathematical problems
      involving area, volume, and
      surface area of two- and
      three-dimensional objects
      composed of triangles,
      quadrilaterals, polygons,
      cubes, and right prisms.

LESSON GOALS

- Understand the relationships between dimensions of a rectangular prism and its perimeter.
- Make a connection between the dimensions of a rectangular prism and its volume.
- Begin to develop a formula for finding the volume of a rectangular prism.

LESSON INTRODUCTION

Hold up some rectangular prisms to show the class. Discuss with students the attributes of a rectangular prism. Distribute a cube to each student and ask if it is a rectangular prism. Explain that a cube is a special rectangular prism. Have students describe the attributes of the cube.

As they share, clarify their thoughts using your rectangular prism. Make of list of these attributes.

TEACHING SUGGESTIONS

Within the bulleted text below are suggestions on how to begin the lesson, introduce essential vocabulary, and question students so that they are prepared to complete the Student Recording Page on their own or with minimal assistance.

- Do the attributes in the list hold true for both the cube and the rectangular prism you have?

- Discuss some of the measurements you can take for a rectangular prism; for example: length, width, height, area of a face, surface area, and volume.

- How would you find the perimeter of one of the faces?

- What does volume mean?

> **Volume** is the amount of space, in three dimensions, that is occupied by an object. Volume is measured in cubic units.

Define, using student language, what volume means. Discuss volume to make sure students can distinguish this measurement from others. Define what a net is with students.

One of the focal points of this lesson is for students to explore the relationship between the growing dimensions of a cube to the perimeter of its face.

You will also want students to begin thinking about how to develop a working formula for finding the volume of a rectangular prism.

> A **net** is a two-dimensional diagram that shows the faces of a three-dimensional solid. When a net is folded along the lines within the diagram, the three-dimensional solid takes shape.

Introduce the lesson to students. Show them the net on Work Pages 3.2 that will be used for Question 1. Have students think about the following questions, *What type of shape do you think it will make? How do you know?* Do not have them share ideas. They will share their ideas in Question 1.

NCTM Correlation

Geometry

Analyze characteristics and properties of two- and three-dimensional geometric shapes and develop mathematical arguments about geometric relationships.

Understand relationships among the angles, side lengths, perimeters, areas, and volumes of similar objects.

Use visualization, spatial reasoning, and geometric modeling to solve problems.

Use two-dimensional representations of three-dimensional objects to visualize and solve problems such as those involving surface area and volume.

Materials

Student Recording Page 3.2

Copies of Net
(Work Page 3.2)

Scissors

Tape

Centimeter ruler

Graph paper

Centimeter cubes

Models of cubes
for summary
- 4 cm × 4 cm × 4 cm
- 6 cm × 6 cm × 6 cm
- 8 cm × 8 cm × 8 cm

Vocabulary

Volume

Net

STUDENT ENGAGEMENT

Instruct students to complete Student Recording Page 3.2. Distribute Work Page 3.2 and tell students that this net is needed for Question 1.

While students begin to work ask them questions about the net, the three-dimensional shape it is making, and things they should look for when creating the box.

Guide students to make a decision about the units to use when measuring the box and have them record the dimensions. Have centimeter cubes available for students to use when finding volume. Leave the approach to finding the volume open to allow students to use strategies they understand. There are several strategies students may use to find volume as suggested in the solutions to this lesson. Ask students about the different strategies they are using to find volume.

As students begin to complete the table and graph, ask questions about patterns they notice, why they think the patterns are occurring, and if they think the patterns are proportional. Continue to ask questions of students while they work to check for understanding.

QUESTIONS FOR STRUGGLING STUDENTS

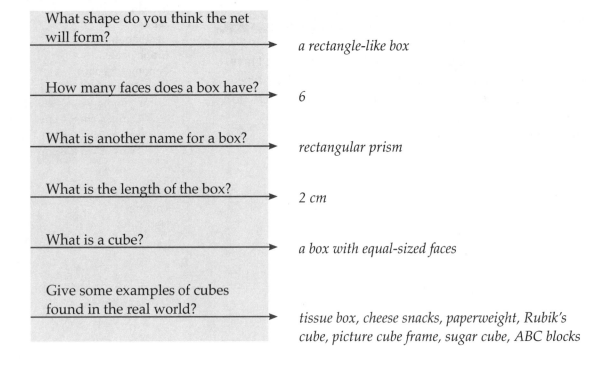

What shape do you think the net will form? → *a rectangle-like box*

How many faces does a box have? → *6*

What is another name for a box? → *rectangular prism*

What is the length of the box? → *2 cm*

What is a cube? → *a box with equal-sized faces*

Give some examples of cubes found in the real world? → *tissue box, cheese snacks, paperweight, Rubik's cube, picture cube frame, sugar cube, ABC blocks*

What are the dimensions of a cube?

length, width, and height

What is volume?

the amount of space in a three-dimensional shape

What does perimeter measure?
What units of measure can be used for perimeter?

length around the shape, in this case around the lid of the box; inches, centimeters, miles, meters, yards, etc.

Are you finding the perimeter of the rectangular prism?

no; just the perimeter of one face

How many dimensions are needed to find volume? What units of measure can be used for volume?

length, width, and height; Volume is measured in cm^3, $in.^3$, m^3, etc.

Why is volume measured in cubic units?

When finding volume, there are three dimensions used.

What relationships do you see in the table? graph?

Answers will vary.

QUESTIONS FOR STUDENTS ON TASK

To find volume how many dimensions are you going to measure?

3; length, width, and height

How long do you think the dimensions are going to be?

about an inch each (actually 2 cm each)

How do you know where to fold the net?

→ *on the dotted lines*

What is a cube?

→ *a three-dimensional shape that is made of 6 identical square faces*

From the table, what is the relationship between length and perimeter of the lid?

→ *For every increase of 2 cm, the perimeter increases by 8.*

Can you use equivalent ratios to describe the relationship between the length and the perimeter of the lid?

→ *There is an equivalent ratio of $\frac{2}{8}$ between the length, width, or height and the perimeter.*

Will that hold true for all rectangular prisms?

→ *Yes; As you increase the dimensions of a figure, you increase the perimeter by the same amount.*

What unit rate would describe the relationship of length and the perimeter of the lid?

→ *$\frac{1}{4}$; For every increase of 1 to a prism's dimensions, there is an increase of 4 to the perimeter of a face.*

How can you find the volume without filling the box with unit cubes?

→ *Fill one layer then multiply by the number of layers it would take to fill the box.*

How is the volume growing as you create the different boxes?

→ *It is increasing.*

How many of the first box fits in the second box? → *eight*

Where do you see this growth in the table? → *It is the growth factor seen in the volume.*

Can you find a rule for the volume of rectangular prisms? → *length × width × height*

QUESTIONS TO EXTEND STUDENT THINKING

If you have different nets for the same box, what will they have in common? → *The nets must have the same number of square units and equal surface areas.*

Can two prisms have the same volume? Explain. → *Dimensions of a prism can be different and the volume can be the same; for example, a prism that measures 4 cm by 6 cm by 2 cm has the same volume as a prism that measures 2 cm by 24 cm by 1 cm. These look very different; one looks more cube-like and the other tall and thin, however each has a volume of 48 cm .*

Is it possible to have the same volume and the same area for the base and have different prisms? Explain. → *Find volume of a prism by finding the area of the base times the height. The area of a triangular base can be the same as the area of a rectangular base; if the two prisms have the same heights, they have the same volume, but would be different prisms.*

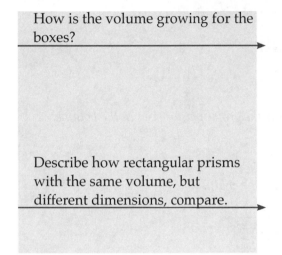

How is the volume growing for the boxes?

by a factor of 8; If the prisms are growing proportionally, the volume grows by that scale factor in each of its dimension. Because volume is three-dimensional, find the cubed amount of the growth. To find the volume, cube the scale factor.

Describe how rectangular prisms with the same volume, but different dimensions, compare.

They will have different surface area, and they will range from long and skinny to more compact or cube-like.

LESSON SUMMARY

Students should have discovered the relationship between the growing dimensions of a cube and the perimeter of a face is a proportional relationship, and the dimensions of a cube to its volume is a non-proportional relationship.

As students begin to investigate volume, they often think there will be a proportional relationship between volume and the dimensions of the figure. They need to understand the dimensions of the figure are increasing by a constant rate, while the volume of the figure is increasing but not at a constant rate. By the end of the lesson, you will have students who have met an essential objective of developing a working formula for finding the volume of a rectangular prism.

Asking the students to create the prism from the net gives students a visual representation of the three-dimensional shape to help them think about volume. The space inside the prism is its volume. At this point in the lesson, students need to make the connection between filling the prism and finding the volume of the prism. Ask students how they found the volume of the prism. As they share their strategies, make connections among the strategies. For example, make the connection between filling the prism to filling the first layer of the prism and then finding how many of those layers it takes to fill the prism.

LESSON SUMMARY (CONTINUED)

When comparing volumes of the different prism, have some models of the prism made to help students see how the volume grows visually. Ask questions so that students assess the situation.

- How many of this cube would it take to fill the next cube and so forth? *8 in each case*

- Where do you see this growth in the table? *If you look at the volume column in the table, you see that there is a scale factor of 8.*

Students might not make the connection between the scale factor of the dimensions and the scale factor of the volume. Students often think they grow by the same scale factor. In this case, because the dimensions are doubling, the volume is growing by a scale factor of 2^3. This relationship is non-proportional.

As students look at the table, make sure they are looking for patterns that occur both horizontally and vertically in the table. About the table, ask students to write down what they noticed. Have students share these ideas. Make a list of these ideas. Someone in the class should suggest finding equivalent ratios. If not, ask students to find a ratio that helps them find the perimeter of a 3 cm × 3 cm × 3 cm cube then a 5 cm × 5 cm × 5 cm cube.

Students should be able to explain where they can find this information on the graph.

As you create the list, have students give you justifications for these patterns. For example, if students notice the perimeter is increasing by 8, ask them if the perimeter will always increase by 8 in. cubes.

Students might also conclude that the perimeter of a face can be found by multiplying the length by 4. Ask students to name a rule that works for all rectangular prisms. Guide students to a rule of $2(l + w)$.

As students suggest rules for finding the volume of a rectangular prism, make a list of these rules so that you can make connections among them.

Students may suggest length × width × height, number of cubes that fills the base × the number of layers, or area of the base × height. Make sure students have at least one rule for finding the volume of a rectangular prism.

Next look at the graphs that students generated, and ask students if they see the patterns found in the tables on the graph. Discuss the relationships found in each of the graphs. These graphs help students see that the relationship between dimensions and volumes is non-proportional. Why does the graph increase at different rates? Make the connections back to the table.

CHECK FOR SUCCESS

☐ Have students write a sentence that summarizes a proportional relationship discovered in this lesson.

☐ Have students write a sentence about a non-proportional relationship from this lesson.

☐ Have students use a formula to find the volume of a rectangular prism that has a length of 3 meters, a width of 5 meters, and a height of 2 meters.

LESSON 2   CANDY BOXES

Sweet Treats has just started selling gourmet candy in gift boxes. The employees need to create boxes for the candy. Angela finds a net on the Internet that folds into a box. She decides to use this as a model for the gift box.

1. Cut and fold the net to form the box. Describe the shape of the box. Are there any clues in the net that helped you determine the shape of the box?

2. What are the dimensions of the box?

3. The owner decides she wants her signature gold ribbon along the perimeter of each box lid. How much ribbon does Angela need for this box?

4. What is the volume of the box? How do you know?

5. The owner likes the shape of the box and the ribbon along the perimeter of the lid, but wants bigger boxes that are similar. Angela decides to make three more boxes. She makes a table that shows dimensions of the boxes, the perimeter of the lid, and the volume of the boxes to give the owner. Complete the table using the descriptions below.

Description of the boxes Angela wants to create:

A Double the original dimensions.

B Triple the original dimensions.

C Quadruple the original dimensions.

Box	Length	Width	Height	Perimeter of Lid (Amount of ribbon needed)	Volume
Original Box					
A					
B					
C					

6. What patterns do you notice in the table?

7. Create a graph showing the side lengths and the perimeter of the boxes.

8. Create a graph showing the side lengths and the volume of the boxes.

9. Compare and contrast the graphs created in Questions 7 and 8.

10. What kind of relationship does each graph show?

1. The net makes a box that is a cube, each face is a square face, two of the triangles join to make a square, and the box has 6 equal faces. The four congruent squares that made me think of a rectangular box, then I noticed triangles and I knew I could put triangles together to form other squares. The grouped triangles completed the six faces I needed to make a rectangular prism. Because all faces are squares, I made the conjecture it was a cube.

2. length = 2 cm; width = 2 cm; height = 2 cm

3. The lid of the box is a square with a side length of 2 centimeters. The perimeter of a square is $s + s + s + s$ or $4s$. The perimeter of the lid is 8 cm. The amount of gold ribbon needed for each gift box is 8 cm.

4. Students may suggest: The volume of the box is how many unit cubes the box holds. Fill the box with centimeter cubes, 8 of the centimeter cubes fit in the box, $v = 8$ cm³
Or
Fill the bottom layer of the box and find that it holds 4 centimeter cubes. It would hold 2 layers, which means it has a volume of 8 cm³.

5.

Box	Length (cm)	Width (cm)	Height (cm)	Perimeter of Lid (cm) (Amount of ribbon needed)	Volume (cm³)
Original Box	2	2	2	8	8
A	4	4	4	16	64
B	6	6	6	24	216
C	8	8	8	32	512

6. Students may suggest:
   - The length increased by 2 cm each time.
   - The width increased by 2 cm each time.
   - The height increased by 2 cm each time.
   - All dimensions increased the same way.
   - The perimeter is increasing by 8 cm each time.
   - Every time the dimensions increase by 2 cm, the perimeter increases by 8 cm.
   - To find the perimeter you can multiply the length by 4.
   - To find the volume you can multiply the dimensions (length, width, and height).
   - Volume is not increasing by the same amount each time.

7.

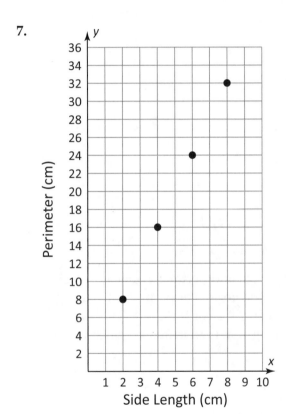

8.

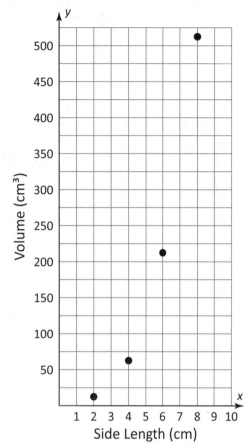

9. One graph shows the relationship between length and perimeter. One graph shows the relationship between length and volume. The perimeter graph is increasing at a constant rate. The volume graph is not increasing at a constant rate. The volume graph increases slowly at the beginning of the graph then increases much faster.

10. If you connect the points on the perimeter graph to see a trend, the graph creates a straight line and that makes it a linear relationship. It would pass through the origin so it shows a proportional relationship also. If you connect the points on the volume graph to see a trend, the graph does not create a straight line so it shows a non-linear and non-proportional relationship.

LESSON 3   DESIGNING FIGURES

Common Core State Standards
Geometry 8.G
Understand congruence and similarity using physical models, transparencies, or geometry software.
3. Describe the effect of dilations, translations, rotations, and reflections on two-dimensional figures using coordinates.

NCTM Correlation
Geometry
Apply transformations and use symmetry to analyze mathematical situations.
Describe sizes, positions, and orientations of shapes under informal transformations such as flips, turns, slides, and scaling.

A **reflection** is a transformation where a figure is changed to be a mirror image of the original figure. In a reflection, there exists a line (might not be included in the graph) over which the original figure is flipped to produce the reflected image. The original image and the new image are congruent.

LESSON GOALS
- Use a coordinate grid to model transformations.
- Describe the effect of dilations and reflections on two-dimensional figures using coordinates.

LESSON INTRODUCTION

As you begin this lesson, ask students questions about graphing on a coordinate grid. Display a coordinate grid showing all four quadrants. Label some points in each of the quadrants and have students name these points by giving their ordered pairs.

On another coordinate grid, draw a simple figure then draw a figure that is similar to the first and one that is not similar. Review the properties of similar figures. Students should know that the measures of the side lengths are proportional and that their corresponding angles are equal.

A transformation in coordinate geometry is the sliding, flipping, turning, or scaling of a figure relative to an original position in the coordinate plane. In this lesson, students will specifically study the transformations of dilations and reflections.

A **dilation** is a transformation where a figure is either enlarged or reduced by a scale factor. Dilating a figure will result in a figure that is similar to the original figure.

Ask students to tell what they know about dilations and reflections. Write the definitions and have students copy each definition. When you feel that students have an understanding of how to correctly identify coordinates of the points and recall what it means for figures to be mathematically similar, introduce the lesson to students.

TEACHING SUGGESTIONS

Within the bulleted text below are suggestions on how to begin the lesson, introduce essential vocabulary, and question students so that they are prepared to complete the Student Recording Page on their own or with minimal assistance.

- Some students might call Figure *A* the pre-image of Figure *B*, so define pre-image to the class.

> In a transformation, the original image is the **pre-image**.

- For students that refer to points as *A* and *A'*, take the opportunity to describe *A'*.

> In a transformation, each point of the pre-image maps onto a new point in the image according to a rule. When the original point is point *A*, the new point is point *A'*. This is read *A* prime. Point *A* and point *A'* are **corresponding points**.

- Review the definition of reflection by having students sketch a reflection of a simple figure (e.g. arrow) on a paper. Ask a couple of students to describe what they did. Have students then fold their paper on a reflection line and hold it up to the light. Ask them what they noticed. Are their images congruent?

- Ask students what remained the same in the transformation. What changed? *The students should say the size stays the same, but the direction changes on the arrow; both arrows are the same distance away from the line of reflection.*

Materials
Student Recording Page 3.3
Coordinate Grid of Dilation
(Work Page 3-3)
Straight Edge
Protractors or angle rulers

Vocabulary
Dilation
Reflection
Pre-image
Corresponding Points

STUDENT ENGAGEMENT

On Student Recording Page 3.3, students are asked to explain some effects of transformations in this lesson by constructing dilations and reflections on a coordinate grid.

Distribute Work Page 3.3 to students. Students will produce the dilations and reflections on this page. Students should work independently on this lesson. Give students the opportunity to discuss the mathematics within the lesson with their peers, but each student should complete the dilations and reflections on their own.

As students work on the lesson, look and listen for students who are identifying patterns and ask them to explain the patterns. You can call on these students during the summary to share with the class. Verify that students see how the figures are growing proportionally, and ask questions to check for understanding.

QUESTIONS FOR STRUGGLING STUDENTS

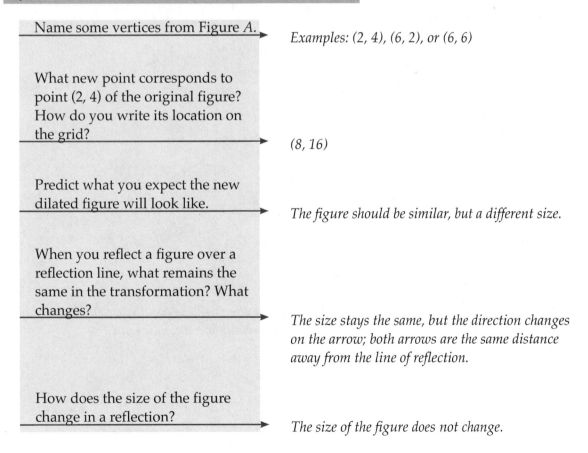

Name some vertices from Figure *A*.

Examples: (2, 4), (6, 2), or (6, 6)

What new point corresponds to point (2, 4) of the original figure? How do you write its location on the grid?

(8, 16)

Predict what you expect the new dilated figure will look like.

The figure should be similar, but a different size.

When you reflect a figure over a reflection line, what remains the same in the transformation? What changes?

The size stays the same, but the direction changes on the arrow; both arrows are the same distance away from the line of reflection.

How does the size of the figure change in a reflection?

The size of the figure does not change.

Identify at least three side lengths on the original figure. What are lengths of those three side lengths? Find the corresponding sides on the new figure. What are the new lengths of the corresponding sides? What patterns do you observe between the original lengths and the new lengths?

Answers will vary, but the length of the sides should remain proportional.

What are the properties of similar figures?

Corresponding angles have to be the same measure and the lengths of the sides of the figures have to be proportional.

Suggest any point in Quadrant I, such as (2, 6).

In what quadrant does the image of this point fall if reflected across the y-axis?

Quadrant II

If this point were reflected across the y-axis, what would be the coordinates of the new point?

(–2, 6)

What patterns do you observe between the original ordered pairs (x, y) and their corresponding coordinates (x′, y′)?

In reflections, the x-coordinate changes to –x and the y-coordinate stays the same.

Repeat above questions for other quadrants.

Name some transformations used in geometry.

reflections, rotations, translations, and dilations

What type(s) of transformations are size-preserving transformations?

reflection, translations, and rotations

How are dilations different from other transformations?

Dilations change the size of the figure proportionally, keeping the image mathematically similar to the original. Reflections, rotations, and translations flip, turn, or slide the figure around, but the size remains the same.

How can you verify if Figure B is a dilation of Figure A?

There has to be a common growth using the same scale factor between corresponding vertices of the two figures.

What creates dilations that enlarge the size of the figure?

When you multiply the corresponding coordinate pairs by a scale factor that is greater than 1, the size of a figure will enlarge.

What creates dilations that reduce the size of the figure?

When you multiply the corresponding coordinate pairs by a scale factor between 0 and 1, the size of a figure will reduce.

What would the scale factor be if the two figures were congruent?

1

QUESTIONS FOR STUDENTS ON TASK (CONTINUED)

The client wanted to increase the lengths of the logo by 250%. What rule would you apply to the original coordinates of the points (x, y)?

→ *(2.5x, 2.5y)*

Suppose the original logo was dilated and the point (5, 4) became (4, 3.2) in the dilation. What do you know about the new image? What scale factor was used in the dilation?

→ *The new image is smaller, and the scale factor is 0.8.*

QUESTIONS TO EXTEND STUDENT THINKING

What happens to the figure's area in dilations?

→ *The area of the image will increase or decrease depending on the scale factor used to perform the dilation. The area increases or decreases by the magnitude of the scale factor squared. If the scale factor growth among the vertices were 3, the area of the new image would be 3, or 9 times, larger than the area of the pre-image.*

What effect does the dilation have on the perimeter of the figure?

→ *The perimeter also increases or decreases by the same scale factor. Each length of a side of the figure is multiplied by a scale factor; the perimeter is the sum of the sides, so it also increases or decreases by the scale factor.*

If a rule for a figure is (x, y), what is the rule for the figure dilated by a scale factor of 5?

→ *(5x, 5y)*

QUESTIONS TO EXTEND STUDENT THINKING (CONTINUED)

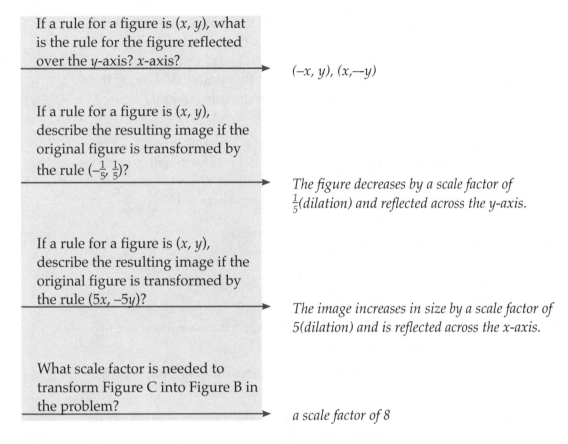

If a rule for a figure is (x, y), what is the rule for the figure reflected over the y-axis? x-axis?

→ $(-x, y), (x, -y)$

If a rule for a figure is (x, y), describe the resulting image if the original figure is transformed by the rule $(-\frac{1}{5}, \frac{1}{5})$?

→ *The figure decreases by a scale factor of $\frac{1}{5}$(dilation) and reflected across the y-axis.*

If a rule for a figure is (x, y), describe the resulting image if the original figure is transformed by the rule $(5x, -5y)$?

→ *The image increases in size by a scale factor of 5(dilation) and is reflected across the x-axis.*

What scale factor is needed to transform Figure C into Figure B in the problem?

→ *a scale factor of 8*

LESSON SUMMARY

Have students describe what dilations are. Ask students to share only one idea, and then move on to another student's idea until you have generated a list describing dilations. Create a chart listing student suggestions. Some examples of suggestions may include corresponding vertices, the growth by the same scale factor, the figures are similar, the side lengths are proportional and/or the angles are equals.

Have students explain their reasoning about how they know Figure B is a dilation of Figure A. Listen for statements that include the items on the list you created. Students should be able to verbalize the role of proportionality in this problem. Verify that students name the vertices of the pre-image that correspond to the vertices on Figure B. Have students name some of the points on the pre-image and name the corresponding points on Figure B.

LESSON SUMMARY (CONTINUED)

Students should recognize that multiplying each of the *x*- and *y*-coordinates of a given figure by the same scale factor creates a new figure that is mathematically similar to the original figure. Ask students how they think the areas of these figures are related. If students are having trouble describing the change in area, you might want to investigate dilations using simpler figures (e.g. different-sized squares).

Begin the summary about reflections by asking students to describe a reflection. Students should be able to verbalize what it means to reflect over the *y*-axis and over the *x*-axis, and the rules for how the coordinates change with these reflections. Make a second chart listing the effects of reflections.

CHECK FOR SUCCESS

☐ Have students explain the effects scale factors have on dilations by answering the following questions.

If the scale factor is 6, how does a dilation affect the coordinates of the pre-image (x, y)? Side lengths? Angles?

If the scale factor is $\frac{1}{4}$, how does a dilation affect the coordinates of the pre-image (x, y)? Side lengths? Angles?

If the scale factor is 1.0, how does a dilation affect the coordinates of the pre-image (x, y)? Side lengths? Angles?

☐ Have students describe how the rule (x, y) would change if the figure were reflected over the *y*-axis? *x*-axis?

Student _____ Class _____ Date _____

LESSON 3 ▸ DESIGNING FIGURES

Design Creations is hired to help other companies with their design needs, such as online advertising and creating company logos. An intern at *Design Creations* was given the client logos on Work Page 3.3 and told to verify that Figure B was a dilation of Figure A.

1. Describe the effects of dilation of a figure.

2. Is Figure B a dilation of Figure A? Explain your reasoning.

3. Name the coordinates of the points that form Figure A. Name the coordinates of corresponding points of Figure B. Write the coordinates in the table.

Coordinates of the points of Figure A							
Coordinates of the corresponding points of Figure B							

4. Describe any patterns you observe. Write a rule that will create Figure B from Figure A.

5. The client decides that the logo, Figure A, is too large for the advertising space and requests a smaller logo. They ask the intern to dilate Figure A by a scale factor of 0.5.

   a. Draw the new figure on your work page and label it Figure C.

   b. What are the coordinate of the points that form Figure C?
   Write the coordinates in the table.

Coordinates of the points of Figure A								
Coordinates of the corresponding points of Figure C								

   c. Describe the change in the coordinates of the points from Figure A to Figure C. Write a rule that will create Figure C from Figure A.

6. The client requests the intern create a reflection of Figure A across the *y*-axis.

   a. What will the logo look like? On your work page, draw a reflection across the *y*-axis of Figure A and label it Figure D.

   b. What are the coordinates of the points that form Figure D? Write the coordinates in the table.

Coordinates of the points of Figure A							
Coordinates of the corresponding points of Figure D							

   c. Describe the change in the coordinates of the points from Figure A and Figure D. Write a rule that will create Figure D from Figure A.

7. Compare dilations and reflections.

1. Dilation is a transformation that changes the size of a figure but not the shape. The new shape remains proportional to the original figure. The original figure is called the pre-image. You can create dilations by multiplying each of the *x*- and *y*-coordinates of a given figure by the same scale factor to create a new figure, which is mathematically similar to the original figure.

2. Yes; Compare the coordinates of the points on Figure A to the corresponding points on Figure B. All of the original (*x*, *y*) coordinate pairs were enlarged by the same factor, or scale factor of 4, to generate the corresponding coordinate pairs. The corresponding angles were the same size. Additionally, the side lengths and increased proportionally. You can also use the grid on the paper to verify proportional growth relationship.

3.

Coordinates of the points of Figure A	(2, 4)	(4, 2)	(4, 3)	(6, 2)	(5, 4)	(6, 6)	(4, 5)	(4, 6)
Coordinates of the corresponding points of Figure B	(8, 16)	(16, 8)	(16, 12)	(24, 8)	(20, 16)	(24, 24)	(16, 20)	(16, 24)

4. All of the coordinates of the points in Figure A were multiplied by a scale factor of 4 to produce the corresponding coordinates of the points of Figure B. The rule is (4*x*, 4*y*).

5. a.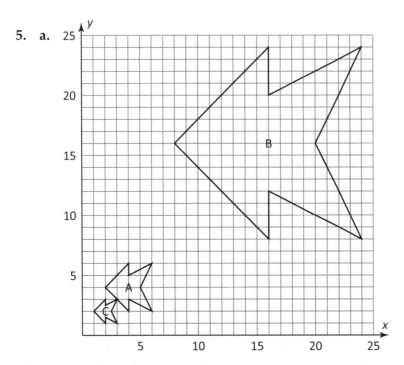

b.

Coordinates of the points of Figure A	(2, 4)	(4, 2)	(4, 3)	(6, 2)	(5, 4)	(6, 6)	(4, 5)	(4, 6)
Coordinates of the corresponding points of Figure C	(1, 2)	(2, 1)	(2, 1.5)	(3, 1)	(2.5, 2)	(3, 3)	(2, 2.5)	(2, 3)

c. All of the coordinates of the points in Figure A were multiplied by a scale factor of 0.5 producing the corresponding coordinates of the points of Figure C. The side lengths stay proportional and the measure of the angles are the same. The rule is (0.5x, 0.5y).

6. a.

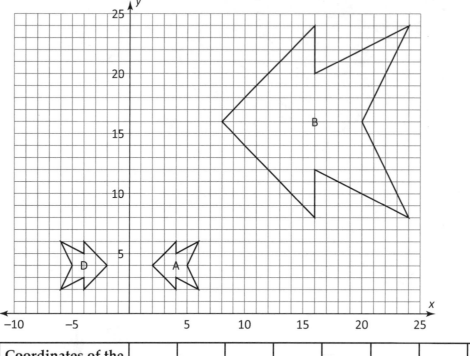

b.

Coordinates of the points of Figure A	(2, 4)	(4, 2)	(4, 3)	(6, 2)	(5, 4)	(6, 6)	(4, 5)	(4, 6)
Coordinates of the corresponding points of Figure D	(–2, 4)	(–4, 2)	(–4, 3)	(–6, 2)	(–5, 4)	(–6, 6)	(–4, 5)	(–4, 6)

c. All of the x-coordinates changed to $-x$. The rule is $(-x, y)$.

7. Dilations create a mathematically similar shape to the original figure. If you multiply any point on the original figure by the same scale factor (greater than 0), you create the dilation. If the scale factor is greater than 1, the original figure will be enlarged. If the scale factor is less than 1, but greater than 0, the original figure will be reduced. Reflections are congruent figures. Sometimes referred to as a flip, a reflection is a transformation that produces a mirror image of the original. Common reflections are vertical reflections and horizontal reflections. To reflect a figure across the y-axis (vertical reflection), any original coordinate, (x, y), will map to the corresponding point, $(-x, y)$ to produce the reflection. To horizontally reflect a figure across the x-axis, change the vertices of the pre-image (x, y) to $(x, -y)$ to produce the reflection. Students' answers should reflect any of the stated ideas.

CHAPTER 4 MEASUREMENT

Common Core State Standards

Ratios and Proportional Relationships 6.RP

Use ratio concepts and use ratio reasoning to solve problems.

3. Understand ratio and rate reasoning to solve real-world and mathematical problems, e.g., by reasoning about tables of equivalent ratios, tape diagrams, double number line diagrams, or equations.

    d. Use ratio reasoning to convert measurement units; manipulate and transform units appropriately when multiplying or dividing quantities.

Ratios and Proportional Relationships 7.RP

Analyze proportional relationships and use them to solve real-world and mathematical problems.

2. Recognize and represent proportional relationships between quantities.

    a. Decide whether two quantities are in a proportional relationship, e.g., by testing for equivalent ratios in a table or graphing on a coordinate plane and observing whether the graph is a straight line through the origin.

    b. Identify the constant of proportionality (unit rate) in tables, graphs, equations, diagrams, and verbal descriptions of proportional reasoning.

LESSON GOALS

- Investigate the relationship between centimeters and inches and determine whether the relationship is proportional.
- Identify proportional relationships in problem situations and solve problems.
- Use ratio reasoning to convert measurement units.

LESSON INTRODUCTION

In this lesson students are asked to investigate the relationship between centimeters and inches. Students will use both the customary and metric systems of measurement throughout this lesson. As you begin the lesson have students measure their desks in centimeters, and then in inches. Record their measurements. Have students explain why they think people found different answers. Some students might suggest rounding issues or human error.

The **customary system** is the main system of measurement used for weights, lengths, and capacities in the United States. For length, the common units are inches, feet, yards, and miles.

The **metric system** is a base-ten decimal system used for measurements. The base unit of measurement for length is the meter. Some of the other units (most common) are the millimeter, centimeter, and kilometer.

Discuss with students that measurement is always only an estimation and can only be as precise as the measuring tools used.

There will be some variation in the measurements but differences should be reasonable.

TEACHING SUGGESTIONS

Within the bulleted text below are suggestions on how to begin the lesson, introduce essential vocabulary, and question students so that they are prepared to complete the Student Recording Page on their own or with minimal assistance.

Introduce the problem to students. Explain that they will be measuring some items in the lesson. They may need to round their measurements.

- Review the rules for rounding.

- Review the meanings of ratio and unit rate.

A **ratio** is a comparison of two quantities. A ratio can be written in three formats: $\frac{1}{4}$, 1:4, and 1 to 4.

- Inform students that when measuring in inches, they should measure to the nearest $\frac{1}{8}$ of an inch. When measuring in centimeters they are to measure to the nearest tenth of a centimeter (millimeter).

A **unit rate** is a rate where one of the measurements is 1. Sample unit rates are: 12 inches:1 foot, $25 per ticket, 4 hours:1 room.

NCTM Correlation
Measurement
Understand measurable attributes of objects and units, systems, and processes of measurement.
Understand both metric and customary systems of measurement.

Materials
Student Recording Page 4.1
Rulers (cm/inch)
Items for students to measure
Graph paper
Optional:
Large gridded paper
Sticky dots
String for line trend line

Vocabulary
Customary
Metric
Ratio
Unit rate

STUDENT ENGAGEMENT

After students have measured 10 items, they are ready to answer the questions on Student Recording Page 4.1. Students should work in pairs, and each student should have the opportunity to measure items in both units of measure.

As students are working on the lesson, have one group record the table on a chart paper to use in the summary. Additionally have a group create a graph on chart paper to use in the summary. If you have some groups graphing inches to centimeters and others graphing centimeters to inches, you should have a chart graph of each to compare and contrast during the summary. As students work, ask them questions about the relationship between their measurements to check for understanding.

Which measurement is longer—an inch or a centimeter? → *an inch*

What object has a length of about 1 inch? → *a paperclip*

What object has a length of about 1 cm? → *a pencil eraser or the width of your fingernail*

How many of the 1-cm objects (e.g. pencil eraser) would it take to equal the length of your 1-inch object (e.g. paperclip)? → *between 2 and 3*

About how many centimeters long do you think a calculator measures? → *Answers will vary.*

About how many inches do you think your pencil measures? → *Answers will vary.*

If you know an estimated length of a paperclip in centimeters, how can you use your estimate to determine the length of 3 paper clips in centimeters? 6 paperclips? → *Multiply the estimated length by 3 to get the measurement of 3 paperclips, and multiply by 6 to estimate the measurement of 6 paperclips.*

How does a ruler (in. and cm ruler) verify these measurements? → *On a ruler there are about 2.5 cm in every 1 in. unit.*

Suppose a group recorded "0" inches as an entry on their table. What is its related value in centimeters?

→ *0 (Have students add this related pair of values to the table.)*

How can you compare two quantities?

→ *Two quantities can be compared using a part to part ratio, a part to whole ratio, a difference, or a percent.*

Show using your hand about what an inch looks like?

→ *Students should show something similar to the distance between two knuckles.*

Show using your hand about what a centimeter looks like?

→ *Students should show something similar to the distance across a fingernail.*

About how many fingernail widths does it take to equal a knuckle length?

→ *between 2 and 3*

Questions for Students on Task

What are unit rates?

→ *a comparison of a quantity to 1 unit of a different quantity ex. miles/hr, gallons/dollar*

What unit rates can you find in this problem?

→ *the unit rate between centimeters and inches*

How can you calculate the unit rates? Explain what your unit rate means in this problem.

Find the ratio between the two measures, then find an equivalent ratio with 1 as the denominator. A unit rate gives me an amount per 1 unit of measure.

How is the unit rate represented in the table of values?

It is the amount of centimeters found in 1 inch.

How is the unit rate represented in the graph?

It is the rate of increase you see in the graph; the steepness of the trend in the graph. For every 1 inch, there are about 2.5 centimeters.

How is the unit rate represented in the equation?

It is the number multiplied by the inches to get a measurement in centimeters.

Is the number of inches and centimeters a proportional relationship? How do you know?

Yes, there seems to be a constant rate of change in the table, although it might be a bit off because of rounding of the measurements.

How do centimeters compare to inches?

There are about 2.5 cm in every inch.

How do inches compare to centimeters?

An inch is about 0.4 of a centimeter.

What do you prefer to measure in—inches or centimeters? Why?

Answers will vary.

Describe any patterns you see in the table.

→ *It seems that for every inch the number of centimeters increases by 2.5.*

What patterns do you see in the graph?

→ *There seems to be a linear relationship.*

If an object measures 5 inches, about how many centimeters would it measure?

→ *about 12.5*

If an object measures 10 cm, about how many inches does it measure?

→ *about 3.5*

Describe the relationship between feet and yards.

→ *There is a constant ratio between feet and yards. It is a ratio of 3:1.*

What patterns would you expect to see in a table of values for this relationship (yards versus feet)?

→ *For every yard, there are 3 feet.*

What patterns would you expect to see in a graph?

→ *a proportional relationship that will increase at a rate of 1 to 3*

What would you expect the equation for the relationship of yards to feet to look like?

→ *y = 3f*

QUESTIONS TO EXTEND STUDENT THINKING

Do you think there is a relationship between pounds and ounces? How would you see it in a table, graph, and equation?

There is a proportional relationship between pounds and ounces. For every pound there is 16 ounces. In the table you would see the ounce increase by 16 for every 1 pound. In the graph you would see the same increase in the steepness of the line for every 1 pound there would be and an increase of 16 ounces. In the equations it would be what you multiply the pounds by to get ounces.

What can you tell about the relationships between other units of measures?

There is a proportional relationship between two units of measure. You use that constant ratio to convert among the units of measure.

If on the Planet Imaginary a "Grainy" is about 4 cm long and you graphed the relationship between a "grainy" and an inch, how would that graph differ from your graph?

The linear relationship would show a steeper slope, but still pass through the origin.

What can you tell about the slope of the line?

It is the constant of proportionality – or unit rate – in this situation.

LESSON SUMMARY

Begin this summary by putting a graph on 1-in. grid paper labeled inches on the *x*-axis with a scale of 1 and centimeters on the *y*-axis with a scale of 2.54. Have each group graph three of the points on the class graph using sticky dots. You will discuss this chart later in the summary.

Ask students what they discovered about the relationship between centimeters and inches. Record what students suggest. Have the group that created the table on chart paper post it. Discuss the measurements listed. How did you find the ratios you recorded? Students should suggest it is the amount of centimeters per inch measured. Record some other measurements on the table by asking students for other items they measured.

- If any groups measure the same thing, how do their measurements compare? Why would the measurements be different? Discuss the unit rates found on the table posted and the unit rates students found.

- What does the unit rate from the table help you see? The unit rate helps to see the relationship between the two units of measures.

- Did everyone have the same unit rate? Why? Students should notice that there might be a variation in their measurements that would cause the unit rates to vary slightly. There should not be a big difference if the unit rates are found.

- Ask students to discuss the relationship between the two units of measure. Could the relationship be a proportional relationship? If so, based on the data what would be the true unit rate between centimeters and inches? Student might suggest the unit rate found most often or they might suggest finding the mean of the unit rates found by all students.

Discuss the graph made by the class at the beginning of the summary. Students should suggest that the points all seem to be linear. Using a string, tape a trend line on the graph. Students should be able to tell you what the line represents and describe a connection between the graph and the table?

Post the graphs you asked students to create during the engagement part of the lesson. Have the groups draw trend lines on these graphs. Compare and contrast the different graphs. Discuss the different ways the graphs are labeled.

- Is one variable dependent on the other? Is it OK to switch the labels of the axes? What happens when we do switch them?

- Compare the scales used. Does having more data on the graph help you decide what kind of relationship there is between the measurements? Do all these graphs share the same points?

Have students compare the graphs they created. Have students draw trend lines on their graphs to compare the trend line to others.

- Do they show a linear relationship? Is this a proportional relationship? How do you know?

- How does the unit rate show up on the graph? Have students show where they see the unit rate in the graph.

Have students show the rise to run relationship on the graph. They may not identify this as the slope yet; however, they should see it as the constant rate of change in the graph.

- What does the point (5, 12.7) on the graph represent?

- Using the graph, if an item measured 12 inches, how many centimeters would it measure?

- Using the graph, if an item measured 36 centimeters, how many inches would it measure?

- What would the point (0, 0) mean on the graph?

CHECK FOR SUCCESS

☐ Place a couple of items along the x-axis starting at the origin. Have students find the length of the items using inches. Based on the graph, students should predict the length using centimeters.

☐ Have students share the equations they wrote in the lesson and explain what they use to write the equations. Record their equations and have the class compare them to the tables. Students can write about the relationship they noticed between the table, graph, and equation.

☐ Have students make conjectures about the relationship between feet and yards and the relationship between kilometers and miles. Have them explain if they think other comparisons have a proportional relationship and why. Have students conjecture about the relationships.

As an extension activity, you can investigate other relationships as projects and create a bulletin board with relationships students have investigated. Once projects are completed, you can have students make generalizations about what they know about the different measurements.

Student _____ Class _____ Date _____

LESSON 1   CENTIMETERS TO INCHES

Lilli came home with an assignment from school. Her teacher, Mrs. Roman, asked the class to investigate the relationship between inches and centimeters. Mrs. Roman told the students to develop a plan that will establish the relationship between 2 units of measure and then use the relationship to solve problems.

Lilli decides to measure 10 items in centimeters and then measure the same items in inches. Do the measurements for Lilli, record the information on the table below, and look for patterns.

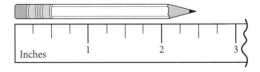

Name of Item	Length (cm)	Length (inches)		
1.				
2.				
3.				
4.				
5.				
6.				
7.				
8.				
9.				
10				

1. Look for 10 different-sized items to measure. List each item on the table. Measure each item to the nearest tenth of a centimeter (millimeter); then measure each item to the nearest $\frac{1}{8}$ of an inch.

2. What patterns do you notice in the table?

3. In the fourth column of the table, write a ratio that describes the two measures. Write an appropriate title for this column.

4. Find a unit rate for each ratio and write it in the fifth column. Write an appropriate title for this column.

5. Describe the pattern, or relationship, between centimeters and inches.

6. Lilli then decided to make a graph comparing the measurements to investigate the relationship more carefully. Create the graph using the information in your table.

7. What patterns do you notice in the graph? Draw a trend line that connects as many points as possible. What do you know about this line?

8. How do the patterns in the graph relate to the patterns in the table of data?

From *It's All Connected: The Power of Proportional Reasoning to Understand Mathematics Concepts, Grades 6–8* by Carmen Whitman. © 2011 Scholastic Inc. Permission granted to photocopy for nonprofit use in a classroom or similar place dedicated to face-to-face educational instruction.

9. Write an equation to use to convert inches into centimeters.

10. Write an equation to use to convert centimeters into inches.

11. Lilli found some neon light strips she wants to hang on two of the adjacent walls of her room. The lights can connect to each other to make one unbroken strip. She has a room that measures 10 ft by 8 ft. The lights are sold in strips that are 28 cm long. Lilli has to buy the strips in lengths of 28 cm. Can she buy enough strips to cover the entire distance of the walls without having any part of a strip left over? Explain.

12. If she buys 10 strips of neon lights, how many feet can she cover?

13. Describe the relationship between inches and centimeters. Where do you see evidence of this relationship in the table, graph, or equation?

1. Answers will vary.
    Example of a partial table:

Name of Item	Length (cm)	Length (inches)		
1. Pencil	16.5	$6\frac{1}{2}$		
2. Book	25.3	10		
3. Floor tile	30.4	12		

2. There are more centimeters than inches; between 2 and 3 times more.

3. Answers will vary.
    Example of a partial table:

Name of Item	Length (inches)	Length (cm)	Ratio (cm:in)	
1. Pencil	16.5	$6\frac{1}{2}$	$16.5:6\frac{1}{2}$	
2. Book	25.3	10	25.3:10	
3. Floor tile	30.4	12	30.4:12	

4. Answers will vary.
    Example of a partial table:

Name of Item	Length (inches)	Length (cm)	Ratio (cm:in)	Unit Rate (cm:in)
1. Pencil	16.5	$6\frac{1}{2}$	$16.5:6\frac{1}{2}$	$\frac{2.54}{1}$
2. Book	25.3	10	25.3:10	$\frac{2.53}{1}$
3. Floor tile	30.4	12	30.4:12	$\frac{2.53}{1}$

5. There is a relationship between centimeters and inches. The constant rate of change increases by about 2.54 cm for each additional inch. There are about 2.54 centimeters of length for every 1 inch of length.

6. Students may graph the relationship as centimeters to inches or inches to centimeters. Both are correct and are to be discussed in the Teaching Suggestions. Student data points will vary because there are different lengths and estimation.

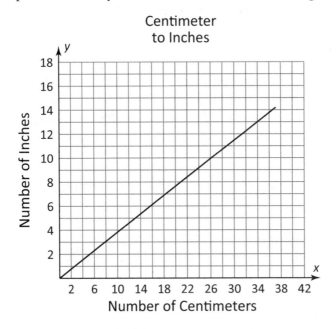

Centimeter to Inches

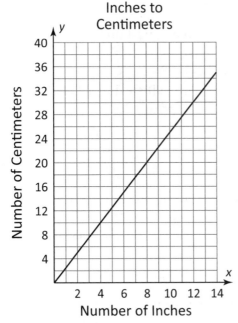

Inches to Centimeters

7. Students may notice that not all their points are on the line, but they are close to the line. This is because of estimating that was used when they did the initial measuring. The data appears to be a linear relationship that passes through the origin, which means it is a proportional relationship. For every 1 inch, the number of centimeters increase by about 2.5.

8. The constant rate of change in the table makes the graph a linear relationship. The coordinates on the graph increase at a rate of about 2.5 cm every time the number of inches increases by 1. Some points might be a bit off because of some estimation that occurred when we first measured the items.

9. $c = 2.54i$; where c represents the number of centimeters and i represents the number of inches

10. $i = \frac{c}{2.54}$, or $i = \frac{2}{5}c$; where i represents the number of inches and c represents the number of centimeters

11. Find the measurement of the walls in inches.
    $(10 + 8) \cdot 12 = 216$ in.
    Then change inches to centimeters using the equation in Question 9.
    $c = 2.54 \cdot 216 = 584.64$
    Then divide 548.64 by 28 because each strip of lights is 28 cm.
    $\frac{548.64}{28} = 19.60$; If she buys 19 strips, she will be short lights; If she buys 20 strips, she will have extra lights.

12. 10 strips; each strip measures 28 cm
    $10 \cdot 28 = 280$ cm
    Then use the equation from Question 10 to change centimeters into inches.
    $i = \frac{280}{2.54} = 110.2362 \approx 110$
    Convert 110 inches into feet (divide by 12) which is 9.1667. This means she can cover a little over 9 ft. (about 9 ft and 2 in.)

13. There is a proportional relationship between the inches and centimeters. For every 1 inch of length measured, there are about 2.54 centimeters. In the table, the unit rate is the relationship between the measures. In the graph; the trend line shows the constant rate of change of 2.54. In the equation, you multiply the number of inches by 2.54 when you want to change the length to centimeters.

LESSON 2 — HOW TALL?

Common Core State Standards
Geometry 7.G
Draw, construct, and describe geometric figures and describe the relationships between them.
1. Solve problems involving scale drawings of geometric figures including computing actual lengths and areas from a scale drawing and reproducing a scale drawing at a different scale.

NCTM Correlation
Geometry
Use visualization, spatial reasoning, and geometric modeling to solve problems.
Recognize and apply geometric ideas and relationships in areas outside the mathematics classroom, such as art, science, and everyday life.
Measurement
Understand measurable attributes of objects and the units, systems, and processes of measurements.
Understand both metric and customary systems of measurement.
Apply appropriate techniques, tools, and formulas to determine measurements.
Select and apply techniques and tools to accurately find length, area, volume, and angle measures to appropriate levels of precision.

LESSON GOALS

- Measure actual lengths with appropriate level of precision.
- Apply the properties of similar triangles.
- Develop and understand a procedure for indirect measurement.

LESSON INTRODUCTION

As you begin, review a right angle and right triangle. Explain to students that a right triangle will be used for the task they will complete in this lesson.

> A **right angle** has a measure of 90˚.

Before students begin this lesson have a discussion about proportional relationships so students know what a proportional relationship is and what it means for two things to be proportional.

> A **right triangle** is a triangle with one right angle.

Students will learn to use proportional relationships as they are related to similar figures to solve problems that involve indirect measurement.

TEACHING SUGGESTIONS

Within the bulleted text below are suggestions on how to begin the lesson, introduce essential vocabulary, and question students so that they are prepared to complete the Student Recording Page on their own or with minimal assistance.

Draw two rectangles as shown below.

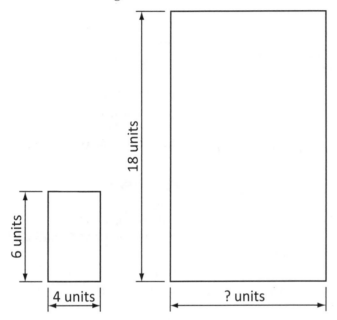

Materials
Student Recording Page 4.2
Meter sticks
Outdoor area containing large objects for measuring (e.g. height of school, flag pole, street lamp, etc.)
Sun

Vocabulary
Right angle
Right triangle
Similar triangle
Indirect measurement
Corresponding
Congruent
Scale factor

- If these two rectangles are proportional, what can be said about their angles? Side lengths?

- If the sides of the rectangles are proportional to each other, what is the missing length?

- If the corresponding sides are proportional and the angles are congruent, how would you describe the shapes?
  mathematically similar shapes

- What has to be true to have similar triangles?
  List the student responses.

TEACHING SUGGESTIONS (CONTINUED)

Introduce the lesson to the students. Clarify that the streamers will be hung from the top rail so that they hang down the backside of the stadium and touch the ground. Use the picture of the stadium to help illustrate. Before allowing students to begin the lesson, ask questions about Sarah's model.

- How do you think it is possible to find the height of a building using shadows? What mathematics will Sarah use?

- If the rays of sunlight run parallel, what statements can be made about the angles in the drawing?

- Help students see that if the imaginary lines of the sun's rays are parallel and that the lines formed by the shadows lie on the same horizon and the lines formed by the object and meter stick are perpendicular to the ground, then the corresponding sides of the triangles are parallel to each other. The angles formed by the heights of the objects and the shadows are right angles. The angles formed by the imaginary lines intersecting the shadows are congruent to each other. Since the measure of any 3 angles in a triangle equals 180° then the other two corresponding angles are equal to each other.

- Be certain that students understand how the situation was set up.

Similar triangles are triangles that have corresponding angles that are congruent and corresponding side lengths that are proportional.

Congruent means having the same size and shape. In this lesson, congruent angles mean the angles have the same measures.

Corresponding angles are the angles in the same location of two similar triangles. **Corresponding sides** are the sides of similar triangles that are between corresponding angles.

Student Engagement

Students are to complete Student Recording Page 4.2. Tell students their challenge is to find the missing lengths in this problem, and use similar triangles to help. Allow students to work on this lesson in groups of 2 – 3 students.

Before allowing students outside, have the students make a plan on how they are going to set up the activity. You might want to take pictures of the area they will be going to so they can decide what they are going to measure before they go. Have them estimate the heights before leaving the classroom. Have students divide the responsibilities so that everyone has a role in the activity.

As they begin to measure, ask students what units of measure they are using and why. You can follow that discussion with other questions listed below to guide students to begin thinking about what measurements are estimations.
- *How precise are these measurements?*
- *What are some variables that will affect how precise your measurement is?*
- *What would happen if you measure the length more than once?*
- *How many times are you measuring a length?*
- *How confident are you in your measurements?*
- *What about the measurement of the missing height?*

Students should suggest that the more times they measure, the more precise they will be able to get the measurement. They should also note that the missing height is an estimate. As students work, ask questions to check for understanding and to verify students have set up the proportions correctly.

Questions for Struggling Students

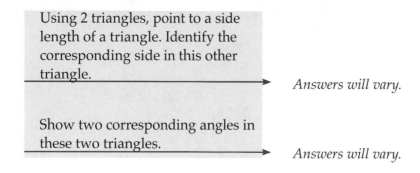

Using 2 triangles, point to a side length of a triangle. Identify the corresponding side in this other triangle.

Answers will vary.

Show two corresponding angles in these two triangles.

Answers will vary.

Make a sketch of what you expect to see when you measure the shadows outside to find the height of our object. What will make up the two triangles? What measurements can you actually take?

→ *Sketches will vary; measurements they can take include lengths of shadows, length of sticks, and angles.*

What can you infer about the corresponding angles on the two triangles?

→ *Their measures are equal to each other.*

What is the sum of all the angle measures of any triangle?

→ *180°*

How is your height problem similar to Sandra's?

→ *The height of a tall object is being estimated using indirect measurement.*

What distance are you trying to find for Sandra?

→ *height of the stadium*

How should the meter stick be positioned to cast the shadow?

→ *perpendicular to the ground*

What units of measure will you use to measure the shadow? Why?

→ *Meters; If the measure is made using centimeters or inches, it will have to be converted to meters.*

Do you think everyone has to use the same unit of measure for this task?

No; the measurements can all be taken in inches or all taken in centimeters. The numbers would be different, but the relationship stays the same.

Compare the meter stick's shadow to the shadow of the tall object. What statements can be made?

The meter stick's shadow will be shorter but, the shadows will be proportional to each other.

QUESTIONS FOR STUDENTS ON TASK

What mathematics will you use today to solve this problem?

Use corresponding parts of similar triangles to set up and solve proportional relationships.

How can you be certain your two triangles are mathematically similar?

Answers will vary.

If you are measuring the shadows of two objects and one is taller than the other, how will their shadows compare?

At any time of day, the taller object will have a longer shadow.

When do you expect to see a long shadow cast by the meter stick?

early or late in the day, when the sun is near the horizon

QUESTIONS FOR STUDENTS ON TASK (CONTINUED)

How do the meter stick and its shadow form a triangle?

→ *The meter stick has to be held perpendicular to the ground. The meter stick becomes the height of the triangle, the angle formed is a right angle, and its shadow becomes the base length of the triangle. If you draw a line from the top of the meter stick to the end of the shadow, that line becomes the longest side of the triangle, or the hypotenuse.*

If the ratio between the stick and its shadow was 4:2 and the object you were measuring cast a shadow 10 m long, what height would you expect the object to have?

→ *20 meters*

What information do you need to know to change meters to feet? Where can you find this information? How do you change meters to feet?

→ *You can use the ratio of* $\frac{1\ m}{3.28\ ft}$ *to find out how many feet are equal to the length in meters.*

How can you find the missing length of a similar triangle?

→ *Set up a proportion between the corresponding sides of the two triangles. You can then find the missing length by finding the scale factor between the corresponding lengths. Next find the missing value that will make the two ratios equal to each other.*

How long should Sandra make each streamer? How confident are you that the streamer will reach the ground?

→ *about 30 meters*

Explain how the angles are congruent between the larger and smaller triangles.

Both the heights (i.e. tall object and the meter stick) are perpendicular to the ground, so a right angle is formed. Since the sun is shining down on the meter stick and the object is being measured at the same time of day, the lines formed from the rays are parallel to each other. The shadows that intersect the sunrays serve as a transversal, which means the angles formed are equal. Because the sum of any three angle measures of any triangle equals 180°, then the other corresponding angles are also equal to each other.

What is indirect measurement?

It is a way to measure the height of a tall object that might otherwise be difficult to measure; such as a very tall tree or a building like the Washington Monument. I use a length I can measure to indirectly measure lengths I cannot.

Later in the day (or earlier this morning) other students also approximated the height of our object. Their shadows were much longer (shorter). How do you think their measurements compared to your measurements?

Their measurements were probably different from mine, but the relationship between their shadows and their objects should be proportional to the relationship between the shadow I measured and the object.

QUESTIONS TO EXTEND STUDENT THINKING (CONTINUED)

Why can you use shadows to make these predictions about height?

→ *If the measurements are taken at the same time of day, the length of the shadows should be proportional because the angle formed by the sun hitting the objects is the same for both objects.*

Are similar figures proportional? Why?

→ *When you have similar figures, the ratio of length to height remains constant throughout all corresponding figures. The side lengths will vary in sizes, but in essence the side lengths are a multiple of that constant ratio. This ratio is the scale factor.*

LESSON SUMMARY

As you begin the summary, have students share their methods of measuring a missing height. Have students tell the class about the items they measured, and if any groups measured the same items have them compare the measurements. If you have many students that measured the same item, you can create a line plot of the calculated height to compare heights.

Discuss with students the role that the time of day played. Compare their measurements to others made at different times of the day. Have students make some conjectures about why different groups found different shadow measurements. Students should suggest that

> **Indirect measurement** is a method used for finding a measurement that you cannot directly (physically) measure. The method uses proportions and similar triangles.

when the sun is closer to the horizon, the shadow cast would be longer than a shadow cast at noon.

- What does taking the measurements at different times throughout the day change? *It changes the measurements of the shadows and the ratio of the two shadows. If later in the day the sun cast a longer shadow for the meter stick, it also casts a longer shadow for the object with the missing height.*

- Besides the sun angle, what else could cause a longer shadow? *the height of the stick; You expect a longer stick to have a longer shadow.*

LESSON SUMMARY (CONTINUED)

Compare the different statements students wrote to explain how they found the missing height. Have one student start the explanation by reading their first statement, and then have other students add to the explanation until all thoughts have been presented. Write a list of student's thoughts that are shared.

Discuss and compare the ratios used to find the missing height.

> A **scale factor** is a number used to proportionately change a quantity. In this lesson the quantity is a measurement.

- Did all students set up the same ratios?

- Is there more than one way to set up the ratios?

- What scale factors were used?

- Did all students use the same scale factor?

- Did every student get the exact same measurement for the height of the stadium?

Discuss how measurements might vary depending on the precision of the calculations. Then discuss why different measures result in the same height of the stadium as in Question 5. Students should reason that the second set of measures might have been taken at a different time of day. Students should also mention that because the sticks used by Sandra and the second group were different heights, the measurements should be different, but the ratios used should still be proportional.

CHECK FOR SUCCESS

- ☐ Have students work with their group to write directions for someone who has not completed this activity. The directions should state how to successfully determine the height of a tall object (e.g. tree) using indirect measurement.

Student _____ Class _____ Date _____

LESSON 2 HOW TALL?

Sandra joined a spirit group at her university this year. This year her university is expanding the seating at their football stadium. They built an additional deck alongside the home section of the stadium. The spirit club wants the freshman class to attach streamers in their school colors from the top railing and down the backside of the stadium for the first game. Sandra has to decide how long the streamers need to be so that they reach from the top railing to the ground. However, she can't get anyone to tell her the height of the stadium.

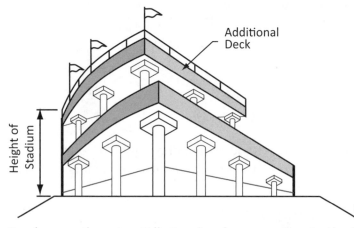

Additional Deck

Height of Stadium

Sarah, a math major, tells Sandra she can estimate the height of the stadium using only one measuring stick on a sunny day. Sarah shows Sandra the following sketch of a model with a note that states:

Triangles are formed by the object, its shadow, and the imaginary line from the top of the object to the end of the shadow.

Sarah then tells Sandra that all she needs is a (meter) stick, shadows, and an understanding of similar triangles to estimate the height of the stadium. Help Sandra find the height of the stadium.

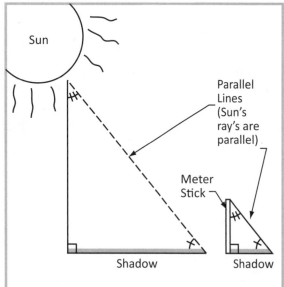

Sun

Parallel Lines (Sun's ray's are parallel)

Meter Stick

Shadow

Shadow

1. How can you tell if two triangles are similar?

2. Using a meter stick and Sarah's method, go outside and find the height of something over 6 ft tall. An example is a building's height, basketball goal, or large tree. Set up a sketch similar to Sarah's to show what measurements need to be taken and what measurements were found. Label all the measurements you make and record the units you used to measure.

3. Illustrate how to use the measurements taken to determine the height of your object. Find the unknown height. Explain how the unknown measurement is found. Does your measurement make sense?

4. When Sandra took measurements at the stadium, she found a stick that (she decided) measured 4 m the shadow cast by the stick was 2.5 m, and the shadow cast by the stadium was 19 m. Draw a sketch of this scenario and label it with the given information. Find the height of the stadium.

From *It's All Connected: The Power of Proportional Reasoning to Understand Mathematics Concepts, Grades 6-8* by Carmen Whitman. © 2011 Scholastic Inc. Permission granted to photocopy for nonprofit use in a classroom or similar place dedicated to face-to-face educational instruction.

Student _____ Class _____ Date _____

5. If one meter equals approximately 3.28 ft, what is the height of the stadium in feet? Show your work.

6. Another group takes their own measurements at a different time of day. Their stick measures 6 ft. The shadow cast by the stick is $3\frac{1}{4}$ ft, and the shadow cast by the stadium is 54 ft. What height did this group get for the stadium? Show your work.

1. When two triangles are similar, they have corresponding congruent angles and corresponding side lengths are proportional.

2. Students should have a sketch resembling two similar triangles consisting of the meter stick, length of shadow cast by the meter stick, object being measured, and the length of the shadow cast by that object. The sketch should also show that the meter stick is at a 90° angle to the ground. Using this information, students should be able to find the missing length, which is the height of the object.

3. If I can have similar triangles, then I know that the corresponding angles have equal measures and that the corresponding side lengths share a common ratio. This means they change proportionally by some scale factor. If I set up the meter stick perpendicular to the ground, then it forms a right angle to the ground. When setting up my meter stick, I place it so that the meter stick, its shadow, and the sunray casting the shadow form a right triangle. The object I am measuring should also be perpendicular to the ground. The sun will cast a shadow on the meter stick and the object I am measuring at the same angle, which means there are corresponding angles formed at the bottom of the triangles. Because the triangles have congruent corresponding angles, then I can compare their side lengths to find the unknown measure. The corresponding side lengths in similar figures share a common ratio, so they are changed by a common scale factor.

4.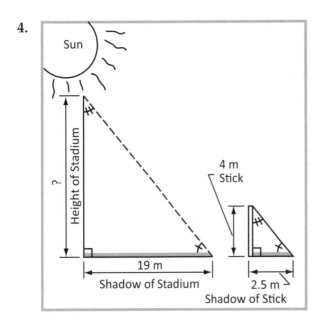

4. (continued)

$$\frac{4 \text{ m}}{2.5 \text{ m}} = \frac{?}{19 \text{ m}}$$

$19 \div 2.5 = 7.6$

7.6 is the scale factor.

$$\frac{7 \text{ m} \times 7.6}{2.5 \text{ m} \times 7.6} = \frac{30.4 \text{ m}}{19 \text{ m}}$$

The stadium is 30.4 m high.

5. I used the ratio $\frac{1 \text{ m}}{3.28 \text{ ft}}$ to find the height of the stadium.

$$\frac{1 \text{ m}}{3.28 \text{ ft}} = \frac{30.4 \text{ m}}{x \text{ ft}}$$

$$\frac{1 \times 30.4}{3.28 \times 30.4} \approx \frac{30.4 \text{ m}}{99.7 \text{ ft}}$$

The stadium is about 100 ft high.

6.

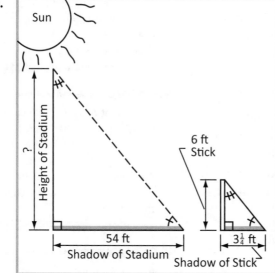

$$\frac{6 \text{ ft}}{3\frac{1}{4} \text{ ft}} = \frac{?}{54 \text{ ft}}$$

$54 \div 3.25 \approx 16.62$

16.62 is the scale factor.

$$\frac{6 \text{ ft} \times 16.62}{3.25 \text{ ft} \times 16.62} \approx \frac{99.77 \text{ ft}}{54 \text{ ft}}$$

The stadium is about 100 ft high.

Common Core State Standards
Ratios and Proportional
Relationships 7.RP
    Analyze proportional
    relationships and use them to
    solve real-world and
    mathematical problems.
    2. Recognize and represent
       proportional relationships
       between quantities.
Geometry 7.G
    Draw, construct, and describe
    geometrical figures and
    describe the relationships
    between them.
    1. Solve problems involving
       scale drawings of geometric
       figures, including
       computing actual lengths,
       areas from a scale drawing
       and reproducing a scale
       drawing at a different scale.
    6. Solve real-world and
       mathematical problems
       involving area, volume, and
       surface area of two- and
       three-dimensional objects
       composed of triangles,
       quadrilaterals, polygons,
       cubes, and right prisms.

NCTM Correlation
Geometry
    Use visualization, spatial
    reasoning, and geometric
    modeling to solve problems.
        Draw geometric objects
        with specified properties,
        such as side lengths or
        angle measures.
Measurement
    Apply appropriate techniques,
    tools, and formulas to
    determine measurements.
        Select and apply techniques
        and tools to accurately find
        length, area, volume, and
        angle measures to
        appropriate levels of
        precision.
        Solve problems involving
        scale factors, using ratio
        and proportion.

LESSON GOALS

- Draw and construct geometric figures using relationships among them.
- Solve problems involving proportional reasoning.
- Calculate measurements for a scale figure.

LESSON INTRODUCTION

This lesson gives students opportunities to work with measurement, scaling, and proportional reasoning. Ask students what they know about scale drawings. Students might suggest that they are drawings of objects that are not drawn using actual measurements.

Discuss briefly how scales are used in building toy models, dollhouses, model buildings, and robots. Show examples if you have them available.

One common application of proportional reasoning is the use of a scale factor in a scale drawing. In this lesson, students will analyze the proportionality of actual measurements and scale measurements.

A **scale drawing** is a drawing that depicts an actual object or area, but has been enlarged or reduced by a certain scale. A scale drawing includes an equation or legend so that a reader can interpret the drawing accurately.

This equation or legend, called a **scale**, states what a specific length in the drawing equals in the actual object or space. A legend is presented using a visual reference of a length on the drawing.

A **scale factor** is a number used to proportionately change a quantity. In this lesson, the quantity is a dimension. A **dimension** is the measurement of a spatial attribute, such as length, width, or height.

TEACHING SUGGESTIONS

Within the bulleted text below are suggestions on how to begin the lesson, introduce essential vocabulary, and question students so that they are prepared to complete the Student Recording Page on their own or with minimal assistance.

Introduce the lesson. Discuss what is known and unknown about the park's partial plans.

- What do you know about the park?

- What information is needed to draw a model?

- Do you think all parks will look the same?

Clarify any questions students have about what needs to be completed for this lesson. Discuss what dimensions are needed to find the areas for these figures. Explain that the drawing they will be creating should be drawn to scale.

Materials
    Student Recording Page 4.3
    Rulers (Inches)
    Paper ($8\frac{1}{2} \times 11$)
    Compass or angle ruler
    Protractors
    Butcher paper/chart paper
Optional:
    1-in. grid paper

Vocabulary
    Scale drawing
    Dimensions
    Scale
    Scale factor

STUDENT ENGAGEMENT

Students are to complete Student Recording Page 4.3. They can work individually or in small groups. If students work in groups, allow them some individual time to make a plan for what needs to be completed. Students will need supplies to make sure the drawings of the models they are creating are correct. You should have 1-in. grid paper available for struggling students.

Students will need to ascertain possible dimensions for the areas provided in the partial plans. With the exception of the square (playground zone), these dimensions will vary, but the areas will remain fixed. As students work, ask questions about the dimensions they have chosen and if other dimensions are possible. Be certain students can explain why other dimensions are possible and why they are using the dimensions that they are. Ask students about the relationship between the drawing and the actual park. Question students about corresponding side lengths. If needed, direct students to draw sketches showing the areas and dimensions of the actual-sized zones. This may help provide structure to the problem. As you monitor their work, make note of the different strategies students are using to share during summary.

QUESTIONS FOR STRUGGLING STUDENTS

Explain the scale on the plan. → *For every inch I draw, it represents 20 ft in the actual park.*

How can you use the 9 inches to find the actual area of the park? → *The scale is 1 inch = 20 ft, so multiply 9 × 20.*

How do you find the area of a rectangle? → *Multiply the length and the width.*

What information was provided about the creative zone? → *The area is 1,800 sq ft. and it is a rectangle.*

What could the side lengths of the actual park measure? → *any two factors of 1,800*

Suppose the creative zone had a side length of 2 ft, what would the other dimension need to be if the area is 1,800? → *900 ft*

What does a rectangle with 2 ft × 900 ft dimensions look like? → *very long and skinny*

Could you design a creative zone with a different set of dimensions that still has an area of 1,800 sq ft? What would the dimensions be? → *Yes; 60 ft × 30 ft*

How do you find the area of a square? → *side length × side length or length × width*

What has to be true about the dimensions of a square? → *The side lengths have to be equal.*

Questions for Struggling Students (continued)

How many different squares can you find that have an area of 6,400 sq ft? List the possible dimensions.	*Just one, 80 ft × 80 ft*
Why is there only one set of dimensions possible for the playground zone?	*Because it has to be a square.*
How do you find the area of a triangle?	$\frac{1}{2}$ *base of the triangle × the height of the triangle*
What must be true about the length and width (base and height) of your rectangle?	*They have to be factors of 1,800.*
What unit of measure will you use to draw your scale drawing?	*inches*
Which zone has the largest area?	*playground zone*
How do the shapes of the park area and the scale drawing compare?	*They are similar; the corresponding side lengths are growing proportionally and the corresponding angles remain equal.*
What is the scale factor of the small model to the large model?	*4*
Is there more than one set of dimensions that can be formed to meet the zone area requirements? How do you know?	*Yes, because the figures can have different dimensions that will produce the same area with the exception of the square.*

Name the corresponding sides of the rectangle by listing their dimensions.

There are many possibilities depending on the dimensions used. One example, the side length of 60 ft in the park's creative zone corresponds to the side length of 3 in. in the model.

Compare the scale of the actual park to the model. What do you notice?

Each side length has been decreased by a scale of 1 in = 20 ft. The ratio of $\frac{length}{width}$ for the model figure is equal to the $\frac{length}{width}$ of the actual figure.

What is the scale factor from the actual park to the model?

Each side length has been reduced by a scale factor of $\frac{1}{240}$.

If you use the scale factor to find the model length, in what unit will your answer be?

Feet, the scale factor does not change the unit of measure.

Will everyone's creative zone share the same dimensions? Explain your reasoning.

No, different dimensions can result in the same area.

Will everyone's playground zone share the same dimensions? Explain your reasoning.

Yes, because it has to be a square.

Will everybody's fountain zone look the same? Why or why not?

No; the base and height can vary between the triangles. A triangle with a base of 3 cm and a height of 4 cm has the same area as a triangle with a base of 2 cm and a height of 6 cm. These triangles have the same area, but are not similar triangles.

Do triangles with the same base and height always create similar triangles? Why?

No, you can have a right triangle with a base of 4 cm and a height of 5 cm or you can create an acute or scalene triangle with the same base and height. The area would be the same, but the triangles would not be similar.

Suppose Vicki decided to change her scale to 2 in. = 40 ft. How would that affect your first drawing?

It would not change it at all because it is equivalent to 1 in. = 20 ft.

How would a scale of 0.5 in. = 20 ft affect your first drawing?

The new-scaled dimensions would be half the size, so the model would appear smaller.

How does a scale factor of greater than 1 affect the drawing?

A scale factor greater than one enlarges the drawing.

How does a scale factor of less than 1 affect the drawing?

A scale factor of less than one reduces the drawing.

How do the perimeters of the model and the actual park compare?

The perimeters grow by the same scale factor.

What other dimensions will work for the fountain zone?

Answers will vary.

What is the difference between a scale and a scale factor?

A scale gives a relationship between two units, such as 1 in. = 20 ft. A scale along with a ruler helps you find original measurements. Scale factor is a number used to multiply a length of a figure to enlarge or reduce it to a similar image.

What is the relationship between the ratio of two corresponding sides and the scale factor of any similar figures?

Because the scale factor tells what you are multiplying by to get the enlargement or reduction and the ratio is measuring the same quantity between corresponding sides; the ratio gives you the scale factor of the larger figure to the smaller figure or vice versa.

Can you produce the area of the creative zone using fractional values for your dimensions? Give an example.

yes; 12.5 ft × 144 ft

Begin by asking students if they think everyone has the same scale drawing. List some things that could be different and why. You can ask either of the following questions to help students identify things that are different.

- Which zones could have different dimensions?

- Are there any zones that should look the same?

With the exception of the square, the dimensions of the zones could be different because different shapes could result in the same area. The scale drawing could also be different because of the location of the zone areas. Have students share the dimensions for the different zones and compare these areas.

As students share the dimensions for the different zones, have them compare these areas. Even if students used different dimensions, the areas should remain equal. When you ask students about the strategies they used to find the dimensions for the model, some might explain the following: 20 ft = 1 in., 60 ft = ? in., 60 ft = 3in.

Others might have used the scale factor to find the model's dimensions.

$$\frac{1 \text{ in.}}{20 \text{ ft}} = \frac{1 \text{ in.}}{240 \text{ in.}}$$

Therefore, the scale factor is $\frac{1}{240}$.

$$60 \text{ ft} \times \frac{1}{240} = 0.25 \text{ ft}$$

$$0.25 \text{ ft} = 3 \text{ in.}$$

Discuss how the playground zone is different from the creative zone.

- Can the playground zone have two different lengths? Can the playground zone have non-whole number dimensions?

- Ask a student to share how they found the dimensions for the scale model. Compare different strategies used by students.

Discuss the fountain zone. The following questions are appropriate to ask.

- Are all the areas on the scale model the same type of triangles?

- What is the same about the fountain zones? What is different? What allows for the variety?

Students should discuss that different bases and the heights can produce the same areas of triangles. In addition, the same base and height can produce different types of triangles. The fountain zone could be shaped to form a right triangle, scalene triangle or other types of triangles as long as the base and height have the correct area.

- What is the relationship between the scale model and the actual park?
  The scale model is a reduction of the park. All model zones dimensions are drawn proportional to the original zones dimensions.

- How do the areas of the actual park compare to the areas in the scale drawings?

Have students look for patterns. This relationship may be difficult to see with the large numbers. If so, draw some rectangles and squares, find the areas, scale the figures up, and then compare the area of the original figure to the area of the scaled figure. Ask students to look for patterns. Students should notice that the areas between the scaled figures and the original figures are growing by the scale factor squared.

Discuss the zones students added to the park. Invite students to share specifics about their zones and explain the calculations made when they were making decisions.

Ask students to share their strategies for finding the dimensions of the larger model in Question 5. Students may have used their original strategies. Another strategy is now available because they have already produced a small model. Students can find the scale factor between the small model and the large model. The small model used the scale 1 in. = 20 ft. The large model will use the scale 1 in. = 5 ft. The scale factor between 20 ft and 5 ft is 4, so students can take all the dimensions of the small model and multiply them by a scale factor of 4 to get the dimensions for the large model.

Discuss with students how a scale factor can either enlarge or reduce a figure while keeping it similar. A scale factor less than one will reduce a figure, while a scale factor greater than 1 will enlarge a figure. A scale factor of 1 creates a congruent figure.

Have students compare the larger models created, and look to see if any zones become distorted. Are zones still similar? Do these models still represent the park accurately?

CHECK FOR SUCCESS

☐ Have students exchange papers and check each other's work. Students should be able to identify if the other student scaled the figure and calculated the areas correctly. Students should also check that the other student adhered to all the guidelines and/or specification.

Student _____ Class _____ Date _____

LESSON 3   PARK

The city is planning a new neighborhood park. Vicki, who works for the city park department, has to present a scale model of the park to the city officials for approval. She finds some partial plans that someone started before cutbacks were made and decides to use these plans for the new park. The plans Vicki found are shown to the right.

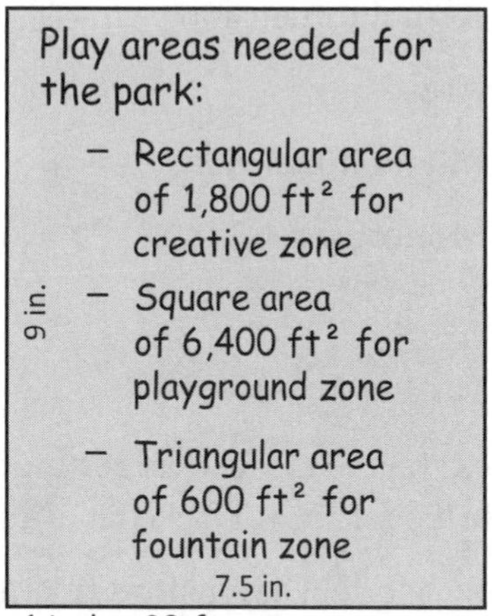

Play areas needed for the park:

– Rectangular area of 1,800 ft² for creative zone

– Square area of 6,400 ft² for playground zone

– Triangular area of 600 ft² for fountain zone

9 in.

7.5 in.

1 inch = 20 ft

1. Find the actual dimensions of the park and play areas.

   Actual Dimensions:

   Park –

   Creative zone –

   Playground zone –

   Fountain zone –

2. Using the scale 1 in. = 20 ft, draw a model of the park. Label each zone of your model in inches.

   Model Dimensions (inches):

   Park –

   Creative zone –

   Playground zone –

   Fountain zone –

3. Add your own circular zone to the park and draw it on your scale drawing. Provide information for your zone. Use 3.14 for π.

   Details:

   Name of Zone –

   Actual dimensions –

   Area –

   Model dimensions –

   Model area-

4. Vicki has to create a larger model of the plan for public display. The scale she selects is 1 in. = 5 ft. What are the dimensions of her new model?

   New Model Dimensions (inches):

   Park –

   Creative zone –

   Playground zone-

   Fountain zone –

   _____zone (circular zone) –

5. Using butcher paper, as a group, create a drawing of the model.

1. Park actual dimensions: 180 ft × 150 ft
   $9 \times 20 = 180$; $7.5 \times 20 = 150$

   Creative zone: Shape must be a rectangle that has an area = 1,800 ft².
   Possible answers include: 30 ft × 60 ft, 20 ft × 90 ft, 10 ft × 180 ft

   Playground zone: Shape must be a square that has an area of 6,400 ft².
   Only one possible answer: 80 ft × 80 ft

   Fountain zone: Shape must be a triangle that has an area of 600 ft.
   Possible answers include: base of 10 ft and height of 120 ft; base of 20 ft and height of 60 ft; base of 40 ft and height of 30 ft.

2. Park model dimensions: 9 in. × 7.5 in.

   Creative zone's model area: $3 \times 1.5 = 4.5$ in.²
   Some possible dimensions for the creative zone include:
   The area of the scale drawing must be 4.5 in.²

   Students may consider scaling the area of the rectangular park to find the new area. Some students may use the information that the area between the scaled figures and the original figures are growing by the scale factor squared. Students may take the area 1,800 and divide it by 400, which is 20^2, to find the area which is 4.5.

Actual dimensions ($l \times w = 1,800$ ft²)	Scale drawing dimensions ($l \times w = 4.5$ in.²)
30 ft × 60 ft	1.5 in. × 3 in.
20 ft × 90 ft	1 in. × 4.5 in.
10 ft × 180 ft	0.5 in. × 9 in.

   Playground zone's model area: $4 \times 4 = 16$ in.²

Actual dimensions	Scale drawing dimensions
80 ft × 80 ft	4 in. × 4 in.

   Fountain zone's model area: $2 \times 1.5 \div 2 = 1.5$ in.²

Actual dimensions	Scale drawing dimensions
base of 10 ft and height of 120 ft	base of 0.5 in. and height of 6 in.
base of 20 ft and height of 60 ft	base of 1 in. and height of 3 in.
base of 40 ft and height of 30 ft	base of 2 in. and height of 1.5 in.

2. (continued)

The drawing shown has been reduced to fit in the space available. Students' drawings need to be the actual size, 9 in. × 4.5 in.

3. Answers will vary. Possible answers for a circle with a radius = 1 in.

Details:

Name of Zone – Merry-go-Round Zone

Actual dimensions – $r = 20$ ft

Area – $A = 3.14(20)^2 = 1,256$ ft^2

Model dimensions – $r = 1$ in.

Model area – $A = 3.14(1)^2 = 3.14$ in.^{2}

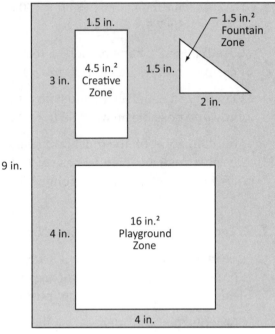

SCALE: 1 in. = 20 ft

4. Answers may vary depending on the dimensions used in Question 2.

New Model Dimensions (inches):

Park – 36 in. × 30 in.
$180 ÷ 5 = 36;\ 150 ÷ 5 = 30$

Divide actual dimensions by 5 to find model dimensions.

Creative zone – 6 in. × 12 in. (may vary)

Playground zone – 16 in. × 16 in.

Fountain zone – 6 in. × 8 in. (may vary)

_____zone (circular zone) – example $r = 4$ in.

5. Depending on the dimensions used, the models may vary.

CHAPTER 5 — PROBABILITY STATISTICS

LESSON 1 ▶ WINNER EVERY TIME

Common Core State Standards
Statistics and Probability 7.SP
Investigate chance processes and develop, use, and evaluate probability models.
6. Approximate the probability of a chance event by collecting data on the chance process that produces it and observing its long-run relative frequency, and predict the approximate relative frequency given the probability. For example, when rolling a number cube 600 times, predict that a 3 or 6 would be rolled roughly 200 times, but probability not exactly 200 times.

NCTM Correlation
Data Analysis and Probability
Understand and apply basic concepts of probability.
Use proportionality and a basic understanding of probability to make and test conjectures about the results of experiments and simulations.
Compute probabilities for simple, compound events, using such methods as organized lists, tree diagrams, and area models.

LESSON GOALS

- Use ratios to describe probability events.
- Find experimental probability and investigate how the relative frequency of the events affects the outcomes.
- Compare experimental probability to theoretical probability using multiple algebraic representations.

LESSON INTRODUCTION

Fill a bag with color cubes. To introduce the lesson select a cube from the bag. Show the cube to the class, then record the color. Return the cube to the bag and select another cube. Record its color. Repeat this several more times. Ask students to predict what color you will select next. Select a cube and see how many students were correct. Ask students what information would help them make a better prediction. Record their responses.

A review of the terms ratio and scale factor is appropriate prior to starting this lesson.

From the experimental probability activities in this lesson, students will use proportions and scale factors, together with ratios of theoretical probability, to make predictions about the number of times to expect a particular outcome.

A **ratio** is a comparison of two quantities. A ratio can be written in three formats: $\frac{1}{4}$, 1:4, and 1 to 4.

A **scale factor** is a number used to proportionately change a quantity. In this lesson the quantity is a measurement.

TEACHING SUGGESTIONS

Within the bulleted text below are suggestions on how to begin the lesson, introduce essential vocabulary, and question students so that they are prepared to complete the Student Recording Page on their own or with minimal assistance.

Ask students if they think each cube has an equally likely chance of being selected. Explain to students that if there are several colors of cubes in the bag and you cannot see them, then each of the cubes has an equally likely chance of being selected.

- Do you think each color has an equally likely chance of being selected? Students should ask to see the cubes in the bag to determine this information. The colors will have an equally likely chance if every color cube has the same quantity in the bag. Show the contents of the bag to the students.

> **Equally likely** means that two outcomes have equal chances of occurring.

- Introduce theoretical probability to students. If the items in the bag have an equally likely chance of being drawn, you can find the theoretical probability by using the following ratio to find theoretical probability.

$$\frac{\text{Number of outcomes you are interested in}}{\text{Number of possible outcomes}}$$

- Discuss what is meant by favorable outcomes. They are the outcomes that give you the desired result.

> In probability, an **event** is a set or collection of possible outcomes.

> **Theoretical probability** is the likelihood of an event based on all possible outcomes. The probability is the ratio of the number of favorable outcomes to the number of possible outcomes.

Materials
Student Recording Page 5.1
Cubes (each group needs 1 blue, 2 red, 3 yellow, and 6 green, more cubes should be available if students need them when scaling the problem)
Opaque containers or bags
Optional:
Calculators (graphing)

Vocabulary
Experimental probability
Theoretical probability
Equally likely
Scale factor
Ratio
Relative frequency
Trial
Outcome
Event

- Introduce the situation of the lesson by reading the scenario about the Spring Festival. Explain to students that they will be conducting an experiment to predict probability. Discuss that experimental probability is found as a result of simulating an event. They will be able to use their experimental data to answer questions and make predictions about the relative frequency over the long run.

> **Relative frequency** is the number of occurrences of an outcome for a specific number of trials.

> An **outcome** is a possible result of an event or experiment.

> As part of an experiment, a **trial** is an action that has an outcome.

STUDENT ENGAGEMENT

Students are to complete Student Recording Page 5.1. Have students work in small groups of 2 to 3 to collect their experimental data. Make sure all students have a role in the experiment. As students begin the trials, observe how students are conducting their experiments. Verify each of the following as you check students' progress and their understanding.

- How are they recording their data?
- Are they keeping track of the number of outcomes in addition to the outcome that occurs?
- What are students doing between each selection of a cube?

Students should try to make their selections truly random. If you observe bias, take the opportunity to talk about what bias is and how it skews the data.

How many colors are in the box?

→ *4*

What outcomes are possible?

→ *blue, red, yellow, or green cube*

Is each outcome equally likely to occur?

→ *No, because each color has a different quantity in the box.*

Do all cubes have the same chance of being selected?

→ *Yes, if you pick them from an opaque container each cube would have an equally likely chance of being selected.*

Which color do you think has the best chance of being selected? Why?

→ *Green, because there are more green cubes in the box.*

What is probability?

→ *Probability describes the chance of something happening. Probability is represented by a number that has a value between 0 and 1 (or 0% and 100%). If the probability is close to 0 (or 0%,) it does not have a good chance of happening. If the probability is closer to 1, (or 100%) it has a good chance of happening. If the probability is 1, it will happen.*

What does a probability of 0 mean?

→ *There is not a chance of it happening.*

Give an example of something with a probability of 0.

→ *Selecting a purple cube from the box.*

What does a probability of 1 mean? Give an example of something that has a probability of 1.

That it will happen; you will pick a cube with 6 faces out of the box.

How many times do you think you would have to select a cube before you get a blue cube? Explain.

about 12 times; there are 12 cubes in the box and one is blue.

If you drew a cube 25 times, how many times would you expect to get a blue?

About 2 times, about 1 out of every 12 times.

How many outcomes can occur using the colored cubes in the box?

12 because there are 12 cubes in the box.

How many favorable outcomes can occur for red?

2 because there are 2 red cubes in the box.

What is the P(red)?

$P(red) = \frac{2}{12} = \frac{1}{6}$

After 50 trials, how many blue cubes did you draw? What is the experimental probability for blue?

Answers will vary.

What are the different ways you could describe or represent that probability?

as a ratio in fraction, decimal, or percent form

If you conducted twice as many trials, what would you expect the probability for blue to be?

About the same probability as on the first trials; I would have twice as many trials and about twice as many blue as I did in my first 50 trials.

What results do you think the other groups are getting for their trials?

Assuming their bags contain the same number and color of blocks, their numbers should be close but there is also a chance that their data might be way off. There is a chance that they may get 5 blue in a row even though there is only one blue in the bag.

What percent of the bag was blue? Red? Yellow? Green?

Blue about 8.3%, Red about 16.6%, Yellow 25%, and Green 50%

Your bag contained three times as many yellow cubes as blue cubes. How does your probability of drawing a yellow compare to the probability of drawing a blue?

P(yellow) $\frac{3}{12}$ and P(blue) = $\frac{1}{12}$; you are three times more likely to draw a yellow cube than a blue cube.

Suppose you continued drawing blocks for 500 trials, what would you expect your data to look like? How would you expect the ratios to change? How would the percents change?

The data will change and the ratio representing the data might vary, but I think it will get closer to the theoretical probability.

Do you think this is a fair game?

Every cube has a chance of being selected but the colors all have a different probability of getting selected. The colors are not equally likely, so the game is not fair.

Why do some people get better prizes than others?

→ *Because some colors will be selected more often, the colors that have a better chance of being selected should get the smaller prizes. You want to give prizes but the prizes cost money and you don't want to assign the biggest prize to the color that has the more likely chance of getting selected.*

Is each outcome equally likely? Explain.

→ *No, green has the best chance, then yellow, red, and blue.*

How is the data you are collecting helpful? How can you use the data to make decisions about the game?

→ *It will help you predict how many of each color will be picked, which will help us determine the quantity of each prize to buy.*

The school has 1,224 students. Suppose each student played the game once, how many times would you expect a blue cube to be drawn?

→ *102; 1 for every group of 12; there are 102 groups of 12 in 1,224.*

How is conducting the experiment going to help decide what prizes Beth should buy?

→ *It will give an estimate of what to expect. You might have to buy some extras of each type of prize but it gives us an idea.*

If the math club wants to increase their profits and give away more of the smaller prizes, what would you have to do?

→ *Add more green cubes to the bag or take some yellow cubes and red cubes out of the bag.*

How could you lower the probability of selecting blue?

Since there is only one blue you cannot take it out, but you could add more of the other colors to lower the probability of selecting a blue.

How do more trials affect the experiment?

The more trials the closer the experimental probability gets to the theoretical probability.

What is theoretical probability?

the number found by listing all the possible outcomes and then finding the ratio of the number of favorable outcomes to the total number of possible outcomes

What is $P(\text{blue}) + P(\text{red}) + P(\text{yellow}) + P(\text{green})$? Would the sum be the same for both experimental and theoretical probabilities? Explain.

The sum of the probabilities should equal 1. Probability is a number with a value from 0 to 1; one representing certainty.

QUESTIONS TO EXTEND STUDENT THINKING

What would happen if you change the number of red cubes in the box?

All the probabilities would change for each color.

How do you know the probabilities you found in Question 1 are correct?

The probabilities should add up to 1.

If one person uses the theoretical probability to analyze a situation and another uses experimental probability to estimate the probability that the outcome will occur, will they get the same answer?

Depending on the number of trials used to calculate the experimental probabilities, they will probably get probabilities that are close to each other but more than likely there will be some variation.

Choose a cube color. Gather the data from at least two other groups. Using the combined data create a scatter plot showing the relationship between number of trials and number of times your chosen color was drawn. Interpret the relationship (if observed) in your scatter plot. If a trend line exists, graph it and give its equation. How are the trend line and the scatter plot related to the probability of your color being chosen? Give reasons to support the graph if you find the relationship is proportional or non-proportional.

Answers will vary.

If someone selects a yellow cube and they do not replace it, how does that affect the probability of the other cubes?

There will only be 11 outcomes so the probability of selecting blue changes to $\frac{1}{11}$, red changes to $\frac{2}{11}$, yellow changes to $\frac{3}{11}$, and green changes to $\frac{6}{11}$.

List some other ways to find theoretical probability.

→ *A tree diagram, making a list, or using an area model can help you find theoretical probability.*

What are some other ways you could simulate this event? How could you use a calculator to set up the same experiment?

→ *Use a random number generator. Select the numbers 1 through 12. Let 1 represent blue, 2 and 3 represent red, 4, 5, and 6 represent yellow, and the numbers 7, 8, 9, 10, 11, and 12 represent green.*

If you added 4 pink cubes to the bag how would that change things?

→ *All the probabilities would change and the total number of outcomes possible will also change. $P(Blue) = \frac{1}{16}$, $P(Red) = \frac{1}{8}$, $P(Yellow) = \frac{3}{16}$, $P(Green) = \frac{3}{8}$, $P(Pink) = \frac{1}{4}$*

LESSON SUMMARY

As you begin the summary, ask students what the difference is between theoretical probability and experimental probability. Students should suggest that experimental probability is based on simulating the situations and that it helps predict outcomes of situations. Theoretical probability is the ratio of all the desired outcomes to the number of possible outcomes. A probability of 1 or 100% means the event is certain to happen. Probability is a number between 0 and 1 (or 0% and 100%) where the closer the probability is to 1, the more likely that outcome will occur. The closer the probability is to 0, the less likely the outcome will occur.

- Ask students to share their thoughts about the chances of each color being selected. What information was helpful? Ask questions about how they collected their data from the experiment.

- Discuss the different ways the students suggest and ask if they think there was any bias in that strategy?

- Ask students how they found the ratios to describe their experiments. Students should know that the ratio is the number of times the color was drawn compared to the total number of trials.

- Are these ratios going to be the same for everyone? There should be some variation however; most should be close to each other.

Collect ratios for each color from a variety of students and compare. Gather some data and recalculate the ratios, how do the new ratios compare to the students' individual ratios. Gather some more data, recalculate the ratios once again and compare the data. Ask students what is happening to the data.

Some students may have compared percents when they were asked to compare theoretical and experimental probability. Ask students to share how they found the percent associated with each ratio. Some students might suggest using a scale factor. They could scale the ratio up to 100 trials then list the percent. Others might have thought of the situation as equivalent fractions. For example, if the ratio for blue were $\frac{2}{25}$, they would have multiplied it by 1 in the form of $\frac{4}{4}$ to get $\frac{8}{100}$, which is equal to 8%. Still others might suggest division, dividing the numerator by the denominator then changing the decimal number to a percent. Make the connections to the three strategies used.

Have students share their response to any effects that performing 50 more trials would have on the data.

- How did you make such predictions? *Students should explain using proportional reasoning, since comparing the number of times a color was drawn, after 50 trials, you should be able to predict 100. If you double the number of trials from 50 to 100, then you would double the number of times each color occurred.*

- How did the students reason about collecting the class data? *Elicit some responses and discuss them. Then make a chart collecting the data they have for 100.*

Blue Cube		
Number of trails	Number of blue cubes selected	Percent
100	8	8%
200	$8 + 5 = 13$	$\frac{13}{200} = 6.5\%$
300	$13 + 14 = 27$	$\frac{27}{300} = 9\%$

LESSON SUMMARY (CONTINUED)

You can recalculate the data after each group to show how the data behaves compared to the theoretical probability; or you might want to collect all of the data and just recalculate once. You may want to use calculators to keep students focused on the task and not on the computation. The objective is to observe how as the number of trials increases; the experimental probability approaches the theoretical probability.

In summarizing the last two questions focus on the reasoning students used. Listen for how students used proportional reasoning to justify their responses.

CHECK FOR SUCCESS

☐ Have students define theoretical probability and experimental probability.

☐ Have students write a description of the trials they performed and explain how the experimental probability changed as the number of trials increased.

☐ Have students conduct a series of trials for flipping a penny. Students should do experiments that consist of 1 flip, 5 flips, 10 flips, 20 flips, and 50 flips. Students summarize their trials and compare how the results compare to the results of the trials they completed on the Student Recording Page.

Student _____ Class _____ Date _____

LESSON 1 — WINNER EVERY TIME

Every year the middle school has a Spring Festival. Clubs set up booths and the community is invited to attend. This year the math club is in charge of the "What's My Color?" booth. Students working at the booth each have a box containing color cubes. Each box has 12 colored cubes: 1 blue, 2 red, 3 yellow, and 6 green.

Everybody wins a prize. The prizes are based on the color selected. Blue gets the best prize; the other colors get smaller prizes with green getting the smallest prize. The club needs to collect data to help them decide which prizes to award.

What is My COLOR?
Exciting New Game

"Best Game at Carnival"
do not miss out! $1.00

1. Based on what is in the box, what do you think about the chances of selecting each of the colors?

   Blue:

   Red:

   Yellow:

   Green:

2. Simulate the game using a bag and 12 colored cubes. Select a cube from the bag 50 times. Replace each cube after you record its color.

   Blue:

   Red:

   Yellow:

   Green:

From *It's All Connected: The Power of Proportional Reasoning to Understand Mathematics Concepts, Grades 6–8* by Carmen Whitman.
© 2011 Scholastic Inc. Permission granted to photocopy for nonprofit use in a classroom or similar place dedicated to face-to-face educational instruction.

3. What is the result of your experiment?

4. If you selected a cube from a box 100 times, predict how many times each color would be picked. Explain your reasoning.

   a. Blue

   b. Red

   c. Yellow

   d. Green

5. What does theoretical probability mean? What is the theoretical probability of selecting each color?

6. How does the theoretical probability compare to the simulation of selecting a cube 50 times from the bag of cubes?

7. Draw 50 more cubes from the bag. What is the experimental probability based on 100 trials? How was your data affected?

8. If the class data was combined into one set of data, how would the ratios of experimental probability compare to the ratios of theoretical probability?

9. The club decides to change the number of cubes in the boxes. Dolores volunteers to change the number of cubes. What should she do if she wants to keep the theoretical probability of selecting each color the same?

10. Iliana wants to have a special box with 60 cubes. She wants the probability of selecting each cube to stay unchanged. How many of each cube needs to go into the box?

11. Becky is in charge of buying prizes. If 360 people play the game, about how many of each prize type should she buy?

From *It's All Connected: The Power of Proportional Reasoning to Understand Mathematics Concepts, Grades 6–8* by Carmen Whitman.

1. Students may suggest:

   Blue: Has the least chance of being selected, because there is only one blue cube.

   Red: May get selected more than blue because it has two cubes in the box.

   Yellow: Will be selected more than red, but less than green.

   Green: Has the best chance of being selected because there are six green cubes

2. Answers will vary.

   Sample Results of Experiment:

   Blue: ||||

   Red: ||||| |||||

   Yellow: ||||| ||||| |||

   Green: ||||| ||||| ||||| ||||| |||

3. (Using data from Solution 2)
   Blue: $\frac{4}{50}$ or $\frac{2}{25}$ Red: $\frac{10}{50}$ or $\frac{1}{5}$ Yellow: $\frac{13}{50}$ Green: $\frac{23}{50}$

4. Students may suggest:

   a. About 8 times; if I pick 100 times I will get a blue cube 4 out of every 50 times I pick, so I thought $\frac{4}{50} = \frac{x}{100}$. $50 \times 2 = 100$, so $4 \times 2 = 8$. I should pick 8 blue cubes.

   b. About 20 times; if after 50 trials I got 10 red cubes then $\frac{10}{50} = \frac{?}{100}$. Since $50 \times 2 = 100$ and $10 \times 2 = 20$, the $P(\text{Red}) = \frac{20}{100}$

   c. About 26 times; since the experiment showed a yellow cube was selected 13 times out of 50 trials, then you expect to pick yellow 26 times out of 100 trials.

   d. About 46 times; since the chance of me picking a green cube is about $\frac{23}{50}$. $\frac{46}{100}$ shows an equivalent ratio out of 100 trials.

5. Theoretical probability: If the outcomes or actions are equally likely then ratio
$\dfrac{\text{Number of outcomes you are interested in}}{\text{Number of possible outcomes}}$ can be used to find theoretical probability.

For example: $\dfrac{\text{How many ways can you get a blue cube}}{\text{Number of possible outcomes}} = \dfrac{1}{12}$

$\dfrac{1}{12}$ is the theoretical probability of selecting a blue club from the bag.

Theoretical probabilities:
$P(\text{Blue}) = \frac{1}{12}; P(\text{Red}) = \frac{2}{12} = \frac{1}{6}; P(\text{Yellow}) = \frac{3}{12} = \frac{1}{4}; P(\text{Green}) = \frac{6}{12} = \frac{1}{2}$

6. Sample solution: when comparing the probabilities I noticed that the experimental probability and the theoretical probabilities were not the same but fairly close.

Color of Cube	Experimental Probability as Percents	Theoretical Probability as Percents	Comparisons
Blue	$\frac{4}{50} = 8\%$	$\frac{1}{12} \approx 8.3\%$	
Red	$\frac{10}{50} = 20\%$	$\frac{2}{12} \approx 16.7\%$	
Yellow	$\frac{13}{50} = 26\%$	$\frac{3}{12} = 25\%$	
Green	$\frac{23}{50} = 46\%$	$\frac{6}{12} = 50\%$	

7. Sample Results of Experiment:

Blue: ЦН1

Red: ЦН1 |||

Yellow: ЦН1 ЦН1 |||

Green: ЦН1 ЦН1 ЦН1 ЦН1 ||||

For 100 trials, add the results from the first trial that drew 50 cubes to this trial that drew 50 more cubes for these results.

$P(\text{Blue}) = \frac{9}{100}; P(\text{Red}) = \frac{18}{100}; P(\text{Yellow}) = \frac{26}{100}; P(\text{Green}) = \frac{47}{100}$

The experimental probability of the red and green cubes got closer to the theoretical probability, while the yellow cube data stayed exactly the same. The blue cube data got a bit farther away from the theoretical probability.

8. The more data there is, the closer the experimental probability will get to the theoretical probability.

9. Dolores can multiply the number of each color cube by the same scale factor to increase the number of each color cube proportionally. For example, if she uses a scale factor of 2, she would increase the blue cubes from 1 to 2, the red cubes from 2 to 4, the yellow cubes from 3 to 6 and the green cubes from 6 to 12. There will be 24 cubes in the bag and the theoretical probabilities and percentages would remain the same.

10. Originally there were 12 cubes in a box. The scale factor to increase from 12 to 60 is 5. She needs to multiply the number of each of the four colors by a scale factor of 5.

Color of Cube	Number of cubes in original bag	Process (Multiply by a scale factor of 5)	Number of cubes for the special box
Blue	1	1×5	5
Red	2	2×5	10
Yellow	3	3×5	15
Green	6	6×5	30

11. Blue: $\frac{1}{12} = \frac{x}{360}$; use a scale factor of 30; therefore the blue cube will be selected 30 times.

Red: $\frac{1}{6} = \frac{x}{360}$; use a scale factor of 60; therefore the red cube will be selected 60 times.

Yellow: $\frac{1}{4} = \frac{x}{360}$; use a scale factor of 90; therefore the yellow cube will be selected 90 times.

Green: $\frac{1}{2} = \frac{x}{360}$; use a scale factor of 180; therefore the green cube will be selected 180 times. Use the ratios describing your experimental probability to find the percentage of times you picked each color.

Common Core State Standards

Statistics and Probability 7.SP
Investigate chance processes and develop, use, and evaluate probability models.

7. Develop a probability model and use it to find probabilities of events. Compare probabilities from a model to observed frequencies; if the agreement is not good, explain possible sources of the discrepancy.

b. Develop a probability model (which may not be uniform) by observing frequencies in data generated from a chance process. For example, find the approximate probability that a spinning penny will land heads up or that a tossed paper cup will land open-end down. Do the outcomes for the spinning penny appear to be equally likely based on the observed frequencies?

NCTM Correlation

Data Analysis and Probability
Understand and apply basic concepts of probability.
Use proportionality and a basic understanding of probability to make and test conjectures about the results of experiments and simulations.
Compute probabilities for simple compound events, using such methods as organized lists, tree diagrams, and area models.

LESSON GOALS

- Develop a probability model of chance.
- Investigate probability of events that are not equally likely.
- Use proportionality to make conjectures about the likelihood of an event using proportional reasoning.

LESSON INTRODUCTION

The lesson is about possible outcomes and their probabilities. Hold up a number cube so students can see it before they answer the following questions.

- If you roll one number cube, what are the possible numbers? *1, 2, 3, 4, 5, and 6*

- Is it equally likely that you will roll any number on the cube? Is it equally likely that you will roll an even number or an odd number? How do you know?

- Is it equally likely that you will roll a number greater than 1? How do you know?

- Define "equally likely." *Two or more events that have the same probability of occurring are equally likely.*

In today's lesson, the students will find products of the number that land face up when two number cubes are rolled and use these products to analyze a came of chance called the *Product Game*.

Students will look at all possible outcomes and their probabilities to determine if the game is fair or not.

The game is played with two players and each player must elect to be the "even" player or the "odd" player. Each player is given a number cube labeled 1 – 6. Both players roll their cubes at the same time. If the product of the two numbers is even, then the "even" player scores one point. If the product of the numbers rolled is odd, then the "odd" player scores one point. The player with the highest score after 30 rounds of play wins.

TEACHING SUGGESTIONS

Within the bulleted text below are suggestions on how to begin the lesson, introduce essential vocabulary, and question students so that they are prepared to complete the Student Recording Page on their own or with minimal assistance.

Model a few rounds of play with the class and write down the results. Review the scoring system for the game the students are about to play. Tell students they will be asked to keep track of the products rolled and their scores during the game. They can decide individually how to do this.

Briefly review with students the difference between theoretical and experimental probability. Allow students to tell their thoughts about each.

- How do you get data for your experimental probability? *by conducting an experiment*

- How do you find theoretical probability? *by analyzing equally likely events that can occur by listing all the possible outcomes; Theoretical probability can be described as a ratio of:*

$$\frac{?}{25} \times \frac{4}{4} = \frac{60}{100}$$

- What type of probability provides estimates of probability? *Experimental probability; If enough trials are completed the experimental probability should get close to the theoretical probability.*

- Will everyone's game come up with the same experimental probability? *No, once again if a large number of trials are conducted you expect to get results close to the theoretical probability.*

- Will everyone get the same theoretical probability for each outcome? *Yes, because it is the ratio of the number of favorable outcomes possible to the total number of all possible outcomes.*

STUDENT ENGAGEMENT

Distribute one number cube to each student. Students should work in pairs (e.g. player verses opponent) to complete this lesson. Students are to complete Student Recording Page 5.2. As students begin playing the game, look for:

- Did students state an opinion before starting the experiment?
- Are students finding the products of the number cubes?
- How are they recording the data they collect?
- Are they following the rules of the game?
- Why did the student choose the method he or she is using to record the data?

You want to give students the opportunity to select their own method of recording data; however, ask them to justify why they have selected that method. Notice if students are recording the products or just even and odd frequencies. Recording products sometimes helps students think about the products that are possible as they experiment with the game. It also helps them verify their scoring.

One aspect of the problem students might struggle with when finding the theoretical probability is accounting for rolling a 3 and a 4 that is counted separately than rolling a 4 and a 3. You can suggest strategies for making sure students account for all 36 possibilities. Putting a dot on one number cube or using different-colored cubes may help them distinguish between the two cubes, as well as emphasizing which cube belongs to the "even" player, and which cube belongs to "odd" player. Press students to find an efficient and organized method to list all the possible outcomes. Suggesting a systematic way, like turning the number cubes to find all outcomes, drawing a tree diagram, or array, might also be helpful. As students play the game and work to complete the recording page, ask questions to check for understanding.

What is a product? → *the answer to a multiplication problem; When 2 factors are multiplied together you get a product.*

In this game, what is the smallest product possible? What is the largest product possible? → *1 is the smallest and 36 is the largest.*

Is every number between 1 and 36 a possible product in this game? → *No, for example there is no way to get 13 as a product if the numbers are 1 – 6 .*

How many ways could you roll the smallest product? How many different ways could you roll the largest product? → *1 way each, 1 × 1 and 6 × 6*

What are some possible products in this game? → *12, 16, 8, 9, 4, 25; All these products have factors included in the numbers 1–6.*

How does Catrina score points? → *If the numbers on the cubes rolled have an even product, Catrina gets a point.*

How does James score points? → *If the numbers on the cubes rolled have an odd product, James gets a point.*

List the possible products that will give Catrina one point. What must be rolled for those products to occur? → *2, 4, 6, 8, 10, 12, 16, 18, 20, 24, 30, 36; They all have at least one even factor.*

List the possible products that will give James one point. What must be rolled for those products to occur?

→ *1, 3, 5, 9, 15, and 25 have two odd factors.*

What is an even number?

→ *A number divisible by 2*

What is an odd number?

→ *Any integer that cannot be divided evenly by 2; the last digit will be 1, 3, 5, 7 or 9.*

What does "fair game" mean? Do you think the game is fair? Why or why not?

→ *Answers will vary.*

Is an even number times an even number always even? If yes, explain why. If not, give an example of when it is not.

→ *Yes, because the product is divisible by 2. Students may use models to represent even and odd numbers to prove their answer.*

Is the product of two odd numbers always odd? Why?

→ *Yes, because the product is not divisible by 2.*

Is an even number times an odd number always even? If yes, explain why. If not, give an example of when it is not.

→ *Yes, because the product is divisible by 2.*

How is 3 × 6 different from 6 × 3?

→ *The products are equivalent but the situations are different. In the first, you have 3 groups of 6, and in the second situation, you have 6 groups of 3.*

Suppose the product rolled is 5. Give all the possible combinations that could have produced this product?

→ *Player A rolls a 1, and Player B rolls a 5 OR Player A rolls a 5, and Player B rolls a 1.*

QUESTIONS FOR STUDENTS ON TASK

What can you tell about the products that two number cubes will produce?

→ *Since the values on the number cubes range from 1 to 6, the products will range from 1 to 36.*

Will every number between 1 and 36 be a product that can be produced in this game?

→ *No, there are some prime numbers in the range of products that cannot be produced with a factor between 1 through 6, for example 7.*

How many products are possible in this game? How can you be certain you accounted for all the possible products?

→ *18; You could list them all.*

List some ways that you can represent the outcomes of the game. How is this list of outcomes useful?

→ *a tree diagram, a list, or an array*

Give an example of proportional reasoning that was used in this problem.

→ *The way proportional reasoning was used in this problem was to scale some situations. For example there were 30 games and P(even) = $\frac{18}{30}$, so to predict the P(even) in 100 games scale P(even) first to $\frac{3}{5}$ then up to $\frac{60}{100}$.*

Why do the experimental probabilities differ from the theoretical probabilities?

The experimental data is based on the trials or simulation you are creating. Experimental data can help you predict outcomes. Theoretical probability is the ratio of possible outcomes you are considering to the number of total outcomes possible. As the number of trials increases, it is expected that the experimental probabilities should approach the theoretical probabilities.

Compare the products 6 and 12. What can you tell about the probabilities of these products?

Both 6 and 12 have a $\frac{4}{36}$ chance of being rolled.

What product(s) would you expect to occur the most and why? What product(s) would you expect to occur the least?

6 and 12, both have 4 ways to get a product of 6; The products that will occur least are 1, 9, 16, 25, and 36 because there is only one way to get these products.

Why do some products have a higher probability of being selected?

Because they have more factors between the numbers 1 and 36.

How can you prove your modified game is fair?

Each person has an equally likely chance of winning.

What are some products that have the same probability of being created with the number cubes?

→ *Students may suggest: 1, 9, 16, and 36 all have the probability of $\frac{1}{36}$.*

What are the advantages and disadvantages of simplifying ratios in probability situations?

→ *If the ratios are representing a probability and they have the same number of total outcomes, it makes it easier to compare the number of favorable outcomes.*

What is the difference between possible and probable?

→ *In the study of probability, possible is often used to describe that an outcome can happen. Probable implies the likelihood of it happening.*

What would be an example of something that is possible but not probable?

→ *If you flip a penny, it is possible for it to land on its edge, but it is not probable.*

Is it possible to have experimental results that are not close to the theoretical results?

→ *Yes; the experimental results are just a predictor of what might happen. It is possible to get results that are a fluke. Anything is possible however it may not be probable.*

What would be a fair game using the product outcomes that would involve scoring based on multiples of numbers?

→ *Catrina gets a point if the product rolled is a multiple of 3 excluding 3. James gets a point if any other product is rolled including 3. This will give each the probability of $\frac{18}{36} = \frac{1}{2}$.*

Name at least two other ways that the game can be modified to make the game fair.

→ *Answers will vary.*

Suppose Catrina and James played a similar game called "The Sum" game. The same rules apply with the exception of when the two cubes are rolled the players find the sum. Explain which player would have the advantage in this game, the "even" player or the "odd" player?

→ *Neither player would have an advantage because the P(even sum) $= \frac{18}{36}$ and the P(odd sum) $\frac{18}{36}$ are equal.*

Create your own fair game including rules and scoring system. Be prepared to justify that your game is mathematically fair.

→ *Games will vary.*

LESSON SUMMARY

Begin the lesson summary by asking students their opinions on the fairness of the game and on what they base their opinions. Have the "odd" players that won raise their hands. Have the "even" players that won raise their hands. Let students share how they recorded their experimental data. Compare and contrast methods. Discuss if some methods give more information about the data than other methods.

- Who can give me their experimental probability for obtaining a product of 6? *Only those who recorded actual rolls or actual products versus tallies of who won a point could provide this data.*

Ask a group to share their data from the experiment with the class. Have the class compare the group's data with the class data. How does it compare? How could you get a better prediction for the data? How could you be more confident in your probabilities?

Students might mention running more trials or collecting the data from every group. Compile the class data and have the students calculate the probabilities. Ask the class what they notice about the individual data as compared to the class data. Students should notice that the class data is getting closer to the theoretical probabilities.

- What mathematics helped you predict what the probabilities would be for 100 rounds played?

Students should recognize the proportional reasoning used to scale their ratios up to 100 rounds. Some students may have used a scale factor, while others might have used equivalent ratios or division. Compare how these strategies are similar.

- What different methods were used to calculate the theoretical probability?

Ask students to share how they found the sample space. Ask questions comparing the different strategies used to determine the sample space.

- How are you certain your method accounted for all the possible outcomes?

- When listing the outcomes, did you consider the factor pair 3 and 4 was not the same as 4 and 3? Why would you have to list both?

Using a grid may help clarify the idea that these are different outcomes. Be sure that students understand if they did not account for all possible outcomes, the probabilities would be incorrect.

As you continue to compare strategies, ask the following questions.

- How are the factors (numbers rolled) represented in each method?

- How are the products represented in each method?

- How are these methods alike? How are they different? Explain which method you prefer and why?

Using a tree diagram ask students to show how a roll of the number cubes is represented. Students should be able to follow the path of a roll to the product it produces. For students that used an array, ask where on the array would they see the roll of the number cubes represented. They should point out one factor vertically and the other horizontally. If a group made a list, ask them to discuss their systematic method used to generate the list and how the list shows the factor pair.

CHECK FOR SUCCESS

☐ Using all representations shared, ask students questions they can answer by reading their representations.

1. What product would you expect to occur the most and why? *Possible answers: 6 or 12 because there are more factors pairs using the numbers 1 through 6 than the other products.*

2. What product would you expect to occur the least and why? *Possible answers: 1; because the only way you can get the product 1 is to multiply 1 × 1.*

3. What is the probability of getting a product of 12? $\frac{4}{36}$

4. What is the probability of NOT getting a product of 12? $\frac{32}{36}$

5. What is the probability of getting a multiple of 4 for a product? $\frac{32}{36}$

6. What is the probability of NOT getting a multiple of 4 for a product? $\frac{6}{36}$

7. What is the probability of getting a product larger than 12? $\frac{17}{36}$

8. What is the probability of getting an even product? Odd product?
   $P(\text{even}) = \frac{3}{4}$ $P(\text{odd}) = \frac{1}{4}$

☐ Have students compare the theoretical probability to the experimental probability. Have them explain if the theoretical probability is close to what they expected it would be.

☐ Have students write an answer to the question, "Why is the game not fair?" *Students should suggest that an even product is rolled more often than an odd product.*

☐ Have students suggest a way to modify the game so that it is fair.

Student _____ Class _____ Date _____

LESSON 2   FAIR OR NOT?

Catrina and James are playing a game. Each player is given a cube numbered 1 – 6. Each player rolls the cube. If the product of the two number cubes is even, Catrina gets a point. If the product of the cubes is odd, James gets a point.

1. Do you think this game is fair? Why or why not?

2. Play the game 30 times with a partner. Record your results.

3. Has your opinion changed about the fairness of the game based on the experiment (playing the game 30 times)? Explain.

4. Based on your data, what is the experimental probability of getting an even product? What is the experimental probability of getting an odd product?

5. Based on your data, how many times would you expect to get an even product if you played the game 100 times? Odd product?

6. List all the possible products for the game.

7. What statements can you make about the likelihood of each event?

8. What is the theoretical probability of rolling two number cubes and getting an even product? What is the theoretical probability of getting an odd product?

9. Based on the theoretical probability, do both Catrina and James have an equally likely chance of winning the game? Explain.

10. Is the game fair or unfair? If not, how can you modify the game to ensure it is a fair game? Justify your decisions.

From *It's All Connected: The Power of Proportional Reasoning to Understand Mathematics Concepts, Grades 6–8* by Carmen Whitman. © 2011 Scholastic Inc. Permission granted to photocopy for nonprofit use in a classroom or similar place dedicated to face-to-face educational instruction.

1. Some students might reason that since a number is either odd or even then the game is fair. Others suspect is it not fair and may give some general statements about how it is easier to roll an even product than odd products.

2. Possible results

Game Played	1	2	3	4	5	6	7	8	9	10	11	12	13	14	15
Even Product	2	4		8	20		8		4	12	16	18	36		
Odd Product			3			15		3						1	9
Who gets points	C	C	J	C	C	J	C	J	C	C	C	C	C	J	J

Game Played	16	17	18	19	20	21	22	23	24	25	26	27	28	29	30
Even Product			12	4	4	10		6		12	4			30	
Odd Product	5	25					5		3			15	1		25
Who gets points	J	J	C	C	C	C	J	C	J	C	C	J	J	C	J

3. Answers will vary. Most students should suggest that the game is not fair because the product of the two cubes rolled is an even number more often.

4. $P(\text{even product}) = \frac{18}{30} = \frac{3}{5}$ $P(\text{odd product}) = \frac{12}{30} = \frac{2}{5}$

5. $P(\text{even product}) = \frac{18}{30} = \frac{3}{5}$ so $\frac{3}{5} = \frac{x}{100}$

    $\frac{3 \times 20}{5 \times 20} = \frac{60}{100}$

    Using a scale factor of 20, I would expect to get an even product about 60 times or

    $P(\text{odd product}) = \frac{2}{5}$ so $\frac{2}{5} = \frac{x}{100}$

    $\frac{2 \times 20}{5 \times 20} = \frac{40}{100}$

    I could scale my first ratio by 20, I would expect to get an odd product about 40 times or $P(\text{odd product}) = \frac{40}{100}$.

6.

		Number on Cube 1					
		1	2	3	4	5	6
Number on Cube 2	1	1	2	3	4	5	6
	2	2	4	6	8	10	12
	3	3	6	9	12	15	18
	4	4	8	12	16	20	24
	5	5	10	15	20	25	30
	6	6	12	18	24	30	36

7. Sample response:

Possible Products	1	2	3	4	5	6	8	9	10
Probability	$\frac{1}{36}$	$\frac{2}{36}$	$\frac{2}{36}$	$\frac{3}{36}$	$\frac{2}{36}$	$\frac{4}{36}$	$\frac{2}{36}$	$\frac{1}{36}$	$\frac{2}{36}$

Possible Products	12	15	16	18	20	24	25	30	36
Probability	$\frac{4}{36}$	$\frac{2}{36}$	$\frac{1}{36}$	$\frac{2}{36}$	$\frac{2}{36}$	$\frac{2}{36}$	$\frac{1}{36}$	$\frac{2}{36}$	$\frac{1}{36}$

The products 1, 9, 16, 25, and 36 have the same likelihood of being selected; each has a probability of $\frac{1}{36}$.

The products 2, 3, 5, 8, 10, 15, 18, 20, 24, and 30 have the same likelihood of being selected; each has a probability of $\frac{2}{36}$.

The product 4 is unique and has the probability of $\frac{3}{36}$.

The products 6 and 12 have the same likelihood of being selected; each have a probability of $\frac{4}{36}$.

Products are not equally likely. There are 18 different products.

The products 6 and 12 are more likely to get rolled as they have the highest probability.

8. $P(\text{even product}) = \frac{27}{36} = \frac{3}{4}$ $P(\text{odd product}) = \frac{9}{36} = \frac{1}{4}$

9. No. Rolling an even product is three times more likely to occur than rolling an odd product, so I would expect Catrina to win three times as many points as James.

10. The game is not fair.
Possible responses will include adjusting the points awarded or modifying the rules of the game, such as:

- Each player gets points according to the product they roll. If you roll an even product, you get 1 point. If you roll an odd product, you get 3 points.
- Catrina gets a point if the product is greater than or equal to 12, or if the product is 1. James gets a point for all other products.

Playing the game this way gives each the same opportunity to win the game.

LESSON 3 TYPICAL ME

Common Core State Standards
Statistics and Probability 7.SP
Use random sampling to draw inferences about a population.
1. Understand that statistics can be used to gain information about a population by examining a sample of that population; generalizations about a population from a sample are valid only if the sample is representative of that population. Understand that random sampling tends to produce representative samples and support valid inferences.

NCTM Correlation
Data Analysis and Probability
Formulate questions that can be addressed with data and collect, organize, and display relevant data to answer them.
Formulate questions, design studies, and collect data about a characteristic shared by two populations or different characteristics within one population.

LESSON GOALS

- Use data from a sample population to make predictions about a larger population.
- Formulate, design, and collect data from a survey.

LESSON INTRODUCTION

While planning for this lesson, it must be decided what components of this problem will be completed during class time and what part will be completed outside of class time. Decide how many days to give the students to conduct a survey and to complete the display of the survey.

As you introduce the lesson to the students, discuss surveys that are produced to gather information. Define a population and sample population so that students understand the need for a survey.

By the lesson's end, students will see how proportional reasoning is used to make predictions and generalizations about a population that is larger than the sub-population used for a survey.

A **sample population** is a subset of a larger population. When a population is too large to study, a sample population that is representative of the larger population is used.

Sampling is the process of selecting an appropriate sample.

Random sampling is the process of selecting an appropriate sample where each individual has an equal chance of being selected.

TEACHING SUGGESTIONS

Within the bulleted text below are suggestions on how to begin the lesson, introduce essential vocabulary, and question students so that they are prepared to complete the Student Recording Page on their own or with minimal assistance.

- What different kinds of information are gathered using surveys?

Have a list of surveys like the following and ask students what kind of data each survey will gather.

Survey	Type of Data Collected
What is you favorite toothpaste?	Types of toothpaste
How many siblings do you have?	Quantity (numbers)
What is your favorite food?	Types of food
What is your favorite soda?	Types of soda or brands
Do you prefer oranges or apples?	Oranges or apples
How much time do you spend on the phone?	Time (numbers)
How many pets do you have?	Quantity (numbers)

- Discuss the difference between categorical data and numerical data.

- Discuss with students examples of questions that will produce categorical data and those that will produce numerical data.

- Have students generate some ideas about what questions to ask in their surveys. They will select three questions to ask. Do they want to collect categorical or numerical data, or both?

Materials
- Student Recording Page 5.3
- Chart paper
- Markers
- Access to 100 students for survey
- Optional:
  - Calculators

Vocabulary
- Numerical data
- Categorical data
- Sample population
- Sampling
- Random sampling
- Representative samples
- Bias
- Scale factor
- Proportion

Categorical data is information given that reflects to a given category. A set of data is said to be categorical if the values can be sorted according to category, such as favorite food or type of gum people chew.

Numerical data are numbers that can be values identified on a numerical scale, such as counts or measurement.

- Think about the questions from the list and consider the types of responses that will be gathered. For example, the survey question, "What is your favorite food?" can provide a large variety of responses. Whereas a question about specific types of food might limit the choices. You can further narrow responses by asking questions like "What do you prefer—apples or oranges?" Think about what kind of responses you will get when you ask your questions. Will the data you get help you define a typical seventh-grade student? As the teacher, you should provide final approval to all survey questions before students begin the survey.

- Discuss with students places they can survey other students. Ask them to generate a list of places that large numbers of seventh-grade students might be in attendance.

- Why is it important to get a large sample of students for your survey? *A larger sample produces a more random sample of a typical seventh-grade student.* Explain to students that they should not just ask their close friends.

- What are some factors to consider so that you select a good representative sample that address bias issues? Which do you feel would be more representative of seventh-grade students—asking a group of students at a math contest or a group of students at a basketball game?

- If 100 students seem too large of a sample for the population, it can easily be scaled down to fit your needs. Students should think about places that revolve around school activities and consider ease of location and time constraints. For example, students could consider a survey location such as the lunchroom, a sporting event, or the front of the school as students arrive or leave school.

A **representative sample** is a sample that is reflective of the general population being studied.

Bias means to influence in an unfair way.

- Students should consider how the time of day, location, or school function might skew their data in their survey. For example, suppose the question was "What's your favorite sport?" Do you think you would get a random sample if the poll was taken at a football game?

- Ask students what methods they might use to evaluate their results. Review the list of things to consider and the requirements for the display. Students should work in groups to complete this task. They will probably need to do some individual work outside of class; however you might want to allow them to work some time on the display in class one day.

STUDENT ENGAGEMENT

As students begin to make decisions about their survey questions and generate plans to carry out their surveys, ensure that the students are taking into account safety and responsibility concerns. Inform students that you must approve of all questions and survey plans before students are allowed to conduct their surveys. When students decide how, when, and where they will conduct their surveys, ask them questions prompting them to scrutinize their surveys for any bias and ensure their samples is representative of a typical seventh-grade student, such as:

- Will the students be at that location randomly?
- Are the students part of a sub-group of seventh-grade students, and if so, does being a part of that group provoke a different response than that of a typical random seventh grader?
- Is it equally likely that any seventh-grade student would be at that event (school function or location, etc)?
- What population of seventh-grade students would not be represented in the survey?

Students should also consider how they will keep track of the data. For example, are they using a questionnaire, keeping tallies, using a spreadsheet, or writing down responses? Whatever plan of action they take, have they taken into account time and efficiency?

How are they going to evaluate their results? Does their method of evaluation match the type of data they have? How will they present the data to the class? Did they use a pie chart, bar graph, or line plot? Does the data show the information needed? For example if they create a bar graph showing only the frequencies of pets owned, could you tell what the pets were? Does their method of presenting their data truly show or reflect a representation of the data?

After their surveys and displays are complete, direct students to answer the questions on Student Recording Page 5.3, which involves making inferences about different-size populations. While students complete their work, notice the mathematics they use. How are they comparing the results and are they considering larger and smaller populations? Do students recognize the proportional reasoning involved? Ask questions to check for understanding and ask them to explain their thinking as they complete their work.

QUESTIONS FOR STRUGGLING STUDENTS

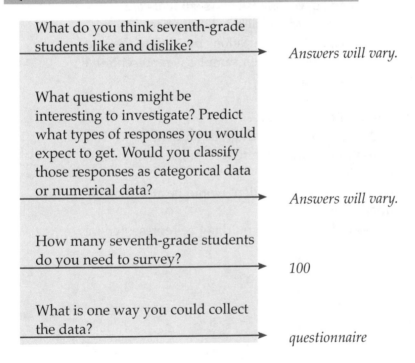

What do you think seventh-grade students like and dislike? → *Answers will vary.*

What questions might be interesting to investigate? Predict what types of responses you would expect to get. Would you classify those responses as categorical data or numerical data? → *Answers will vary.*

How many seventh-grade students do you need to survey? → *100*

What is one way you could collect the data? → *questionnaire*

Name some ways to display the data.

→ *bar graph, frequency graph, table*

What kind of numerical information can you gather from your survey?

→ *a ratio of people that like something, the mode of something they like if there are choices*

What kind of data does numerical data produce?

→ *numbers; for example the number of cats students own*

What kind of data does categorical data produce?

→ *words that describe a category, i.e., favorite color*

If you were able to poll twice as many people, how might that have changed your data?

→ *The results would be closer to a true representation of a typical seventh grader.*

How many times larger is the population of seventh- grade students for the entire school compared to your sample?

→ *Answers will vary.*

QUESTIONS FOR STUDENTS ON TASK

What kind of questions produce categorical data?

→ *sample answers: What is your favorite soda? What is the color of your eyes? Do you prefer mornings or evenings?*

What kind of questions produce numerical data?

→ *Sample answer: How many sodas do you drink in a day? How many letters are in your name? How many doors are there in your home?*

QUESTIONS FOR STUDENTS ON TASK (CONTINUED)

Why did you select this data representation (i.e. circle graph, bar graph) to summarize your data?	*Answers may vary.*
What information can be readily seen in your choice of representation? What information cannot be readily seen with your choice of representation?	*Answers are dependent on the representation.*
How will you use your information from the survey to predict information about other populations?	*Take the information and scale it to support a new population.*
What mathematics are you using when you make predictions?	*proportional reasoning*
Why does making inferences about populations from a sample population involve proportional reasoning?	*Surveys gather information from a group of people and use it to predict, based on the size of that group, how a smaller or larger group might respond.*
How confident are you that the inferences you made about the larger populations are valid?	*It depends on the sample surveyed. If all students were rural students in a rural area it might not truly be representative of an urban population.*

Will all sets of data have a mean, median, and mode? Explain.

→ *No; categorical data does not have a median or mean.*

If applicable, calculate the mean, median, and mode of your data sample. How would you expect these measures of center to change for a larger population?

→ *The measures of center should stay the same.*

QUESTIONS TO EXTEND STUDENT THINKING

How would surveying a small group of 15 students affect the results of the study?

→ *Asking a small group of students is not be a good idea. The survey should help to describe a typical seventh grader. If there is only a small group of students, it is not an effective sample.*

Summarize your data.

→ *Look at ratios in the data to decide what is typical. Scale the values in the sample data by the scale factor needed to attain the total population numbers and make conclusions about the population using the ratios that occurred in the sample data. Find the mode of the data to tell which happens most often.*

Could you use the mode to describe categorical and numerical data?

→ *Yes, the mode tells what occurred most often.*

Could you use the median to describe categorical and numerical data?

→ *Categorical data is not organized by order and the median tells you the halfway point of data. So, the median does not help analyze categorical data. The median could describe numerical data.*

Have students share the methods they used to collect their data. Ask others if they used the same method or another method to collect data. Make a list of the various methods used. Have students share their conclusions describing what they think a typical seventh-grade student is based on their surveys. Ask students to look for bias in the sampling as students share their ideas and make conclusions.

- Did some groups ask the same question? If so, look at the results of their surveys; are they similar? How are they different? What caused the differences? If you joined the results of two or more surveys would your inferences change? Could the location or timing of where the survey took place have affected the data? What factors may have caused the differences?

> A **scale factor** is a number used to proportionately change a quantity. In this lesson the quantity is a measurement.

- Summarize the inferences made by the students. Does the data support their statements? Did the students interpret their data correctly? Think about the questions asked and the sample population surveyed. How representative are their samples? How would the region of the country affect any of the results? Can students use this data to describe a typical seventh grader in their school, town, state, and country?

> A **proportion** is an equation that states two ratios are equal.

- Go to the questions asked on the Student Recording Page. What strategies did students use to answer these questions? How did they use their data to make inferences about their class and the other populations of 250, 750, and 360,000 seventh-grade students? Did they use equivalency, scale factor, or did they solve a proportion? Display the different strategies used and help students make connections between them. If students do not have different strategies, pose the following examples and ask students to look for similarities and differences.

Example 1:

Survey said 60 out of 100 prefer gum.

$$\frac{\text{Prefer gum} \to 60}{\text{People Asked} \to 100} = \frac{? \to \text{Prefer Gum}}{25 \to \text{Class Size}}$$

$$\frac{?}{25} \times \frac{4}{4} = \frac{60}{100}$$

(Finding equivalent fractions)

$x \times 4 = 60$

$x = 15$

15 out of 25 should prefer gum.

Example 2:

$$\frac{60 \times \frac{1}{4}}{100 \times \frac{1}{4}} = \frac{15}{25}$$

Used scale factor of $\frac{1}{4}$
15 out of 25 students should prefer gum.

- Have students give examples of how their surveys may not provide a representation of other populations. An example might be if students surveyed seventh-grade students in a rural area about their favorite hobby and they answer "horseback riding." That is not likely a typical hobby for seventh-grade students in New York City. What are some other factors that could affect the comparison to other populations? *Gender, regional climate, economics, culture and experiences.* How could you modify the survey to get a better representation? *Students may suggest asking seventh-grade students in other parts of the city, state, or country.*

- Compare and contrast the representations of the data. Do some graphs offer more information than others? Do pie charts offer the same information as line plots or bar graphs? What information can be readily seen from each type of data representation? If it is believed that the survey is asked of a truly random group, then the information can be used to describe a larger or smaller population using proportional reasoning.

CHECK FOR SUCCESS

☐ Have students explain how to use proportional reasoning to make predictions about a different-sized population than the one surveyed.

☐ After all surveys are discussed, have students write a list of statements about the typical seventh-grader from the results shared in class.

☐ Have students explain what the following statement means: "As the random sampling of seventh-grade students increases, so does the validity of the inferences made."

Student _____ Class _____ Date _____

LESSON 3 — TYPICAL ME

Students at Grant Middle School are trying to define their seventh-grade students. Recently the school has noticed groups of seventh-grade students with very interesting characteristics. Zane and Will, who are also seventh-grade students, decide to conduct a survey to characterize the typical seventh grader.

Create and conduct your own survey of 100 students in the seventh grade. Create a display showing your results.
Things to consider:

- Where will you survey the students?
- What questions will you ask of seventh-grade students?
- How will you record the data?
- What data representation best summarizes the collected data?

Display requirements must include:

- The three questions asked and the type of data collected (categorical versus numerical)
- Where the data was collected
- How the data was collected
- Conclusions formed from the data collected

After you have completed the survey and the display of your data, answer the following questions using your data.

1. Based on your survey data, what can you conclude about seventh-grade students at your school?

From *It's All Connected: The Power of Proportional Reasoning to Understand Mathematics Concepts, Grades 6–8* by Carmen Whitman. © 2011 Scholastic Inc. Permission granted to photocopy for nonprofit use in a classroom or similar place dedicated to face-to-face educational instruction.

Student _____ Class _____ Date _____

2. How many students are in your math class? Based on your survey results, what statements can you make that should describe the students in your class? Be specific about how many students in your class will have the characteristic.

3. Suppose there are 250 students in the seventh grade in the school. Use the ratios from your data to make conjectures about a typical group of seventh-grade students in the school.

4. If there were 750 students in the seventh grade in the surrounding area, what would your data indicate about the population you are studying (theses students)?

5. Suppose there are 360,000 students in the seventh grade in the state of Texas. What would your data indicate about the seventh-grade students in the state of Texas?

Students should select three questions to ask on their surveys. Survey suggestions:

Do you have your own laptop?

Do you have an iPod/MP3 player?

Do you do something after school?

What is your favorite movie?

What is your favorite subject?

What is your favorite sport?

What is your favorite type of clothing?

What is your favorite dessert?

What is your favorite type of music?

Do you prefer a brush or comb?

Do you prefer singing or dancing?

Do you prefer gum or candy?

Do you wear perfume/cologne?

How many pets do you own?

How many siblings do you have?

Do you own a cell phone?

Do you play a sport?

Do you own a pet?

Do you ride or walk to school?

What is your favorite animal?

What is your favorite food?

What is your favorite television show?

What is your favorite ice cream flavor?

Do you prefer mustard or ketchup?

Do you prefer burgers or pizza?

Do you prefer nights or mornings?

Are you left-handed or right-handed?

How many letters are in your first name?

How much do you exercise?

How many televisions are in your home?

How many times a day do you send a text, on average?

What is a typical time you go to bed at night?

How many hours a day do you watch TV?

Do you know the words to more than five songs?

1. Sample results:
    Questions asked to 100 students in the seventh grade:
    - Do you prefer burgers or pizza? 30 preferred burgers, 70 preferred pizza
    - Do you prefer gum or candy? 60 preferred gum, 40 preferred candy
    - How many letters are in your first name? 13 had 3 letters, 17 had 4 letters, 35 had 5 letters, 15 had 6 letters, and 20 had 7 letters.
    - Do you prefer mustard or ketchup? 80 preferred ketchup, 20 preferred mustard
    - What is your favorite ice cream flavor? 30 preferred Chocolate, 5 preferred Strawberry, 25 preferred Rocky Road, 10 preferred Bubble Gum, 2 preferred Coffee, 7 preferred Cookies and Cream, 10 preferred Pistachio Almond, 11 preferred Butter Pecan

2. Number of students in classes will vary. Based on the size of your classroom, have the students take their data and use proportional reasoning to adjust their data to describe their classmates.

    Shown below are alternative ways students might reason through this question.
    Do you prefer burgers or pizza? 30 preferred burgers, 70 preferred pizza

    $\frac{30}{100} = \frac{?}{25}$ The students could use a scale factor of $\frac{1}{4}$, which will result in 7.5 students. So, about 8 students will be expected to choose burgers.

    $\frac{30}{100} = \frac{3}{10}$; $\frac{3}{10}$ of 25 is the same as $\frac{3}{10} \cdot 25 = 7.5$.

3. Students should show methods using proportional reasoning to describe 250 students.

4. Students should show methods using proportional reasoning to describe the 750 students.

5. Students can use original data or use already scaled data to reason through this problem for a population of 360,000.

LESSON 4 ARMS AND FEET

Common Core State Standards
Statistics and Probability 8.SP
Investigate patterns of
associate in bivariate data.
1. Construct and interpret
    scatter plots for bivariate
    measurement data to
    investigate patterns of
    association between two
    quantities. Describe
    patterns such as clustering,
    outliers, positive or
    negative association, linear
    association, and nonlinear
    association.

NCTM Correlation
Data Analysis and Probability
Select and use appropriate
statistical methods to analyze
data.
  *Discuss and understand
  the correspondence
  between data sets and their
  graphical representations,
  especially histograms,
  stem-and-leaf plots, box
  plots, and scatter plots.*

LESSON GOALS

- To graph a relationship between two sets of data and interpret the relationship.
- Graph a scatter plot.

LESSON INTRODUCTION

As you begin this lesson, hand out Work Page 5.4 and show students the scatter plot, "Distance Traveled by Car."

- What kind of a graph is this? *a scatter plot*

- What is a scatter plot? What information does a scatter plot give you? *Listen to students' answers, but be certain that by the end of the discussion the information given in the definition box has been stated to students.*

- What do you notice about this graph? *This graph shows how long it took a car to travel a given distance.*

> A **scatter plot** is a graph that shows the relationship between two variables. A scatter plot may show that a relationship exists, but cannot prove that one variable is causing the other. The scatter plot gives you an indication that two things might be related, and if so, how they move together.

- What two variables are being explored? *time traveled in hours and distance traveled in miles*

- What can you say about the points on the graph? *It seems that for every hour cars travel about 65 to 75 miles. They seem to be increasing together. As time increases, the distance increases as well.*

When one studies the human body, many amazing proportions can be discovered. One of these proportions of the human body will be the subject of the scatter plots created and studied in the lesson.

TEACHING SUGGESTIONS

Within the bulleted text below are suggestions on how to begin the lesson, introduce essential vocabulary, and question students so that they are prepared to complete the Student Recording Page on their own or with minimal assistance.

After looking and the scatter plot and discussing information that is displayed on the scatter plot, move the discussion to trend lines.

A **trend line** is a line added to a scatter plot that shows a relational trend of the two sets of data.

Trend lines are often added to a scatter plot to see how the data is related. A trend line can be drawn so that about half the data points are below the line and about half are above the line. The trend line helps to see the relationship between the two sets of data.

- Using the string or pasta, have the students form a trend line on Work Page 5.4. What trend line matches the data shown on the graph? $y = 70x$

- When the two variables are unrelated, it is described as having no association.

- What kind of association does this graph have? *a positive association*

- Have examples of more scatter plots with positive and negative associations to share with students. Do not label these scatter plots. Ask students to identify possible relationships that can be shown by these graphs and have them identify the type of association.

- Show Work Page 5-7 once again. Choose specific points on the graph and ask students to interpret the points. Ask students to predict the distance traveled based on some given points representing time traveled and vice versa.

Materials
Student Recording Page 5.4
Work Page 5.4
· Graph paper
String/pasta for trend line
Optional:
Ruler (if students are collecting their own data)

Vocabulary
Scatter plot
Positive association
Negative association
Clustering
Outliers
Linear and non-linear association

When two variables increase or decrease together, they are described as having a **positive association**.

When one variable decreases as the other increases, the data shows a **negative association**.

- Discuss outliers and clusters informally at this point. These should be discussed further in a later lesson as this is more of an introduction lesson to scatter plots.

> An **outlier** is a data point that is separated by the rest of the data.

- Introduce the lesson to students and talk briefly about any other measurement relationships they know about. You may want students to collect their own class data instead of using this data. If so, the questions that follow can still be asked about their own class data.

> Data points in a scatter plot that are close in proximity are considered a **cluster**.

STUDENT ENGAGEMENT

Students should complete Student Recording Page 5.4 independently in this lesson. As students are working on this lesson continue to ask questions about the relationship between the forearm and foot length data. Select points that they have graphed and ask them to interpret the data points. Additionally ask them questions about the relationship among the points.

- What do you notice as you graph the points? What patterns do you observe? *The points are all close to each other and some of the data pairs are the same, which means their forearm and foot lengths are equal.*
- How do the data points relate to the line you graphed? *Some of the points are on the line, some are above the line, and some below the line.*
- Describe the line you have graphed. *The line is a proportional linear relationship whose constant rate of change, slope, is 1.*
- What does it mean in terms of this context? *Forearm length is equal to foot length. Students should notice that their data points all hover around the line, which shows a linear association.*

As students work on the questions, ask questions to check for understanding.

> A scatter plot that has data points that closely approximate a line has a **linear association**.

> A **non-linear association** is an association that is not linear.

Questions for Struggling Students

What are the variables in this situation? → *forearm length and foot length*

Measure your forearm in centimeters. Can you estimate your foot length based on any patterns you observe in the table? → *Answers will vary.*

What variables will you graph on the scatter plot? → *length of forearm in centimeters and length of foot in centimeters*

How will you label your axes? → *length of forearm and length of foot*

What variable goes on the x-axis? → *length of the forearm*

What variable goes on the y-axis? → *If I graph forearm on the x-axis then the length of the foot would go on the y-axis.*

Does it matter which variable you put on which axes? Why? → *No; it does not matter since one variable is not dependent on the other variable.*

What data values are possible for this context? What is the maximum value recorded in your list of data? → *Positive lengths; the maximum value in the data is 29.*

What scale should you use for the graph? → *1 grid unit = 1 cm*

What do you think the data in the table will look like when represented on the graph? → *It will be close to a straight line.*

What information is known about person C? Where would that information be represented on the graph?

→ *The forearm measures 24 cm and foot measures 23 cm. It would be represented at the point (24, 23) if the x-axis was the forearm length.*

What does the point (20, 19) mean in this context?

→ *forearm length 20 cm, foot length 19 cm*

What does the equation $y = x$ mean in this context?

→ *In the context, it represents Robert's mother's statement that the length of the forearm is equal to the length of the foot.*

How can you tell from the table which students' data points will fall on or closest to the trend line?

→ *If the number pairs are the same, they fall on the line.*

What does the point (22, 22) mean?

→ *A person has a forearm that measures 22 cm and a foot that measures 22 cm. These are equal.*

What does the point (0, 0) mean in this context?

→ *no length; no forearm or foot*

Would the point (22, 8) seem to belong in this set of data? Explain why or why not.

→ *It seems like a person with a forearm length of 22 cm would not have a foot length that measures 8 cm. Therefore, I do not think it belongs in this set of data.*

How many students are in the class data?

→ *Answers will vary.*

Based on the table of data, what do you expect the scatter plot to look like?

→ *points that hover around the line $x = y$*

Do you think your data is linear?

→ *No, it is not because there is not a constant rate of change in the table.*

Based on the table of data, is there a positive association, negative association, or no association?

→ *Positive, because the data seems to be increasing together.*

Name three other data points that are reasonable for this situation.

→ *(23, 25), (21, 21), (24, 23)*

Give one point (x, y) that you would not expect to see in this relationship. Explain your thinking.

→ *(22, 2) because there is no one with feet that measure 2 cm.*

Is the relationship that Robert's mother describes a proportional relationship? How do you know?

→ *Yes, because she says that the two lengths are equal to each other. It would be a linear relationship that passes through the origin.*

How do you know that this linear relationship passes through the origin?

→ *If you have no forearm length, it is assumed you have no foot length, except for special circumstances which are not being considered.*

Can the axes on a scatter plot have different scales?

→ *Yes, sometimes there is a large or small difference on only one of the variables so you do not necessarily want to use the same scale. If one scale represents a person's height and the other scale represents his finger length, you would not want to use the same scale on both axes.*

What does the equation $y = x$ mean in this scenario?

→ *That represents the relationship that Robert's mother mentioned about the length of the foot being the same as the length of the forearm.*

What can you tell about the points that are on the line?

→ *The points represent people that have the same forearm and foot length.*

How can these points be represented symbolically?

→ *$y = x$ or foot length = forearm length*

What can you tell about these people? (point to coordinates below the line) How can this be represented symbolically?

→ *They have longer forearms than their feet. $x > y$ or $y < x$ or forearm > foot length*

Suppose you collected data from a third grade class. What would you expect to be the same? Different?

→ *The relationship would be around the line but the cluster of points would be closer to 15 cm.*

Do you think all points along the $y = x$ line represent reasonable data for this situation?

→ *yes, disregarding special circumstances*

If you knew a person's foot length, what could you say about his or her forearm length?

→ *The person's forearm length would be close to the length of his or her foot.*

If you knew a person's forearm length what could you say about his or her foot length?

→ *The foot length would be close to the length of their forearm.*

QUESTIONS TO EXTEND STUDENT THINKING

What are some examples of a relationship between variables that would have a positive association?

→ *Study time and grade; walking pace and distance traveled*

What are some examples of a relationship between variables that would have a negative association?

→ *Age of a car and the value of the car; car engine size and gas mileage*

What are some examples of a relationship between variables that would have no association?

→ *Height of a person and intelligence; gender and musical talent*

We used the relationship that Robert's mother mentioned to compare the data, how would you find a trend line in other scatter plots?

→ *A trend line should pass through the center of the scattered data, so that about half of the data points are above the line and about half are below the line.*

Today's trend line was the line $y = x$. Can you give another scenario that you would expect to be modeled by the line $y = x$?

→ *Apples bought at $1.00 per pound*

What does it mean when it is said that there is a strong linear relationship in a scatter plot?

→ *It means that the two variables you are comparing have a relationship with each other; as one variable changes the other variable will change in a predictable way. A scatter plot will have a straight trend line comfortably fitting through the data.*

If you think the data is modeled by the trend line $y = x$, what would $y < x$ mean in this situation?

→ *The point is below the line on the graph.*

What would $y > x$ mean in this situation?

→ *The point is above the line of the graph.*

If a scatter plot had a negative association, what can you tell about its trend line?

→ *The line would have a negative slope.*

How could you find the median length of the forearms and feet using the scatter plot?

→ *For each data point find the x values of the ordered pairs then find the middle of the set. Do the same thing for the y values of the ordered pair.*

Students should each have a scatter plot. Start by asking students what they think about what Robert's mother said about forearms and feet. Have the students share their opinions. Ask them to back their opinions with mathematics. Have students share their graphs as they explain their opinions. Ask students questions about how they chose their scale and what the graphs depict. Ask what on the graph showed the relationship Robert's mother stated. Students should know the relationship is shown by the trend line.

- How can you describe the relationship between the forearm and foot length described by Robert's mother? *Students should recognize that the relationship is linear and proportional.*

- Is the scatter plot or actual data proportional? *No, for each unit increase in one variable, there is not a constant change in the other variable. Some of the points lie on the trend line, but not all do.*

You can expand on the students' answers by further explaining that there are some students who share a common forearm length but different foot lengths. However, the scatter plot does reflect a strong linear association, which means the points all cluster around the trend line that shows a linear relationship. Ask about the associations found in the scatter plot. Students should be able to describe the difference between positive, negative, and no association and how they can make the interpretation from a graph or table of values.

Ask students to share what they know about points on, above, and below the line. Ask students if they noticed any strange points on the graph. Again, discuss outliers informally with students.

- How did you determine which data points were outliers?

- Most students at this point are "eyeballing" points that are outliers.

Point out that they compared their data to what Robert's mother mentioned so that the line drawn through the data served as the trend line. Students should discuss that scatter plots often show a trend that can be represented by a line that passes through the center of the points graphed, so that about half of the points are above the line and about half are below the line. Discuss with students that if a pattern exists, then there is an association or relationship between the variables. If a relationship exists, then the plot can be used to make predictions about the data.

Lesson Summary (continued)

Make a list of attributes describing scatter plots.

- How does a scatter plot help to look at data? Attach this list to an example of the scatter plot and post in your room as they study more about patterns of associations between two quantities.

Check for Success

☐ Have students write a description of the difference between positive, negative, and no associations? Tell them to include how to tell from looking at a graph or a table of values.

☐ If students used the given data for this lesson, have them measure their own forearm and foot lengths now. Then they should predict where their data will fall on the scatter plot. Will the data be on, above, or below the trend line? Have the students graph the data and answer the following two questions. Is your foot length equal to your forearm length? How close to the trend line are you?

Student _____ Class _____ Date _____

LESSON 4 ARMS AND FEET

One day Robert and his mother were shopping. Robert needed socks so his mother told him to make a fist with his hand. She wrapped a sock around his fist to see if the heel and the toe of the sock met. It did so his Mom said, "Yes it fits." Robert asked his Mom if there were any other facts she knew about body relationships. She mentioned your height should be approximately equal to 7 lengths of your head; your thumb is about the same length as your nose, and the measurement of your forearm from the wrist to the elbow is approximately equal to the length of your foot. Robert told these facts to his math teacher and she decided to investigate the relationship between the forearm and the length of the foot.

Here is the data on the length of forearm and foot length that Robert's class collected.

Student (Assign a letter name)	A	B	C	D	E	F	G	H	I	J	K	L	M
Length of forearm (cm)	22	27	24	23	26	26	23	25	19	27	26	24	24
Length of foot (cm)	23	28	23	23	27	26	22	28	20	25	25	16	25

Student (Assign a letter name)	N	O	P	Q	R	S	T	U	V	W	X	Y	Z
Length of forearm (cm)	25	27	20	21	29	25	22	17	24	21	18	26	25
Length of foot (cm)	25	26	19	22	29	23	22	24	24	20	17	28	26

1. Construct a scatter plot of the data. Describe any patterns or relationships you notice.

2. Robert's mother told him that the length of the forearm was equal to the length of the foot. Using x for the length of a forearm and y for the length of a foot, what equation represents this relationship?

3. Graph your equation on the same coordinate grid with your scatter plot.

4. Describe the graph of the equation.

5. What does the y-intercept mean in this context?

6. What can you say about the data in the scatter plot?

7. How is the scatter plot useful in identifying a relationship?

8. Does the scatter plot have a positive or negative association? How do you know?

9. What statements can you make about the data points that fall on the line?

10. What can you say about the points that are below the line?

11. What can you say about the points that are above the line?

12. Do you notice any clustering in the scatter plot? What can you say about it?

13. Would you say the scatter plot has a linear or non-linear association?

14. Does the data appear to have any outliers? Explain why or why not.

15. If a person's foot length was 12.5 cm, what can you tell about the length of his or her forearm?

16. What can you say about the comment that Robert's mother made about forearms and feet?

1. If you used the data given, below is a scatter plot of that data.
   Patterns students may notice:
   The data seems to be grouped together.
   Some people's forearm lengths are the same as the lengths of their feet.
   There are about the same number of people that have a longer foot than their forearm as the number of people that have a foot that is shorter than their forearm.

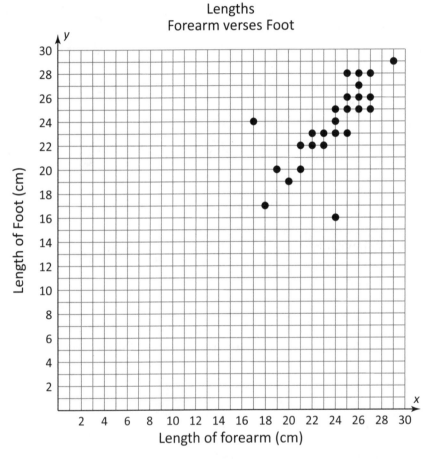

Lengths
Forearm verses Foot

2. $y = x$

3.

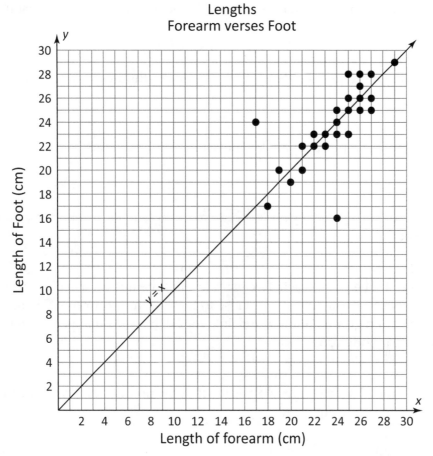

Lengths
Forearm verses Foot

Length of Foot (cm)

Length of forearm (cm)

4. It is a linear graph. For each unit increase in one variable, there is a constant change in the other variable. It is the graph of a proportional relationship. The graph of $y = x$ shows a straight line passing through the origin that increases 1 cm in foot length for every 1 cm increase in forearm length.

5. The y-intercept is located at $(0, 0)$, which can be interpreted in this context as relating 0 cm of forearm length to 0 cm in foot length.

6. It seems to have a strong linear relationship as the points all hover near the line. Some points are below the line. Some points are above the line and some points are on the line.

7. It allows you to see if and how the two types of data are related. If some sort of a pattern is evident, then predictions can be made based on the pattern. If predictions can be made, then there should be a relationship between the two variables.

8. The scatter plot has a positive association because as one quantity increases the other quantity increases.

9. The points on the line represent people whose forearm lengths are equal to their foot lengths.

10. The points below the line represent people whose forearm lengths are longer than the lengths of their feet.

11. The points above the line represent people whose forearm lengths are shorter than the lengths of their feet.

12. Students may suggest: The points seem to cluster around the line $y = x$. This means that the length of your forearm seems to be close to the length of your foot. There seems to be a cluster or a group around the point (26, 26). It seems that people in the class may have similar body proportions.

13. It seems to have a strong linear relationship as most of the points are close to the line formed by the linear relationship $y = x$.

14. The point (17, 24) appears to be an outlier because the person's forearm is 7 cm shorter than his or her foot. Similarly, the point (24, 16) appears to be an outlier because the person's forearm is 8 cm longer than his or her foot.

15. A person with a foot length of 12.5 cm should have a forearm length that is about 12 or 13 cm.

16. There seems to be a strong relationship between the length of a person's forearm and the length of his or her foot. For some people these lengths were equal to each other and for most, they were close to each other. In general, the class data closely approximated a 1:1 ratio; meaning for every 1 cm of forearm length there was approximately 1 cm of foot length. This trend was represented graphically as well because most of the data points seem to fall along the line $y = x$. This correlation seems to support Robert's mother's statement that the length of your forearm is the length of your foot. I would say that the length of your forearm gives you a pretty good indication of the length of your foot.

WORK PAGES

WORK PAGE 3.1 FOR USE WITH *WHAT'S MY SIZE?*

WORK PAGE 3.2 FOR USE WITH *CANDY BOXES*

WORK PAGE 3.3 FOR USE WITH *DESIGNING FIGURES*

WORK PAGE 5.4 FOR USE WITH *ARMS AND FEET*

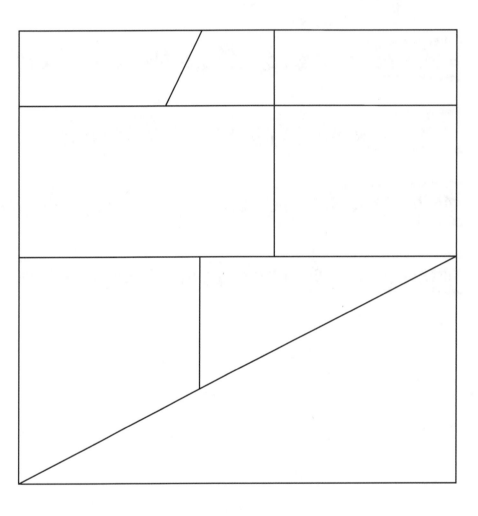

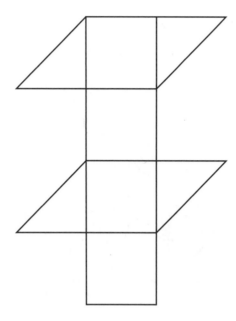

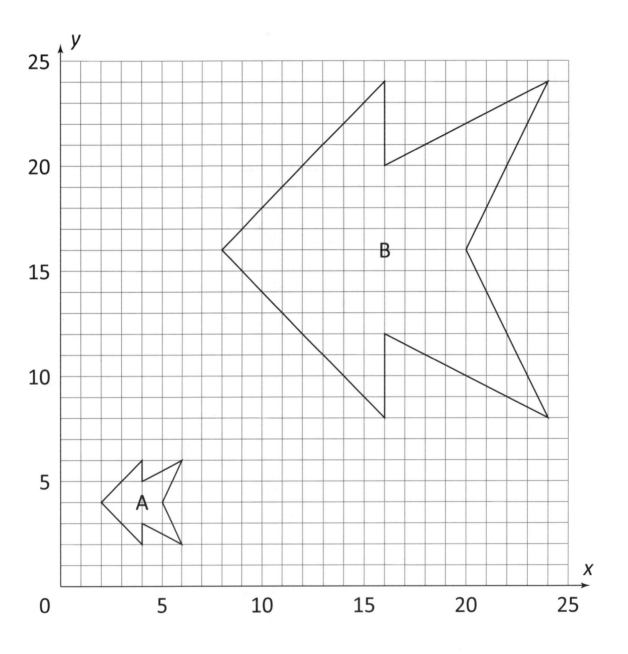

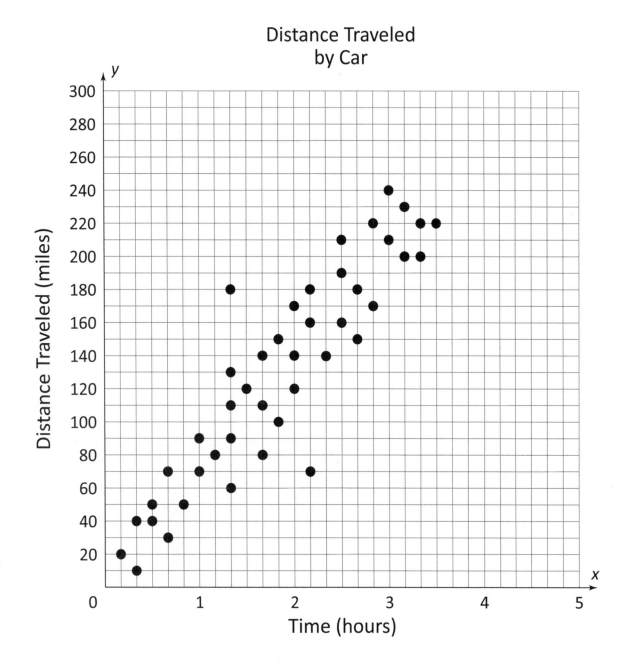

Distance Traveled
by Car